From Desolation to Reconstruction

Studies in International Governance is a research and policy analysis series from the Centre for International Governance Innovation (CIGI) and Wilfrid Laurier University Press. Titles in the series provide timely consideration of emerging trends and current challenges in the broad field of international governance. Representing diverse perspectives on important global issues, the series will be of interest to students and academics while serving also as a reference tool for policy-makers and experts engaged in policy discussion. To reach the greatest possible audience and ultimately shape the policy dialogue, each volume will be made available both in print through WLU Press and, twelve months after publication, online under the Creative Commons License.

From Desolation to Reconstruction
Iraq's Troubled Journey

*Mokhtar Lamani and
Bessma Momani, editors*

Wilfrid Laurier University Press

Wilfrid Laurier University Press acknowledges the financial support of the Government of Canada through the Book Publishing Industry Development Program for its publishing activities. Wilfrid Laurier University Press acknowledges the financial support of the Centre for International Governance Innovation. The Centre for International Governance Innovation gratefully acknowledges support for its work program from the Government of Canada and the Government of Ontario.

Library and Archives Canada Cataloguing in Publication

From desolation to reconstruction : Iraq's troubled journey / edited by Mokhtar Lamani and Bessma Momani.

(Studies in international governance)
Co-published by Centre for International Governance Innovation.
Includes bibliographical references and index.
Also available in electronic format.
ISBN 978-1-55458-229-7

1. Iraq—Politics and government—2003–. 2. Iraq—Social conditions—21st century. 3. Postwar reconstruction—Iraq. 4. Iraq War, 2003–. I. Lamani, Mokhtar II. Momani, Bessma, 1973– III. Centre for International Governance Innovation IV. Series: Studies in international governance

DS79.76.F76 2010   956.7044'3   C2009-906527-4

ISBN 978-1-55458-232-7
Electronic format.

DS79.76.F76 2010a   956.7044'3   C2009-906528-2

Cover design by David Drummond. Cover photo, showing homeless Iraqi families taking shelter at the al-Rashid military base, by Paula Bronstein, Getty Images, Inc. Text design by Catharine Bonas-Taylor.

© 2010 The Centre for International Governance Innovation (CIGI) and Wilfrid Laurier University Press

This book is printed on FSC recycled paper and is certified Ecologo. It is made from 100% post-consumer fibre, processed chlorine free, and manufactured using biogas energy.
Printed in Canada

Every reasonable effort has been made to acquire permission for copyright material used in this text, and to acknowledge all such indebtedness accurately. Any errors and omissions called to the publisher's attention will be corrected in future printings.

No part of this publication may be reproduced, stored in a retrieval system or transmitted, in any form or by any means, without the prior written consent of the publisher or a licence from The Canadian Copyright Licensing Agency (Access Copyright). For an Access Copyright licence, visit www.accesscopyright.ca or call toll free to 1-800-893-5777.

Contents

Acknowledgments vii

List of Abbreviations ix

1 Introduction 1
Mokhtar Lamani and Bessma Momani

2 Iraq under Siege: Politics, Society and Economy, 1990–2003 13
Peter Sluglett

3 Inching Forward: Iraqi Federalism at Year Four 35
David Cameron

4 The Struggle for Autonomy and Decentralization: Iraqi Kurdistan 53
David Romano

5 Armed Forces Based in Iraqi Kurdistan: A Lens to Understand the Post-Saddam Era 75
Maria Fantappié

6 The Extinction of Iraqi Minorities: Challenge or Catastrophe? 95
Mokhtar Lamani

7 Iraq's Economy and Its Brain Drain after the 2003 Invasion 117
Joseph Sassoon

8 IRFFI: A Multi-Donor Initiative 135
Carla Angulo-Pasel

9 Iraq's Tangled Web of Debt Restructuring 155
Bessma Momani and Aidan Garrib

10 The Iraq War and (Non)Democratization in the Arab World 175
Rex Brynen

11 Debating the Issues: A Roundtable Report 191
Carla Angulo-Pasel

12 Reinventing Iraq: Binding the Wounds, Reconstructing a Nation 211
Nathan C. Funk

List of Contributors 221

Index 225

Acknowledgments

Without the kind support of The Centre for International Governance Innovation (CIGI), its leaders, and its staff, this volume would not have been realized. CIGI's support for a meeting in April 2009 of leading minds on Iraq helped synthesize the ideas in this volume. As a result, we would like to thank the participants of the April 2009 workshop on Iraq for their time and effort in helping to produce this book. In addition to the authors in this volume, we would like to thank Marie-Joelle Zahar, Matteo Legrenzi, Mark Sedra, Marc Lemieux, Michael Bell, John Packer and Hussain Shaban who all participated in the workshop and were instrumental in providing feedback and comments to all of the authors.

CIGI is a vibrant and diverse environment for the exchange of ideas and we would like to thank the people involved in planning the workshop and ultimately this volume. Research assistants who helped facilitate writing portions of this book include Anton Malkin, John Roden and Fadi Dawood. Briton Dowhaniuk, Matt Eason, Deanne Leifso, Chafic Khouri and Jessica Hanson all helped in making this a team effort. Our greatest thanks go to Carla Angulo-Pasel for her logistical and intellectual support for this project from beginning to end.

We would like to dedicate this book to the five million Iraqi orphans. No volume could ever do justice to the pain and suffering of the Iraqi people, and we honour their stories and their lives in tackling the topic of Iraq in this volume.

Abbreviations

9/11	September 11, 2001
ALUBAF	Arab International Bank
AQI	al-Qaeda in Iraq
BACB	British Arab Commercial Bank
BBC	British Broadcasting Corporation
BNL	Banca Nazionale del Lavoro
CIA	Central Intelligence Agency
CIDA	Canadian International Development Agency
CPA	Coalition Provisional Authority
CRRPD	Iraq Commission for Resolution of Real Property Disputes
DFAIT	Department of Foreign Affairs and International Trade, Canada
DPA	Dayton Peace Agreement
DSA	Debt Sustainability Analysis
EPA	Emergency Post-conflict Assessment
EU	European Union
FCC	Facility Coordination Committee
G7	Group of 7
G8	Group of 8
G20	Group of 20
GAO	United States Government Accountability Office
GDP	gross domestic product
GWOT	Global War on Terror
HRW	Human Rights Watch
ICDC	Iraqi Civil Defense Corps
ICG	International Crisis Group
ICI	International Compact with Iraq
IDMC	International Displacement Monitoring Centre
IDPs	internally displaced persons
IDRO	Iraq Debt Reconciliation Office

IFI	international financial institutions
ILCS	Iraq Living Conditions Survey (ILCS)
IMF	International Monetary Fund
IRFFI	International Reconstruction Fund Facility for Iraq
IRIN	Integrated Regional Information Networks
ISCI	Islamic Supreme Council of Iraq
ISRB	Iraqi Strategic Review Board
KDP	Kurdistan Democratic Party
KDPI	Iranian Kurdish Democratic Party
KRG	Kurdish Regional Government
LCCG	London Club Coordination Group
MDTF	Multi-Donor Trust Fund
MNF	multinational force
MoPDC	Ministry of Planning and Development Cooperation
NATO	North Atlantic Treaty Organization
NDS	National Development Strategy
NGOs	non-governmental organizations
OPEC	Organization of the Petroleum Exporting Countries
ORHA	United States Office of Reconstruction and Humanitarian Assistance
PLO	Palestine Liberation Organization
PUK	Patriotic Union of Kurdistan
SBA	Stand-by Agreement
SCIRI	Supreme Council for the Islamic Revolution in Iraq
SIDA	Swedish International Development Cooperation Agency
SIGIR	Special Inspector General for Iraqi Reconstruction
SOITM	Iraqi Turkmen Human Rights Research Foundation
TAL	Law of Administration for the State of Iraq for the Transitional Period
TOR	Terms of Reference
UAE	United Arab Emirates
UBAF	Union de Banques Arabes et Françaises
UK	United Kingdom
UN	United Nations
UNAMI	United Nations Assistance Mission for Iraq
UNDG	United Nations Development Group
UNDG-ITF	United Nations Development Group Iraq Trust Fund
UNDP	United Nations Development Programme
UNESCO	United Nations Educational, Scientific and Cultural Organization

UNHCR	United Nations High Commissioner for Refugees
UNICEF	United Nations Children's Fund
UNIFEM	United Nations Development Fund for Women
UN OCHA	United Nations Office for the Coordination of Humanitarian Affairs
UNSC	United Nations Security Council
UNSCOM	United Nations Special Commission on Disarmament
US	United States
WB-ITF	World Bank Iraq Trust Fund
WHO	World Health Organization

1
Introduction

*Mokhtar Lamani and
Bessma Momani*

Throughout most of the Ottoman Empire's rule, Iraq's "imagined communities"—composed of overlapping identities of tribes, ethnic groups and religious groups—were self-sufficient, that is, out of the reach of the empire's power and administration (Zubaida, 2002: 205). After the notorious "Tanzimat" policies of the mid-nineteenth century, the Ottomans tried to regain control of the three Iraqi provinces. Following the demise of the Ottoman Empire, Iraqi communities would again witness the British and the Arab nationalists attempt to centralize power by crafting a common Iraqi state identity. The construction of the Iraqi state was a concerted exercise in political manufacturing, created to ensure internal coherence among a decentralized and fractured people. Iraqi nationalists, allied to elite networks of political officials, the military, urban notables and industrialists, played an important role in defining and perpetuating the myth of the Iraqi state as an Arab nation that would protect its citizens from the undue influence and intervention of foreign powers (Simon, 2004). This Iraqi brand of Arab nationalism was championed by the short-lived installation of King Faisal, and continued through the authoritarian rule of Saddam Hussein.[1]

The United States' (US) invasion and occupation of Iraq in 2003, however, led to not only the breakdown of social order but also to the breakdown of Iraq's manufactured state identity. In the absence of a broad civil society movement and ideological cohesiveness to aggregate the Iraqi peoples' interests, it was not surprising that Iraqis organized along ethno-sectarian lines (Wimmer, 2003: 119). The process of organizing people into ethnic political parties, it has been shown, can lead to a radicalization of interests, further cementing perceptions of "otherness," and the permeation of ethnic consideration into all aspects of governance, from education policies to tax policies (Horowitz, 2000: 8). When ethnic divisions are further fermented by social disorder, there is an added risk of a breakdown in "civility" that can lead to violence, the dehumanization of the other and the escape of people into familiar ethnic neighbourhoods (Horowitz, 2000: 12). The rise of Baghdad's walled-in city throughout 2006–2007, and the ethnic cleansing within these Bantustan-like communities, reflects this radicalization of ethnic identity in its ugliest form.

The American hope had been that through power-sharing mechanisms of federalist arrangements and strong regional governments the Iraqi state could meet the needs of ethnic groups without reverting to ethnic politics (Brancati, 2004: 14). The Bush administration's rush to implant democracy in Iraq proved to be not only premature but totally irrelevant, as time did not permit the rise of broad-based, non-ethnic-based political parties (Wimmer, 2003: 124). Moreover, the international and US domestic pressure to restore power to Iraqis and bring about Iraqi sovereignty were factors that helped produce the unintended consequence of further cementing the ethno-political dynamics of Iraq's new institutions. Many among the international political community, regional governments and local leaders would like to see Iraqis striving for a legitimate, democratic and unified state. The question is how to achieve this ideal while centrifugal forces are pulling the country toward a decentralized state marred by ethnic and sectarian politics.

The post-2003 Iraqi state, consequently, with its recognized borders and sovereign status, is a shell that needs internal repair to build state legitimacy and to capture the people's imagination of an Iraqi identity. It remains to be seen how the new Iraq will fare with the after-effects of US withdrawal, with the political future of Kurdistan (and the very foundation of federalism and decentralization at stake), with the new oil law and with the unique status of Kirkuk and the Ninawa province. Having said that, no serious reconstruction can be achieved without a sustainable security, and security cannot be achieved without an inclusive political project of a real, national reconciliation, engaging all Iraqis without any exclusion. The challenges are abundant, and this book is an attempt to build a discussion on how to surmount Iraq's most daunting obstacles.

Iraq and Security: Examining the Literature

Since the US invasion of Iraq, there has been a plethora of academic and journalistic books written on the invasion, occupation and post-occupation of Iraq. Many bestselling and popular books have been written on the war, recalling what went wrong or right and often recalling the narratives of policy makers, military personnel and journalists. These books have often been written to enhance understanding of the implications of Iraq's role in preserving regional and global security, with an emphasis on structural variables in, or consequences to, the international political system. Consequently, the impact of the occupation and post-occupation period at the domestic societal level has often been ignored. In general, three trends can be observed in the literature on Iraq: (1) the examination of US and international decision making in the case for invading Iraq and in the justification for the subsequent occupation; (2) the description of the follies and challenges of the US occupation through firsthand accounts from within the internationally secured Green Zone and through the eyes of international journalists in the country; (3) and the examination of Iraq's ethnic and religious constituencies and their link to external or regional factors, spanning ideological and political influences. Although the literature reviewed here is by no means exhaustive, and the academic and journalistic literature in Arabic is vast and more critical than those examined here (such an exercise is far beyond the scope of this book), the purpose of this introductory chapter is to discuss some of the bestselling books on the subject and to note the lack of analysis of the societal impact of the occupation and post-occupation periods.[2]

In the first category, journalists and former military officials have filled pages and volumes with explanations of the bureaucratic and foreign-policy machinery involved in making the case for war to the people of the United States (see Ricks, 2009). For example, soon after the US invasion, Bob Woodward, with unparalleled access to the US cabinet, described in his book *Plan of Attack* the conflicted personalities behind the negotiations and debate to invade Iraq (2004). Similarly, scholars and public affairs writers have examined the debates and public dialogues, global and within the United States, to make the case that some public officials manipulated the information age to make the case for a predetermined and pre-planned war (Abele, 2009). Jaramillo (2009) goes further to argue that cable news networks had packaged the war in a sanitized and "pretty" form to make the perception of war a more palatable one for the US domestic audience. The tone of these works and many others implies that the US military worked to implement a difficult plan of regime change in the context of a vulnerable US domestic audience, inhospitable Iraqi governmental machinery and, more importantly, a hostile regional environment (Abele, 2009). As US public support for the war in Iraq began to wane, with the 2007–2008 US presidential debate raging (which included an active debate on the form and timing of withdrawal from Iraq), a number of books dedicated to finding a suitable exit strategy were released (see Waltz and Mills, 2009). Others note how the US influence on Iraq would continue, either directly or indirectly, well after the withdrawal of the US military (Ricks, 2009). The case for perpetuating a US presence in Iraq has similarly been made on the grounds that if the United States was to withdraw, then the doom of either regional chaos or the undermining of US national security would be realized (Duffield and Dombrowski, 2009).

The second category of books written on Iraq includes those written by individuals who have ventured inside the country to reveal the realities on the ground, and particularly to reveal the follies and challenges of administering the occupation. Paul Bremer's memoir accounts for the challenges in crafting a representative Iraqi government and makes the case for the implementation of the controversial policy of de-Baathification (the ousting of Baath Party officials from government positions) (2006). In contrast, journalist Chandrasekaran (2007) discusses the irrational and ideological bent of decision making within the Green Zone to point out the mismatch between idealized neo-conservative policies and Iraqi realties and needs—such as the institution of a smoking ban during a time of intense conflict and upheaval in Baghdad. Dobbins et al. (2009), for example, examine the inability of the US-led coalition government to keep civil peace despite attempts to restore public infrastructure, reform the statist economy and modernize the judicial system. Former US official Larry Diamond (2005) also argues that the US occupation will have a lasting negative effect on Iraq because the US officials were short-sighted and overly ideological in planning for Iraqi democratic and political transformation, such that the transition to an independent Iraq required a rollback of policies that could ensure the political compromises needed in an already fractured country. Other than these officials' memoirs, a number of journalists make rare insights into Iraqi society, often noting the great human toll of the war on ordinary citizens (see Fassihi, 2008; Rosen, 2006; Shadid, 2005).

In the third category, academic historians and specialists on Iraq have weighed in and provided analysis of what went wrong in Iraq and lessons for the future of state building. Many highlight the incompatibility between the fragmented nature of Iraqi society and the decentralized Iraqi state, or the lack of an elite consensus in forging a democratic process (see Dawisha and Dawisha, 2009). Using a historical narrative, Dodge compares the US occupation to the British Empire's attempt to consolidate Iraq into a state more than 80 years ago. He notes that both hegemons have had grand visions of a transformed Iraq and both failed to appreciate the local circumstances in crafting the Iraqi state (Dodge, 2005). Herring and Rangwala detail the US plans for Iraqi state building, which did not take into account—and even further exacerbated—internal Iraqi divisions. These divisions had contributed to a devastating outcome during the post-invasion political reconstruction. The authors argue that the fragmented Iraqi state proved incapable of coping with the insurgency and the multiple simultaneous demands on the government, leading to a situation that eventually spiraled out of control (Herring and Rangwala, 2006). On the security front, many academies also use the Iraqi case to argue for the appropriate measures in counterinsurgency operations. Often noting the United States' emphasis on force protection, they point to a trade-off that involved a higher loss of civilian life and consequently a visceral response of insurgency movements (Smith, 2008: 144). A growing body of academic literature and military analysis details the nature and ideological leanings of the insurgency, and the risks and challenges in appropriately dealing with the Iraqi insurgency, particularly in the context of humanitarian law (see Hashim, 2006; Cordesman, 2006; Biddle, 2006).

While much of the examined literature describes and analyzes Iraq's state security and threats to sovereignty, as well as that of its neighbours, the underlying academic purpose of this volume is to bring to light a number of new empirical studies and forward-thinking pieces on Iraq. Iraqi society is often neglected in books on Iraq, many of which have either a realist or critical bent to their analysis. Alternatively, in this book the editors are inspired by the "Copenhagen School" of security studies—a European school focused on examining alternative paradigms to security studies—and of the work of its pioneer, Barry Buzan. This volume makes the case that Iraqi societal security has been threatened further by the US invasion. In *People, State, and Fear*, Buzan argues that societal security entails the protection of traditional language, culture, religion and national identity (1991: 122–23). Prior to the invasion, the Iraqi state did not provide societal security for many of its minorities but it did guarantee an *Iraqi* form of societal security. The hegemony of the Iraqi state was derived in part from creating these "memories of state," where the Baathists rewrote Iraqi history to raise the valour and cultural importance of the centre (Davis, 2006: 272). In many ways, the Iraqi state derived its strength from a centrist Baghdadi narrative that then forced all Iraqis to participate in its body politic (Tripp, 2007: 1). The political process of the Baathist Iraq often involved persecuting people who did not conform to the centrist vision of an *Iraqi* identity (Tripp, 2007: 2).

Taking the Copenhagen model further, it has been proposed that, in the ideal, a secure society is one that has a shared sense of collective identity (Weaver, 1993: 17)—be it manipulated or manufactured. Historically, the Iraqi political centre has maintained control of its Iraqi identity through the domination of, what Charles Tripp identifies as, "three spheres of political life": patrimonial relations, political economy and violence (2007: 5–7). The Baghdadi manipulation of these spheres of political life had accorded the centrist government a form of Iraqi societal security. These interrelated spheres of political life were lived through networks of patron–client relations, including the use of tribal politics, the state's distribution of political spoils from oil revenues to those loyal to the regime's narrative of the state and the use of violence to suppress and bring fear to those who challenged the centrist interpretation of social order. After the US invasion and occupation, this centrist model was challenged. Specifically, when political and societal loyalty shifted to the micro-level—to the religious sect, tribe or region, for example—there was a further erosion of societal security.

The occupation and dismantling of governing structures has also contributed to this erosion. The romanticized notion of Iraqi societal security had already been beleaguered by eight years of war with Iran and twelve years of economic sanctions. In other words, an *Iraqi* culture, language and collective identity have in essence been corroded. The idealized or romanticized version of a pluralist, secular and nationalistic Iraq has been destroyed. Regardless of the longer-term prospects, the process of erosion in Iraq's societal security structure has brought great human suffering and pain to many Iraqis. The objective of this book is to explain these phenomena and to provide ideas and solutions for moving forward.

The Plan of This Book

The future of Iraq is clearly an uncertain one; however, our intent in this book is to reflect on the issues and concerns of building a viable Iraqi state. The chapters are empirically rich and cover new policy areas, including those missing from the existing collections on Iraq today. We begin the book with a brief look into Iraq's modern social and political history. Peter Sluglett looks at the background of Iraq's invasion of Kuwait and what started the isolation of Iraq from the international community. Sluglett recounts the attempted Shi'a uprising in Iraq's south and in Kurdistan in the early 1990s and the impact of the revolt on these communities' politics in a post–Saddam Hussein Iraq. This chapter's nuanced description of Iraq before the US invasion helps set the context of the book.

David Cameron reflects on the challenges of building an Iraqi constitution. An expert in federalism, Cameron points to the link between having a strong constitution and an effective federal Iraqi state. Cameron demonstrates the pressure of Iraq's Shi'a Arabs to centralize the state and how achieving this may prove to be a challenge for the Iraqi constitution. He notes how Iraq's ethno-sectarian groups have differing interests on the future of federalism and how the resultant tension are bound to raise thorny constitutional issues for Iraq's politicians.

David Romano looks at the situation of Iraq's Kurdish community and the struggles they have faced in pursuing autonomy. Romano reviews the delicate balance in Kurdistan's political scene—its predisposition to ethno-national independence and its simultaneous support for a unified Iraqi state. Building trust among Arabs and Kurds is a century-old challenge that further inspires Kurds to maintain their autonomy and pursue a decentralized Iraqi state. Based on field research and interviews in Kurdistan, Romano debunks notions that the Kurds are waiting for the demise of the Iraqi state to create independence, but he notes that the Kurds are a traumatized people and that their pursuit of a decentralized Iraq is seen as an important prerequisite to their participation in a federal Iraq.

Maria Fantappié examines two of the major armed forces currently based in Iraqi Kurdistan and two of Iraq's military academies to highlight changes and continuities in Iraq's security dynamics since 2003. Fantappié looks at the emergence of the regional centre in Erbil and its relations with the central Baghdad government. Based on field research in Iraq, she analyzes the Kurdish regional government's struggle for autonomy from Baghdad. She shows how the Kurdish regional authorities are trying to keep their position as an integral part of Iraq for as long as they continue to profit from this collaboration. This strategy is particularly evident in the Kurdistan Regional Government's (KRG) attempt to keep an important role within the establishment of the new Iraqi army, as evidenced by the two Iraqi military academies based in Zakho and Sulaymaniyah.

Mokhtar Lamani examines the plight of Iraq's minorities. Tracing the rich mosaic of Iraq's Mesopotamian heritage, Lamani highlights the pressure and suffering of Iraq's lesser-known ethnic groups. The particular situations of Yezidis, Mandeans, Christians, Turkmen and other minorities are examined. Based on personal interviews with representatives of these groups both within and outside of Iraq, Lamani recommends a constitution that enshrines equal citizenship for the Middle East.

This book provides three chapters on economic factors in Iraq's future reconstruction, an important but often forgotten dimension of this conflict. Joseph Sassoon begins with a discussion of Iraq's economic development after the US invasion and reflects especially on the failed post-invasion policies and resulting brain drain of Iraq's professional class. The loss of this middle class further hampers Iraq's political and socio-economic development. Providing new evidence and data on the socio-economic situation of Iraqis is a key contribution of the chapter.

Carla Angulo-Pasel examines the International Reconstruction Fund for Iraq (IRFFI) as a multi-donor approach to Iraq's reconstruction effort. Based on interviews with the 2005–2007 chair of the IRFFI Donor Committee, Angulo-Pasel reflects on the challenges involved in the coordination of this multilateral initiative and Canada's experience as a primary stakeholder in the Donor Committee. Angulo-Pasel finds that the IRFFI has made significant contributions in fostering international cooperation on Iraqi state building, but notes the lessons that can be learned from the process—lessons that should be implemented to further maximize its positive impact.

Bessma Momani and Aidan Garrib examine the international negotiations on Iraq's official and private debt. After the United States pressured the International Monetary Fund (IMF) to give Iraq a favourable debt sustainability assessment, the stage was set for Iraq to receive generous debt relief from its other official and private creditors. The Paris Club, representing many of Iraq's European government creditors, applied IMF formulas to determine Iraq's debt forgiveness and restructuring terms. The London Club, representing private creditors, had no choice but to follow suit. Without progress on Iraqi political reconciliation, however, and without being able to dispel suspicions that Iraq's politics are dominated by Iranian influence, many of the Gulf neighbours with large unsettled loans to Iraq were reluctant to forgive Iraqi debt.

Rex Brynen begins his chapter with a review of one of the leading explanations offered by the Bush administration to justify its invasion of Iraq. Brynen suggests that the democratization of Iraq has had a limited demonstration effect across the region and may have even soured further political reform efforts. The spread of radical elements within Iraq and throughout the region were further spurred by the US invasion of Iraq. This has had a negative effect on mainstream Islamist movements that participated and pushed for political reform throughout the region.

Carla Angulo-Pasel reflects on a roundtable discussion of academic experts who convened to discuss a number of important issues in Iraq today. The roundtable examined participants' views on Iraq's Internally Displaced Persons (IDPs) and refugees. Entitlements to basic services, rights of return and repatriation and property rights are relevant issues for millions of Iraqis living outside the country. The issues of citizenship in Iraq and the feasibility of federalism, given the state's ethnic heterogeneity and associated competing interests, were also examined. Benefiting from the roundtable's comparative expertise, the panelists examined the lessons that have been learned from cases comparable to Iraq—such as the Balkans—and the potential these lessons may have held for the development of the 2005 Iraqi constitution. In addition, participants exchanged views concerning the role for middle powers, like Canada, in Iraq.

In the final chapter Nathan C. Funk provides a concluding reflection. While acknowledging the fact that Iraq still has a long way to go to improve its domestic political arrangement and to build strong relations with its neighbours, Funk provides us with an optimistic assessment of the future, reflecting on a post-conflict Iraq and its place in the region.

Our hope is that this book will be of value to academics, students, policy makers and journalists who are interested in understanding the present desperation of life in Iraq. Although the contributors have been rigorously challenged by their peers and the editors to contribute to a volume with a unified purpose, the views expressed in this volume are the authors' own. We hope that the chapters will stimulate new debates and ideas on Iraq's future and its place in global governance. At the Centre for International Governance and Innovation, we strive to identify and contribute policy-relevant ideas to advance global governance. Indeed, as this volume attests, Iraq presents real and complicated challenges to peace and good governance in the Middle East and beyond.

Notes

We would like to thank the research assistantship of Anton Malkin, Fadi Dawood and John Roden and the initial copy-editing of Deanne Leifso.

1 Some would argue that this form of exclusionary politics was abandoned briefly during Bakr Sidqi's rule in 1936–37 and during Abdelhakim Qassem's communist rule from 1958 to 1963 (Wimmer, 2003: 116).
2 Based on selected examination of both the amazon.com bestseller list and Google Books popular lists.

Works Cited

Abele, Robert P. (2009). *Anatomy of a Deception: A Reconstruction and Analysis of the Decision to Invade Iraq*. Lanham, PA: University Press of America.
Bremer, Paul and Malcolm McConnell (2006). *My Year in Iraq: The Struggle to Build a Future of Hope*. New York: Simon and Schuster.
Biddle, Stephen (2006). "Seeing Baghdad, Thinking Saigon," *Foreign Affairs*. Vol. 85, No. 2: 2–14.
Brancati, Dawn (2004). "Can Federalism Stabilize Iraq?" *The Washington Quarterly* Vol. 27, No. 2: 7–21.
Buzan, Barry (1991). *People, States, and Fear: An Agenda for International Security Studies in the Post-Cold War Era*. Hemel Hempstead, UK: Harvester Wheatsheaf.
Chandrasekaran, Rajiv (2006). *Imperial Life in the Emerald City: Inside Iraq's Green Zone*. New York: Knopf.
Cordesman, Anthony H. (2006). "The Iraq War and Its Strategic Lessons for Counterinsurgency." Washington, DC: Center for Strategic and International Studies, 1–16.
Davis, Eric (2005). *Memories of State: Politics, History, and Collective Identity in Modern Iraq*. Berkeley, CA: University of California Press.
Dawisha, Adeed and A.I. Dawisha (2009). *Iraq: A Political History from Independence to Occupation*. Princeton, NJ: Princeton University Press.
Diamond, Larry Jay (2005). *Squandered Victory: The American Occupation and the Bungled Effort to Bring Democracy to Iraq*. New York: Times Books.
Dobbins, James, Seth Jones, Siddharth Mohanadas and Benjamin Runkle (2009). *Occupying Iraq: A History of the Coalition Provisional Authority*. Santa Monica, CA: The Rand Corporation.
Dodge, Toby (2005). *Inventing Iraq: The Failure of Nation Building and a History Denied*. New York: Columbia University Press.

Duffield, John and Peter Dombrowski (2009). *Balance Sheet: The Iraq War and U.S. National Security*. Palo Alto, CA: Stanford University Press.

Fassihi, Farnaz (2008). *Waiting for an Ordinary Day: The Unravelling of Life in Iraq*. New York: Public Affairs.

Hashim, Ahmed S. (2006). *Insurgency and Counter-Insurgency in Iraq*. Ithaca, NY: Cornell University Press.

Herring, Eric and Glen Rangwala (2006). *Iraq in Fragments: The Occupation and its Legacy*. Ithaca, NY: Cornell University Press.

Horowitz, Donald (2000). *Ethnic Groups in Conflict*. 2nd edition. Berkeley, CA: University of California Press.

Jaramillo, Deborah L.(2009). *Ugly War, Pretty Package: How CNN and Fox News Made the Invasion of Iraq High Concept*. Bloomington, IN: Indiana University Press.

Ricks, Thomas E. (2009). *The Gamble: General David Petraeus and the American Military Adventure in Iraq, 2006–2008*. New York: Penguin Press.

Rosen, Nir (2006). *In the Belly of the Green Bird: The Triumph of the Martyrs in Iraq*. New York: Free Press/Simon and Shuster.

Shadid, Anthony (2005). *Night Draws Near: Iraq's People in the Shadow of America's War*. New York: Henry Holt.

Simon, Reeva (2004). *Iraq between the Two World Wars: The Militarist Origins of Tyranny*. New York: Columbia University Press.

Smith, Thomas (2008). "Protecting Civilians... or Soldiers? Humanitarian Law and the Economy of Risk in Iraq." *International Studies Perspectives*. Vol. 9, No. 2: 144–64.

Tripp, Charles (2007). *A History of Iraq—3rd Edition*. Cambridge: Cambridge University Press.

Waltz, Michael and Nicolaus Mills (2009). *Getting Out: Historical Perspectives on Leaving Iraq*. Philadelphia, PA: University of Pennsylvania Press.

Wimmer, Andreas (2003). "Democracy and Ethno-religious Conflict in Iraq." *Survival*. Vol. 45, No. 4: 111–34.

Zubaida, Sami (2002). "The Fragment Imagine the Nation: The Case of Iraq." *International Journal of Middle East Studies*. Vol. 34: 205–15.

2

Iraq under Siege
Politics, Society and Economy, 1990–2003

Peter Sluglett

During the 12 years between the allies' defeat of Iraqi forces in January–February 1991 and the invasion of Iraq by the United States in March 2003, Saddam Hussein managed to consolidate, even to enhance, his regime's long-standing reputation as a major pariah of the contemporary state system, although in these latter years he no longer attracted the covert support of the United States, which he had enjoyed for much of the period before the invasion of Kuwait in 1990. The 1990s and early 2000s were terrible times for the people of Iraq, who, unless they were part of the elite or were somehow able to escape the country, endured a catastrophic decline in living standards, personal freedom and security and a massive deterioration in the fabric of their social and economic life.[1] Almost all of Iraq's national revenue came from oil, and it was only occasionally (most notably between 1998 and 2001) that oil production, whose capacity had been severely damaged in the course of the fighting in 1991, approached pre-1990 levels.[2] Even this modest achievement was offset by the lowest world oil prices posted since the early 1970s—well below $30 a barrel in real terms between 1992 and 2000, and as low as $12 in 1999.[3]

Although Iraq was effectively besieged by the outside world for some 12 years, it is difficult to escape the conclusion that the greater part of the blame for this state of affairs lay squarely at the feet of the Government of Iraq. If it wished to relieve the people's suffering, it had only to resign, or less drastically and more realistically, to abide by various United Nations (UN) resolutions, which, given that Iraq had invaded and attempted to annex Kuwait, were not especially draconian. The four conditions on which the UN insisted were: the identification and elimination of Iraq's weapons of mass destruction; the demarcation of Iraq's frontier with Kuwait, to be accompanied by acceptance of Kuwaiti sovereignty; the release of Kuwaiti and other nationals held in Iraq; and the establishment of a Compensation Commission that would assess the damage done to Kuwait in 1990–91 and pay for it with a levy of 30 percent on Iraqi oil revenues. By the time of the invasion in 2003, under great international pressure, Iraq had complied fully with only one of these conditions, the recognition of the frontier with, and the sovereignty of, Kuwait. In much the same spirit, the principles of an oil-for-food program, which should have obviated most of the necessity for food rationing, had been put on the table by UN negotiators as early as 1991 but had been continually rejected by the government of Iraq as an intrusion on its sovereignty.[4]

An important consequence of the long siege was that it was virtually impossible for individuals and groups outside of Iraq (including the opposition in exile and Western intelligence agencies) to have a clear idea of what was going on inside of the country. Journalists could not go anywhere without official minders, and the various security services were justifiably feared for their ferocity and ruthlessness. In terms of control and surveillance, Iraq under Saddam Hussein more nearly resembled the opaqueness of Cambodia under Pol Pot, contemporary North Korea or Myanmar/Burma, than twentieth-century China or the last decades of the former Soviet Union.[5] At the same time, perhaps paradoxically, law and order gradually broke down over the 1990s and 2000s, and as Iraqis were exposed to increasing arbitrariness and could no longer rely on the conventional institutions of the state, they turned toward pre-state organizations such as family, tribe, kin and sect to protect them from the state and from each other. Since the Communists had effectively been killed off or driven abroad decades earlier, it was only the clandestine Shi'i parties (especially al-Da'wa) that put up any serious opposition to Saddam Hussein and the Ba'th between 1991 and 2003.

When the Americans invaded Iraq in 2003, the neo-conservatives in the administration of President George W. Bush found comfort and justification from a group of (mainly) secular Shi'is in exile in Washington, led by Ahmad Chalabi. Chalabi was just the kind of person that US policy makers envisaged putting in charge of the new democratic Iraq, which they imagined would spontaneously rise from the ashes of the previous regime, who argued that the Americans and American tutelage would be welcomed with open arms. Chalabi himself had left Iraq in 1958 at the age of 10: Ayad Allawi had not been to Iraq since 1978, and other members of the opposition like Kanan Makiya and Ali Allawi had left in the mid-1970s, long before the general breakdown of the social and moral order that took place in the 1990s and early 2000s. None of them seems to have understood the profound changes in Iraqi society that a combination of the effects of the failed Kurdish and Shi'i uprisings of 1991, the UN sanctions and Saddam Hussein's steadily increasing paranoia had wrought upon Iraqi society.

The Iraqi state collapsed, or was not present, in much of southern Iraq (and more so in Kurdistan) throughout the 1990s and early 2000s, as a result of the factors that have already been mentioned and more generally because of "the regime's withdrawal from the social sphere" (Harling, 2008). Given the absence or deterioration of educational facilities, young people had few employment prospects, and they were no longer accepted into the army. They lacked the capital or social contacts necessary to migrate in search of greater opportunities and so "menial jobs and criminal activity appeared to be their only horizon" (Harling, 2008). Such individuals, in their 20s and early 30s, would later become attracted to the Sadrist Movement, just as they had been to the populist message of Muhammad Sadiq al-Sadr: "By eradicating the Islamist parties in the early 1980s, isolating the *marja'iya* and retreating itself from society, the regime generated huge appeal for the particular form of religious-based mobilisation engineered by Sadr in the 1990s [and continued by his son in the period after the invasion]" (Harling, 2008). In general, Iraqi Shi'i society "displayed a relatively high degree of social organisation, in comparison with both the Sunni and the progressive component of Iraqi society ... this specificity largely contributed to its ascendency in post-2003 Iraq" (Harling, 2008). Needless to say, none of the Bush administration's appointees in charge of planning the Iraq invasion in Washington, between late 2001 and early 2003, were seriously encumbered by any real knowledge of the recent history and politics of the Middle East, let alone any appreciation for the kind of nuanced developments in Iraqi society that have just been described; none of their Iraqi interlocutors were familiar with them either. This ignorance, together with a highly simplistic (if tenaciously held) (mis)understanding of the role played by sectarianism in Iraqi politics, lies at the heart of many of the more egregious blunders perpetrated by the occupying forces after 2003, both civilian and military. In order to understand developments in the 1990s and 2000, it is necessary to go back to the period before the invasion of Kuwait and the events of 1990 and 1991.

Perceptions and Misperceptions: The Background to Iraq's Invasion of Kuwait[6]

In 1988, after "winning" the war against Iran on behalf of "the Arab nation," Saddam Hussein found himself in something of a cul-de-sac. His armed forces had increased enormously, from about 200,000 to one million men, with his sophisticated weaponry in the same proportion. The war had also been extremely costly in terms both of casualties and damage to physical infrastructure. Demobilization of the vast army was politically difficult because of the damage done to the economy, which meant that there would be limited employment opportunities for those who were released. It was time, then, for Saddam Hussein to assert himself once again and to assume the "leadership of the Arab nation" that he thought to be his by right.

The decision to invade Kuwait most likely had four principal roots. First, Saddam Hussein's almost pathological ambition and his desire to carve out a major leadership role for himself within the Arab world, which the rather humdrum post-war realities were preventing; second, the fact that he had created an enormous military machine that could not easily be immobilized; third, the sense that the great changes taking place in Eastern Europe in the late 1980s would mean that neither he nor "the Arab masses" could continue to rely upon the broad support of the Soviet Union and its allies; and, finally, the decision was almost certainly based on a false set of premises and an extremely limited understanding of what the world outside of Iraq and the world outside of the Middle East would tolerate.

Three important points should be made here. In the first place, in spite of the fact that Iraq had one of the most, vicious and tyrannical regimes in the Middle East at the time, Saddam Hussein always managed, at least until he invaded Kuwait, to attract a following both within Iraq and in the rest of the Arab world. Some of this following was opportunistic, but Saddam Hussein's stridently anti-imperialist, and until 1984—when Iraq restored its diplomatic relations with the United States—anti-Zionist, rhetoric also found an echo in the streets and refugee camps in the Arab world, especially in Jordan, the West Bank and Gaza, as well as among certain Arab intellectuals (see Makiya, 1993: 231–327). Secondly, there was a sense, in both Arab and Western business circles, that however ruthless Saddam Hussein might be, he "got things done," somewhat in the spirit of an earlier dictator who "at least" made the trains run on time. Finally, although he would have lost the war with Iran had it not been for the arms and support he received from the West, the folk memory in the region was sufficiently selective (or short-term) for it to be widely believed that, unlike most other Arab rulers, he had never been afraid to stand up to the West.

It had long been clear that the Soviet Union was too concerned about its relations with the West to throw its weight behind any Arab policy or manoeuvres that might crucially threaten Israel (see El Hussini, 1987). Nevertheless, since no Arab state or combination of Arab states had seriously entertained such ideas since 1973, this particular constraint had become less important, as Soviet assistance was still crucial in a variety of other ways (see Smolansky with Smolansky, 1991). It was not until 1986 that the United States and the West felt it prudent to make high-technology weaponry available to Iraq, enabling it to defeat Iran in 1988 and invade Kuwait in 1990. Until then, and indeed long afterward, almost all of Iraq's basic weaponry came from the Soviet Union; as long as the "old guard" remained in power in Moscow, Iraq could always count on deliveries of Soviet military *matériel*. Between 1985 and 1989, Iraq spent nearly $12 billion on arms, of which nearly $7 billion came from the Soviet Union. France, Iraq's second major supplier, provided just over $2 billion of arms over the same period. Hence, the new atmosphere of *glasnost* and *perestroika* of the latter 1980s, culminating in the collapse of the regimes in Eastern Europe and the Soviet Union, was highly unsettling to Saddam Hussein.

There were other ominous developments. Since the latter part of the 1980s, Iraq had openly enjoyed close relations with the United States and other Western countries, partly because of its value as a market for armaments and for more conventional consumer goods, and partly because of the Ba'th's stance first against communism and then against Iran. The United States supplied a large proportion of Iraq's agricultural needs; in addition, there had been spectacular increases in Iraq's oil exports to the United States over the 1980s. In 1984, 1.2 percent of Iraq's oil (10.1 million barrels) went to the United States; in the first seven months of 1990 alone (the invasion of Kuwait took place on August 2) the proportion was 32.2 percent, or 514.5 million barrels, just under 9 percent of all United States oil imports (OPEC, 1991: Tables 51, 56). In addition, throughout most of the 1980s, the United States and the West had sedulously built up Iraq's strategic arsenal (often in contravention of their own export regulations) and were guarded in their criticism of Iraq's human rights record.

When the clouds began to gather early in 1990, Saddam Hussein seemed to come to the conclusion that this close relationship was coming to an end. Hence, beginning in February 1990, he launched a virulent campaign against the United States and Israel, presenting himself as the only steadfast Arab leader capable of defending the Arab nation against the West and its allies in the region. The logical extension of such policy was the invasion of Kuwait.

One of the major unanswered questions of this whole episode is why Saddam Hussein continued on a course of action in which he could not conceivably have prevailed instead of making a fairly honourable retreat.[7] Nasser's seizure of the Suez Canal was often mentioned in comparison, but Nasser was taking over a waterway owned and run by foreigners that ran through his own country, in which he himself was extremely popular. In contrast, Saddam Hussein was invading the territory of a small and defenceless neighbour, which had spent much of the previous decade paying his debts; this aside, there was no particular sense in which Kuwait was engraved on every Iraqi's heart.[8] Most Iraqis were heartily sick of military adventures and had little enthusiasm for fighting after eight years of war with Iran. Furthermore, while the Kuwaitis had certainly been grumbling at the prospect of being asked to pay for Iraqi rearmament for the foreseeable future, there was no reasonable sense in which they could have "threatened" Iraq.

Much has been made of the encouragement that Hussein may or may not have received from April Glaspie, the American ambassador in Baghdad, and from President George H.W. Bush. From the published accounts of her meetings with Saddam Hussein in late July 1990, it seems clear that Glaspie (an Arabic-speaking career diplomat) *did* underestimate the seriousness of the situation and put an over-optimistic gloss on the substance of her meetings in the reports that she sent to Washington. However, although she may have gone so far as to give the impression that the United States would look the other way if Iraq went about adjusting its borders by taking over Kuwait's part of the Rumayla oilfield, or quietly annexing the small islands of Bubyan and Warba (which Iraq had long been anxious to lease in order to expand its coastline on the Gulf),[9] it was surely the height of wishful thinking on Hussein's part to imagine, as has sometimes been asserted, that he was being given an American go-ahead for a full-scale invasion or annexation of Kuwait.[10]

Reaction to the invasion of Kuwait on August 2, 1990 was swift: in broad terms, no Arab state supported Iraq, but some, notably Jordan, Yemen and Yasser Arafat and the PLO, hesitated to condemn the action outright. The United Nations Security Council quickly passed a number of resolutions condemning Iraq, calling for its immediate withdrawal from Kuwait and declaring punitive trade and financial sanctions. On August 7, President Bush ordered an immediate airlift of American troops to Saudi Arabia; on August 8, Iraq proclaimed that Kuwait was an integral part of Iraq (it was to become Iraq's nineteenth province on August 28), and Turkey and Saudi Arabia closed the pipelines running across their territories from Iraq. Arab and Asian guest workers began to pour out of Kuwait across Iraq toward the Jordanian border. The price of oil rose steadily, from about $20 per barrel before the crisis to above $40 by mid-September 1990; neither Iraq nor Kuwait were exporting oil.

At the end of November 1990, the United Nations issued Resolution 678 authorizing member states to use all means necessary to oblige Iraq to withdraw from Kuwait by January 15, 1991. Over the next few weeks, several mediation efforts were made, but Hussein remained adamant. During the autumn of 1990, the United States put together an anti-Iraq coalition of 30 states, including Egypt and Syria, almost all of which sent token detachments to Saudi Arabia. In the end, the coalition forces mustered some half a million troops. When Saddam Hussein failed to respond to the ultimatum in Resolution 678 by the end of January 1991, the United States and its allies began to bomb various "strategic" targets within Iraq, causing large numbers of civilian deaths and considerable damage to the country's infrastructure. Iraq retaliated by launching Scud missiles at targets in Israel and Saudi Arabia. After five weeks of bombing, a ground offensive was launched on February 24, which ended with Iraqi troops being driven out of Kuwait and the destruction of much of the regular Iraqi Army on February 27 when a ceasefire was declared.

The Risings in the Shi'i South and Kurdistan

Shortly after the ceasefire, uprisings against the Iraqi regime, encouraged by the US and Britain, broke out in southern Iraq and in Kurdistan (see Romano, 2006: 204–206). By March 4, Kurdish Peshmerga forces had taken Sulaymaniyah, and by March 24 were in control of most of Kurdistan, including the towns of Arbil and Kirkuk. Although the "rebels" in the south gained control of large areas between the end of February and the beginning of March, units of the Republican Guard responded with exceptional brutality and were soon able to regain the upper hand in

Basra, Najaf and Karbala. In the southern cities, the insurgents captured and killed local Ba'thist officials, members of the security services and their families. When the Republican Guard regained control of the southern cities, it carried out indiscriminate mass executions of the population. Many tanks were painted with the slogan "*La shi'a ba'd al-yawm*" (No Shi'is [will survive] after today) and there was widespread destruction of Shi'a shrines in the Holy Cities. The complexity of these events is illustrated in an article by Peter Harling, who notes that one of the principal flash points of the largely Shi'i intifada in the south against the regime in 1991 was the Sunni enclave of Zubayr. He also lists the names of prominent Shi'i Ba'thists in the south who made use of their local knowledge and connections to put down the rising (Harling, 2007: 168–69).

The failure of the risings also reflected the general unpreparedness and disunity of the opposition. The difficulties of mobilizing are obvious; nevertheless, the opposition remained unable to capitalize on the clear weakening of morale in the army and on the increasingly sorry state of the economy. In the autumn of 1990, for example, "for the first time under Saddam's rule, feeding the people [had become] a serious problem" ('Abd al-Jabbar, 1994: 101). With hindsight, it is difficult to escape the conclusion that President Bush might have been wiser to have brushed aside the reservations of his Saudi and Turkish interlocutors in 1991 and ordered General Schwarzkopf to march on to Baghdad. History has not vindicated his judgment that it was somehow "safer" (in regional and strategic terms) to maintain Saddam Hussein's regime in power than to intervene in support of the risings against the regime, which might well have succeeded.

Sanctions and the United Nations Inspections

United Nations Resolution 661 of August 6, 1990 "froze Iraqi financial assets abroad and banned imports and exports, allowing only medical supplies to be imported without restrictions, and, in humanitarian circumstances, foodstuffs" (UNSC, 1990). As Sarah Graham-Brown has explained in great detail, the original sanctions regime was modified after the ceasefire in April 1991; although Iraq was still not allowed to export oil, it was permitted to import foodstuffs and "materials and supplies for essential civilian needs" (under Resolution 687) (1999: 56–104). Clearly, it was never envisaged that the sanctions would be in place for 12 years, and the long passage of time had a number of unforeseeable consequences. At least in theory, the severity of the sanctions was considerably reduced by various United Nations Resolutions that eventually permitted Iraq, under UN supervision, to sell first $2 billion net (Resolution 986) and then $5.26 billion gross, $3.55 billion net (Resolution 1153), worth of oil in exchange for food every six months.[11] Resolution 1153 also accepted the principle that some of the money (up to $300 million) could be used for replacement and repair of the oil facilities. In October 1999, the Security Council raised the revenue cap to $8.3 billion.

Attempts to introduce oil-for-food arrangements had begun on the United Nations side as early as 1991 but had been rejected by Iraq since they were to be accompanied by on-site monitoring, and also required Iraqi acceptance of the presence of the United Nations Special Commission on Disarmament (UNSCOM), set up in May 1991. Before January 1996 (when it reluctantly accepted Resolution 986), Iraq held out for, but could not obtain, the comprehensive lifting of sanctions. The continuing revelations of the extent of Iraq's nuclear, chemical and conventional weapons arsenals, which were brought to light both by high-level Iraqi defectors and by the work of UNSCOM, made the lifting of sanctions unlikely.

The overriding argument against sanctions—that their indiscriminate nature punishes the innocent and has little effect on the guilty parties in the regime itself—was persuasive at the time and is even more persuasive with hindsight. Various international organizations wrote heart-rending reports of the effects of the shortages of basic foodstuffs and medicines; the monthly ration was reduced by 40 percent in October 1994, infant mortality rose alarmingly and severe malnutrition among young children was widely reported by both internal and external observers. The provision of education and health care deteriorated noticeably; in education, large numbers of teachers left the profession, with the result that fewer children could go to school, while diseases associated with poverty virtually eliminated over the previous decades (such as kwashiorkor, tuberculosis and respiratory and digestive illnesses), began to reappear after 1991. In January 1996, a middle-ranking civil servant earned ID 5,000 a month; a chicken cost ID 4,000. Many families were forced to sell most of their property and possessions. By 1996, some three million Iraqis had left the country to live abroad (mostly via Iran and Jordan; the Syrian border was reopened in June 1997).[12] On the other hand, those close to Saddam Hussein and his circle made fortunes from the organization of the rationing system and from speculation in foreign currency, illegal oil sales and other forms of profiteering.

Sarah Graham-Brown has carefully described the great difficulties facing the various international aid agencies and the NGOs, as well as the tensions between them and the major coordinating body, the United Nations High Commissioner for Refugees (UNHCR), and the other United Nations agencies charged with weapons inspection and with supervising the sanctions. Neither the NGOs nor the United Nations agencies could have reasonably foreseen that the crisis would drag on, so while accusations of "short-termism" are not without foundation, the failings of these humanitarian organizations were due almost entirely to a combination of the ambiguous (and often inconsistent) political will of the international community and the obstructive policies of the Iraqi regime.[13] These obstacles were not unrelated to the difficulties faced (or caused) by the UNSCOM teams and the fact that inspection and aid were being carried out by different branches of the same organization.

Kurdish Politics since 1991

The creation of a "safe haven" under international protection over most of the Kurdish area in 1991 led to the gradual withdrawal of Iraqi civil and military authorities from the region and, in time, to the creation of a de facto Kurdish autonomous region. Elections to a regional government were held in May 1992; the closeness of the vote (a more or less even split between the Kurdistan Democratic Party [KDP] and the Patriotic Union of Kurdistan [PUK]) resulted in Mas'ud Barzani of the KDP and Jalal Talabani of the PUK as joint leaders of the politico-administrative entity that emerged.

The Kurdish government's difficulties were compounded by a series of personal, regional, national and international problems. In broad terms, the two leaders presided over followings that were largely defined by region, and, in addition, they had been brought up in very different ideological schools. Barzani (b. 1946) had inherited the leadership of the KDP from his father, Mulla Mustafa, who symbolized an old-fashioned Kurdish identity that was (simplifying a more complicated reality) more "tribal" than "political," and whose over-reliance on Iran and the United States could be said to have been largely responsible for the Kurds' disastrous defeat in 1975. In contrast, Talabani (b. 1933) and his father-in-law, Ibrahim Ahmad (1914– c. 2003) of the PUK, represented what they claimed to be a more progressive political line, in the sense that Ahmad and Talabani were both critical of Mulla Mustafa's political judgment, trying to find common ground with the Ba'th in the late 1960s and early 1970s, and being extremely wary of Barzani's close ties with the United States and the Shah.[14] Thus Ahmad and Talabani broke away from Barzani's KDP to found the PUK in Damascus in 1976. While Mas'ud Barzani inherited his father's tribal supporters (who showed little interest in changing or reforming the archaic social structures that persist in parts of the region), Talabani's followers tend to come from more educationally sophisticated and socially aware strata in the larger cities of the east and south of the area. Of course, given the checkered history of the relations of both the KDP and the PUK with the Iraqi Communist Party, attempts at neat classifications of this kind cannot always account for actions taken by the two leaders to serve some temporary interest or other. A further overarching problem is the intense and mounting suspicion that "Kurdish autonomy" provoked in the chanceries of Iraq's two northern neighbours, Turkey and Iran, both fearful of the domino effect this might have had on their own Kurdish populations;[15] to simplify a complex reality, both states, particularly Turkey, continue to intervene in Iraqi Kurdish affairs.

On several occasions, the bitter rivalry between the two men and their followers has seriously threatened the survival of the autonomous region. The executive, which was supposedly responsible for the day-to-day administration of the region, was composed of equal numbers from both parties, but could not bring itself to act in unison, and patronage and corruption were rife on both sides. Given that both the KDP and the PUK command large numbers of armed men, and that there were plenty of other former Peshmerga and/or *jash* irregulars whose support could be bought or traded by either side, the potential for infighting can easily be imagined. In the summer of 1996, at Talabani's invitation, Iranian troops entered the area controlled by the PUK; in August, Barzani called for assistance from Baghdad to remove them. Forty thousand Iraqi troops were sent to Arbil, which they captured from the PUK with the assistance of the KDP. After the capture of Arbil, Iraqi intelligence sought out and executed opponents of the regime who had taken refuge there, together with some of those attached to a rather rudimentary organization funded by the CIA, which, it had been hoped, would overthrow the regime in Baghdad. Iraqi forces retreated, but the message was clear: no independent entity could survive in Kurdistan as long as Saddam Hussein remained in power, given the intense and apparently endemic factionalism of those who controlled the region. On the other hand, a new order did emerge in Kurdistan between 1991 and 2003, involving a degree of political and economic independence from Baghdad that now seems irreversible.

Shi'i Politics since 1991

Given that they form the largest group in the population, it is hardly surprising that "the Shi'is" are no more politically monolithic than "the Kurds." One of the more persistent outsider misconceptions about Iraqi politics is the belief in a fundamental "from-time-immemorial" division between Sunnis and Shi'is (see Farouk-Sluglett and Sluglett, 2001: 190–200; and Sluglett, 2007), and that since the coming into being of the Islamic republic of Iran in 1979, a principal objective of the Shi'is has been the creation of an Islamic state in Iraq that would have a close relationship with Iran. Most Iraqi Shi'is consider themselves Iraqi Arabs first and foremost (as is clear from the experience of the Iran–Iraq War), and deeply resent the ghettoization to which successive regimes have subjected them. An important feature of developments since 2003 has been the rise of serious and often deadly *intra-* Shi'i conflicts, which reflects the differing experiences and objectives of different classes within the community.

In spite of comprising over half of the population, the Shi'is have always been discriminated against by Iraqi governments, especially under the Ba'th, beginning with the mass expulsions of Shi'is to Iran in the 1980s,[16] and culminating in the terrible revenge taken by the Republican Guard after the intifada in the South in 1991 and the subsequent forcible uprooting of a substantial proportion of the population of the southern marshes (see Sluglett, 2002a). Partly as a result of Iraqi air and ground attacks on the South and the virtual genocide being waged against the Marsh Arabs, the Western allies imposed a no-fly zone south of 32° N at the end of August 1992. The bogey of an "Islamic Republic of Iraq" was embraced with something akin to relief by Saudi Arabia, Turkey and the United States in 1991 as an excuse for retaining what they imagined would be a more subdued Saddam Hussein in power.

In brief (and it should be remembered that many of those who are Shi'i by birth are completely secular in outlook), the principal political divisions among Iraqi Shi'is are *Hizb al-Da'wa*; the organization formerly known as The Supreme Council for the Islamic Revolution in Iraq (SCIRI) and now known as the Islamic Supreme Council of Iraq (ISCI); and the Sadrists, a less formal organization associated with Muqtada al-Sadr and his Mahdi Army that emerged after the US invasion in 2003.[17] The word "political" is used deliberately since the influence of the *marja'* Ayatollah Sistani, although considerable, is not diffused through an organized political party (Nasr, 2007: 70–72). It is difficult to estimate the influence that Sistani still wields, but he has never supported the principle of *wilayat al-faqih* (mandatory clerical rule), the basis of the legitimacy of the Islamic Republic of Iran put forward first by Ayatollah Khomeini and his successor (since 1989), Ayatollah Khamene'i. *Hizb al-Da'wa* is the oldest of these movements, founded by clerics in Najaf in the late 1960s (see Farouk-Sluglett and Sluglett, 2001: 195–200), and is associated particularly with the charismatic Muhammad Baqir al-Sadr. Partly a reaction against secularism (especially, before the rise of the Ba'th, against communism), partly a call for the Islamization of politics addressed to Muslims in general rather than to Shi'is in particular, it seemed to present a major threat to the Ba'th regime, especially after Sadr's public espousal of the cause of the Iranian Revolution in 1979. SCIRI, closely associated with the Iranian regime, was founded by Muhammad Baqir al-Hakim in Iran in November 1982, to function as an umbrella organization of Iraqi Shi'is in exile in Iran, whom Iran intended to install in government in Baghdad when it "won the war against Iraq"; its militia, the Badr brigades, became notorious for torturing Iraqi prisoners captured during the war (Cockburn, 2008: 53). In general, SCIRI/ISCI, now led by 'Ammar al-Hakim (since the death of his father 'Abd al-'Aziz in August 2009) has always been more "clerical" and retained closer links to Tehran than *al-Da'wa*, whose leader is the current Prime Minister Nuri al-Maliki and which is less equivocally supportive of the notion of *wilayat al-faqih*.

In comparison with these two groups, which are both associated with the clergy attached to the shrines and *madrasas* of Karbala and Najaf, the much newer movement led by Muqtada al-Sadr is widely supported by the "Shi'i masses." Much of its appeal lies in its claim to represent the dispossessed and the fact that Muqtada is the son of Muhammad Sadiq al-Sadr, who was assassinated along with two other senior clerics by the regime in 1999.[18] The followers of Muqtada, mostly poor and uneducated, lacked the means or the opportunity to leave Iraq for Iran or Syria, still less the United Kingdom or the United States, and of course there were no longer any secular parties that might otherwise have accommodated these strata of the population.

Iraqi Politics between 1991 and 2003

In a formal sense, Iraqi politics changed little between the invasion of Kuwait and the invasion of Iraq by US forces in 2003. A despotic, beleaguered ruler ran a state that he impoverished to the utmost degree with the assistance of a few long-time associates and close family members, tacitly if not always enthusiastically supported by many of his neighbours (see Tripp, 2007: 259–67). Since the Ba'th Party had been in power (at least in a formal sense) since 1968, and Saddam Hussein himself had been in sole charge since 1979, no effective alternative authority with widespread recognition or appeal was ever able to build itself up either inside or outside of the country. No exiled Lenin, no imprisoned Mandela, was waiting to take over the leadership. In this dismal scenario, Saddam Hussein was greatly assisted by external forces, including the Iranian Revolution; the slight rise in oil prices in 1999–2000—when Iraqi oil production increased—the gradual crumbling of the alliance against him from the more gung-ho days of 1990–91, and the long period of close relations with the West, which enabled him to build up a ruthlessly efficient security service as well as a formidable arsenal of conventional weapons and weapons of mass destruction. In addition, the slow progress of the Arab–Israeli peace process, especially during the governments of Binyamin Netanyahu and Ariel Sharon, and the relentless dashing of Palestinian hopes, occasionally produced demonstrations evoking the anti-Western and pro-Palestinian stance of Saddam Hussein.

For many Iraqis in exile in 1990–91, the invasion of Kuwait was a time of great anticipation. At last, the tyrant had overreached himself and would get his comeuppance. Such views were of course dismissed by Arab nationalists of various hues who, with a blithe disregard for their hero's ambiguous past, saw Saddam Hussein's defiant posturing as a major step toward the realization of the Arab nation, or the liberation of Palestine or whatever fantasy appealed to them most. On the whole, most Iraqis knew better, having lived under the Ba'th since 1968. Since the war and the failure of the intifadas that followed, the opposition gave the impression of being driven from pillar to post, unable to unite around a common goal and splitting into ever smaller *groupuscules*.[19] Hence, the only viable organizations to emerge after 2003 were Shi'i political parties.

At its apex, the regime itself was not without its problems. Coup attempts were regularly reported: in January, February and June 1992; in

September and November 1993; March, May and June 1995; and June and December 1996. Some of the plots involved senior members of Republican Guard units composed principally of members of the Dulaym, Jubbur and 'Ubayd tribes (from the Sunni heartland of western Iraq), and terrible vengeance was taken on these units in the spring and summer of 1995. There were also a number of high-level defections, perhaps the most spectacular of which was the departure to Jordan with their husbands and children of two of Saddam Hussein's daughters in August 1995. One of the sons-in-law—the two were brothers, and second cousins of Saddam Hussein—was Hussein Kamil al-Majid, formerly Minister of Defense and Military Industries, who was presumably able to give his debriefers in Amman accurate details of the regime's military capacity. In an act of extraordinary folly (apparently Hussein Kamil was cold-shouldered by most of the Iraqi exile community in Amman, and was also rather disappointed at not being adopted as heir apparent to the Iraqi presidency by the United States), the two sons-in-law returned to Iraq with their families in February 1996, where they and several other male members of their family were shot the next day, evidently on the orders of their father-in-law (see Baram, 1998: chapter 1). One consequence of this was the increase in the public visibility of Saddam Hussein's eldest son, 'Udayy, whose provocative behaviour seems to have been one of the main reasons behind the Kamels' defection.[20]

Inevitably, the upheavals within previously loyal and reliable tribes, the defections and the internecine family feuding somewhat reduced Saddam Hussein's support base, although not sufficiently to cause him to lose control. Charles Tripp has identified three groupings within the family who had strained relations with the president: Saddam Hussein's three maternal half brothers (Barzan, Sab'awi and Wathban); the al-Majids, his paternal cousins (that is, his sons-in-law the brothers Hussein Saddam Kamil, 'Ali Hasan al-Majid—"chemical 'Ali," the perpetrator of *al-Anfa*—and the latter's brother Abd al-Hasan), and his sons, 'Udayy and Qusayy. 'Udayy, who was involved in several quarrels with his father (most spectacularly after having shot his bodyguard, Sabah Mirza, in October 1988) and with other members of his father's extended family, was severely injured in an assassination attempt in December 1996; Qusayy, his younger brother, was also the target of an assassination attempt early in 1997. After 1998, there was a certain amount of backtracking by the president away from excessive reliance on family and kin networks and toward reinstating some of the previous importance of the Ba'th Party.

During the war with Iran in the mid-1980s, the regime had begun to turn toward the market economy, partly in an attempt to promote efficiency, but also to disencumber itself of part of the massive state sector. As in Eastern Europe, the bureaucratic backbone of the various state enterprises was composed of party members and party officials (Communist in Eastern Europe, Ba'thist in Iraq), who gradually found themselves either demoted or unemployed. Some of the slack was taken up by the military mobilization of the Iran–Iraq War and the invasion of Kuwait. At the same time, the regime started assiduously courting the tribes, bestowing favours on tribal leaders[21] and seeming to forsake the Ba'th Party. However, in the dire social and economic circumstances of the late 1990s and early 2000s, the Party enjoyed a brief return to favour, earning the president's praise for its attempts to monitor prices and for overseeing the fair distribution of supplies. In 1998, a number of older party loyalists were promoted, including some who had been associated with Saddam Hussein since the time of his attempt on the life of 'Abd al-Karim Qasim in 1959. In spite of this, the president still relied to the very end on his kitchen cabinet of faithful aides who were always at his side: Tariq 'Aziz, his mouthpiece to the rest of the world, 'Izzat Ibrahim al-Duri and Taha Yasin Ramadan.

Conclusion

The absence of statistics, and the general difficulty of access to Iraq since the beginning of the war with Iran, means that it is difficult to carry out any kind of broad analysis of the economy for the decade or so before the regime's overthrow. Saddam Hussein showed enormous agility in resisting and countering any threats to his personal rule by resorting to different expedients and seeking support from a variety of different groups. Yet it is almost impossible to discover how Iraq was actually run on a day-to-day basis, how the bureaucracy functioned, how essential services were maintained and so forth. It is not inconceivable that the sanctions and the severe circumstances in which Iraq found itself actually suited the regime's Machiavellian purposes, since it could always claim that its own benevolent intentions were being thwarted by the evil designs of the international community.

What seemed certain was that there could be no internal peace or reconciliation in Iraq until Saddam Hussein and his henchmen ceased to be in power. However, short of what actually happened in 2003, there were no particularly compelling reasons to suggest that such a change would be possible; the opposition within Iraq lacked both the means and the opportunity to effect its removal on its own. At the time of the invasion, Saddam Hussein was 66 and had no known health problems. 'Udayy's unpredictability and physical disabilities following the assassination attempt made him an unlikely successor, and given the generally strained relations between father and son, it seemed improbable that he would have been his father's nominee. For similar reasons, it was even less likely that 'Udayy would have been able to gather a significant body of supporters for any coup attempt of his own. The regime always rested on very fragile foundations; longevity does not necessarily imply stability. Saddam Hussein was able to stay in power because of his total monopoly of the means of coercion, power and patronage. Most of those who enjoyed the fruits of Saddam Hussein's long rule knew that they would not continue to do so if their patron disappeared, which gave them every reason not to break ranks.

However it was done (and it was done in an almost criminally incompetent fashion; see Sluglett, 2006; 2008), the ending of the regime in Baghdad was an essential precondition for the restoration of peace and stability in Iraq. It is difficult to argue with the general proposition that Iraq is better off without Saddam Hussein. In spite of the false claims by the US administration of the existence of weapons of mass destruction, of the regime's involvement with al-Qa'ida or of its alleged uranium purchases in Niger, there is no sense in which Saddam Hussein was unjustly demonized, or that his regime was made out to be worse than it actually was. Regardless of what has happened since 2003, there is no doubt about the nature and the extent of the atrocities that he committed against the people of Iraq.

It could be argued that the greatest mistake of Desert Storm in 1991 was that it was brought to an end before any definite settlement was reached. Given the United States' past record of military intervention, it is hard to accept the pious hand-wringing of officials to the effect that the administration would somehow have fatally exceeded its brief if the US military had forced the regime to surrender. On the contrary: the US would have gained kudos and respect for having supported widely popular risings in both the north and the south. It is too early to assess the possible long-term consequences of the disastrous aftermath of the US invasion, although after years of US occupation some semblance of security seems to be emerging in Iraq.[22] For most Iraqis, the end of one nightmare has been followed by the beginning of another, with no imaginable benchmark to suggest when the second might end. But, as Larry Diamond remarked in 2004, "in post-conflict situations in which the state has collapsed, security trumps everything: it is the central pedestal that supports all else. Without some minimum level of security, people cannot engage in trade and commerce, organize to rebuild their communities, or participate meaningfully in politics" (Diamond, 2004). Some five years later, it is difficult to imagine how long it will take before Iraqis can take part in such activities without fear, however fervently we hope that time will soon come.

Notes

1. Charles Tripp estimated that core support for the regime came from "500,000 or so [individuals] including dependants; these were the people whom Saddam Hussein needed to convince both that his leadership was better for their interests than that of any imaginable alternative and that they would lose everything if he were to be overthrown" (Tripp, 2007: 259).
2. For oil prices, see "Crude Oil Production, Iraq; Thousand Barrels per Day." http://www.economagic.com/em-cgi/data.exe/doeme/paprpiq.
3. See Energy Information Administration (2008). "Annual Oil Market Chronology," July. http://www.eia.doe.gov/emeu/cabs/AOMC/Overview.html.
4. The principal UN resolutions, 661 (August 6, 1990) and 687 (April 8, 1991), specifically excluded foodstuffs and medical and humanitarian supplies from the sanctions regime. The oil-for-food arrangements meant that Iraq's oil revenues could only be spent on food and medical supplies.
5. In the last decades of the Cold War, political dissidents like Andrei Sakharov, Natan Shcharansky or Václav Havel were sent into internal exile or imprisoned (Sakharov was exiled to Nizhny Novgorod between 1980 and 1986; Shcharansky was jailed between 1978 and 1986 and Havel between 1979 and 1984) rather than being murdered or tortured to death, the fate of most opponents of the Iraqi regime between 1970 and 2003.
6. Much of what follows is adapted from Marion Farouk-Sluglett and Peter Sluglett, *Iraq since 1958: from Revolution to Dictatorship*, 281–310.
7. Much the same question might be asked about his actions in 2003.
8. cf. "[President 'Abd al-Karim] Qasim committed his greatest error in 1961 when he attempted to divert the Iraqi people's attention away from domestic problems by resorting to the timeworn tactic of Iraqi leaders in trouble: reviving the claim to Kuwait" (Mufti, 1996: 139).
9. For details of these negotiations/requests between 1965 and 1990, see Schofield, 1991 and Sluglett, 2002b.
10. At the meeting on 25 July, Glaspie told Saddam Hussein that she had been instructed to ask him about his intentions *vis-à-vis* Kuwait (*The New York Times*, 1990). His reply was vague and long-winded, and it is clear that she did not press him to give any specific undertakings. While she does not seem to have expressed herself forcefully enough, it is difficult to argue that she was deliberately egging him on, except in the very limited sense outlined above. It is also

most unlikely that the United States, faced with the cataclysmic changes taking place in Eastern Europe and the former Soviet Union, was eager for a confrontation with Iraq (Kessler, 2008: A15).
11 The $1.71 billion difference was appropriated by the United Nations for war reparations, Turkish pipeline transit fees and so forth.
12 It is worth noting that this process had begun well before 2003.
13 As time went on, the "united international front" against Iraq gradually began to crack, largely because a number of major businesses had either lost lucrative business deals in Iraq or were eager to pursue new ones. Thus French, Italian, Russian and Spanish oil companies were vying for concessions in various unexploited oil-bearing areas in the mid-1990s, and the Australian consortium Broken Hill Proprietary (BHP), was later found to have been exploiting the oil-for-food arrangements for its own benefit and was seeking an exclusive contract for the exploitation of the Halfaya field in 1996–97 (Marriner, 2006). For more details see: "Record of Conversation: Mr. Downer and BHP Billiton," 23 July 2003, available from http://www.ag.gov.au/www/inquiry/offi.nsf/indexes/images/AWB.0269.0014.pdf.
14 Jalal Talabani became President of Iraq in April 2005.
15 The Kurds form about 23 percent of the population of Iraq and Turkey, about 10 percent of the population of Iran; about 50 percent of the world's Kurdish population lives in Turkey. See McDowall (1996) for the broad historical context; for more recent developments, see Romano (2006), which covers events in all three countries.
16 See Farouk-Sluglett and Sluglett 2001, chapter 6. The Shi'is had begun to benefit from the general climate of secularism in the 1950s and 1960s, but lost out to a combination of Islamic fundamentalism and the desire of the Ba'th to control every aspect of Iraqi political and social life. There was the added quirk that they could be made out to be an Iranian "fifth column" if circumstances required.
17 In *The Shia Revival: How Conflicts within Islam will Shape the Future*, Nasr plays down the importance of *al-Da'wa*, but otherwise gives a readable account of the differences between the various groups (2007: 185–210).
18 "Sadiq al-Sadr believed that by withdrawing from the world the Shi'i hierarchy had abandoned their own people, whose sufferings, already great, had become a great deal worse after 1991. His plan was to persuade the regime that he was under its control so that he could build a mass movement, making Shi'ism once more relevant to the spiritual, psychological and economic needs of the faithful" (Cockburn, 2008: 82–83).
19 In "Saddam Hussein et la débâcle triomphante; Les ressources insoupçonnées de Umm al-Ma'ârik," Peter Harling develops the interesting argument that it is possible to interpret the actions of the regime as directed "non pas au dépassement mais à la pérennisation de la crise, qui devient la condition paradoxale de la stabilité du pouvoir" (2007: 158).
20 Baram says that "Uday commandeered Husayn Kamil's corner of the market in military procurement" (1998). Tripp writes that "Udayy took over Kamil's share of the oil smuggling business" (2007: 267).
21 Such government appointees were popularly derided as *shuyukh al-tisa'inat*, the *shaykhs* of the 1990s.

22 A sceptical observer might wonder whether the beneficiaries of the "Sunni Awakening" in the province of Anbar, whose success in dealing with al-Qa'ida has been hailed as such a major achievement, might not be tempted to turn their US-supplied weapons against their fellow citizens when the time comes for the US to leave.

Works Cited

'Abd al-Jabbar, Faleh (1994). "Why the Intifada Failed," in *Iraq since the Gulf War: Prospects for Democracy*, edited by Fran Hazelton. Pages 97–117. London: Zed Press.

Baram, Amatzia (1998). *Building toward Crisis: Saddam Husayn's Strategy for Survival*. Washington, DC: Washington Institute for Near East Policy.

Cockburn, Patrick (2008). *Muqtada al-Sadr, the Shia Revival, and the Struggle for Iraq*. New York: Scribner.

Diamond, Larry (2004). "What Went Wrong in Iraq?" *Foreign Affairs*. Vol. 83, No. 5: 34–56.

El Hussini, Mohrez Mahmoud (1987). *Soviet–Egyptian Relations 1945–85*. Basingstoke: Macmillan.

Farouk-Sluglett, Marion and Peter Sluglett (2001). *Iraq since 1958: From Revolution to Dictatorship*. 3rd ed. London: I.B. Tauris.

Graham-Brown, Sarah (1999). *Sanctioning Saddam: The Politics of Intervention in Iraq*. London: I. B. Tauris.

Harling, Peter (2007). "Saddam Hussein et la débâcle triomphante. Les ressources insoupçonnés de Umm al-M'ârik." *L'Irak en perspective. Revue du monde musulman et de la Méditerranée*. Vol. 117–118: 157–78.

––––––– (2008). "Building on Sand? Buttressing the Saddam-era Body of Knowledge." Unpublished paper presented to the colloquium on "Writing the History of Iraq: Historiographical and Political Challenges," Geneva. November 6–8.

Kessler, Glenn (2008). "Ex-Envoy Details Hussein Meeting." *The Washington Post*. April 3: A15.

Makiya, Kanan (1993). *Cruelty and Silence: War, Tyranny, Uprising and the Arab World*. London: Cape.

Marriner, Cosima (2006). "BHP Billiton Embroiled in Iraq Oil-for-Food Scandal." *The Guardian*. January 23.

McDowall, David (1996). *A Modern History of the Kurds*. London: I. B. Tauris.

Mufti, Malik (1996). *Sovereign Creations: Pan-Arabism and Political Order in Syria and Iraq*. Ithaca, NY: Cornell University Press.

Nasr, Vali (2007). *The Shia Revival: How Conflicts within Islam Will Shape the Future*. New York: Norton.

The New York Times, International (1990). "Excerpts from Iraqi Document on Meeting with U.S. Envoy." September 23. Available at: http://chss.montclair.edu/english/furr/glaspie.html.

Organization of Petroleum Exporting Countries (OPEC) (1991). *Annual Statistical Bulletin*. Vienna.

Romano, David (2006). *The Kurdish National Movement: Opportunity, Mobilization and Identity*. Cambridge: Cambridge University Press.

Schofield, Richard (1991). *Kuwait and Iraq: Historical Claims and Territorial Disputes*. London: Royal Institute for International Affairs.

Sluglett, Peter (2002a). "The Marsh Dwellers in the History of Modern Iraq," in *The Iraqi Marshlands: A Human and Environmental Study*, edited by Emma Nicholson and Peter Clark. Pages 223–39. London: Politico's Press.

——— (2002b). "The Resilience of a Frontier: Ottoman and Iraqi Claims to Kuwait, 1871 to 1990." *International History Review*. Vol. 24: 783–816.

——— (2006). "The Blunder Books: Iraq after Saddam." *Middle East Journal*. Vol. 60, No. 2: 361–68.

——— (2007). "The Implications of Sectarianism in Iraq." *Journal of Middle Eastern Geopolitics* (University of Rome). Vol. 2, No. 1: 45–53.

——— (2008). "Imperial Myopia: Some Lessons from Two Invasions of Iraq." *Middle East Journal*. Vol. 62, No. 4: 593–609.

Smolansky, Oles M. with Bettie M. Smolansky (1991). *The USSR and Iraq: The Soviet Quest for Influence*. Durham, NC: Duke University Press.

Tripp, Charles (2007). *A History of Iraq*, 3rd ed. Cambridge: Cambridge University Press.

United Nations Security Council (UNSC) (1990). *The Situation between Iraq and Kuwait*, Resolution 661. August 6. New York.

3
Inching Forward
Iraqi Federalism at Year Four

David Cameron

It is difficult to conceive of a more disastrously mismanaged international initiative than the United States' (US) invasion and occupation of Iraq. Seizing the opportunity offered by the tragedy of 9/11, President George W. Bush and his ideologically committed colleagues went after the dictator they wanted to unseat, rather than pursuing the terrorists who had attacked the US. The Americans left the Afghan job unfinished, with Osama bin Laden still plying his trade from hideouts somewhere along the Afghan–Pakistani border. They went instead after Saddam Hussein, resting their case for invasion on a tissue of fabrications. Not finding al-Qaeda in Iraq, American policy inadvertently created it there, as well as much of the agony Iraqis have gone through since 2003.

Astonishingly, however, US policy has been present at the creation of some good developments in Iraq. Some real progress has been made, so much so that it is just possible to imagine that Iraq will stand up as America stands down. But, how could this be? The establishment of a stable, constitutional regime in Iraq after the Americans leave would be a colossal achievement. This may not happen, but one can voice the possibility without being thought a fool. If it does happen, it will be a matter of high moment—both for students of regime change and democratic transition and for future policy makers—to understand how such a result could appear at the end of such a botched process.

The Iraqi Constitution was drafted in the summer of 2005 and approved by a national referendum in October of that year. Four years on, it is too soon to render anything like a settled judgment on the success or failure of this remarkable and painful effort to establish constitutional government in Iraq. The most one can hope to do is offer something of a progress report, and sketch out, at least provisionally, the direction in which the country is moving. This I hope to do in this chapter, focusing in particular on the federal dimension of Iraq's constitutional arrangements. First, I offer some reflections on the link between constitutional government and federal government with reference to Iraqi political experience. Next, I share some thoughts on the Iraqi experience with federalism to date. Finally, I outline a scenario indicating how the next phase in Iraq's federal development might unfold.

Constitutional Government and Federal Government

The link between constitutional government and federalism is very strong, but the arrow of dependence runs one way. One can easily imagine the existence of constitutional government without the presence of the federal principle; it happens all of the time. But—if constitutional government is government by rules—it is difficult to think of how a federal system of government could work for any length of time in the absence of a constitutional order. Federalism is, in this sense, derivative in character, contingent upon the existence of a constitutional regime. This is because it is necessarily a government of rules, with a constitution at its core. Rules for relating the federal units to one another and to the centre require a written constitution and an autonomous umpire, like the courts, at the very least to oversee the operation of the federal units and to settle disputes among them.

The trappings of a democratic constitutional political system are normally part and parcel of an operating federal regime—constitutionalism, the rule of law, the respect for rights, democratic elections and the like. In federal government, as in other constitutional regimes, the conflicting ambitions of politicians are confined by a system of enforceable rules. The main difference with federalism is that the struggle for power is territorially dispersed, rather than concentrated on one central hierarchy. It is difficult to imagine a durable federation to which the constitutional shibboleth, "a rule of laws, not of persons," is inapplicable.[1] Thus, an appreciation of what is happening in federal Iraq needs to be set in the context of what is happening in constitutional Iraq.

For many years, Iraq was an authoritarian dictatorship that offered little scope for normal politics or for the fashioning of the arts of political activity. Like most authoritarian regimes, Saddam Hussein's was highly centralized, with power concentrated in the president and policy very much the product of the personal will and preferences of Saddam himself. The underlying social and cultural diversity of the society was given little means of expression, and the Sunni population in general and the members of Saddam's Tikriti tribe in particular were given privileged roles in Iraq's governing institutions—the army, the police, the oil and gas industry and the public service.

Iraq was, then, a country with little experience with the rules-based systems employed elsewhere to create the public space within which democratic politics could be carried on. Still less, it was a society with a sense of what it meant to disperse and decentralize political power in recognition of the social, cultural and linguistic diversity of the political community. Iraq, potentially a federal society in its social composition, was the very antithesis of a federal country in its political structure.

Very rapidly after the fall of Saddam and then the effective collapse of the Iraqi state—inexplicably tolerated by the United States—the underlying diversities of Iraqi society, and the cleavages that defined them, surfaced, often in a toxic form, as people, finding themselves in a condition of radical insecurity, resorted for survival and protection to the primordial loyalties of family, tribe and sect.[2] This reality shaped political parties, election outcomes and governance in the early years. It also shaped constitutional politics.

Another factor has been in play. Iraqis did not wrest political power from a dictator; the chance to start again did not come as a result of a freedom struggle but as a result of geopolitics. The global superpower, mauled by al-Qaeda in 9/11, decided to invade Iraq and overturn Saddam Hussein's government. The people of Iraq were delivered an ambiguous opportunity for a fresh start—freedom of a kind, but under the provisional control of an occupying power. Psychologically, this must have been deeply troubling for Iraqis and their political leaders; cooperating or not cooperating with the Americans were each problematic in their own way.

The elections of January 2005 produced the interim government and set the stage for the constitutional negotiations of the following summer. The outcome of the constitutional talks was influenced by several factors, including pressure, largely from the Americans, to complete the job quickly, the aggressive and focused participation of the Kurdish representatives, the active engagement of the Shi'a leadership in the talks and the relative absence of Sunni representatives from the constitutional negotiations. To a significant degree, the outcome was pre-figured in the vector of political forces within which the talks were conducted.

The constitution was agreed to by the negotiators in August 2005 and approved in a referendum on October 15, 2005. The referendum process, although controversial, nevertheless ultimately attracted broad public participation, and, but for the relatively slight Sunni participation, gave the country's founding document a fair degree of legitimacy. A commitment was made, largely to give some reassurance to the Sunni community, that changes could be made to the constitution to address their concerns, employing the original rules for ratification. The recommendations of the Constitutional Review Committee, charged with this task, have not yet been acted upon.

The negotiation of the 2005 Iraqi Constitution was a considerable achievement. However incomplete or imperfect the product, and however much the negotiations took place under the watchful eye of the Americans, it was strikingly impressive that a fragile interim political regime, functioning in the midst of endemic and crippling violence, was able to fashion a bargaining and ratification process that produced a constitutional outcome in such a short space of time. Anyone who observed the action in that summer and fall of 2005 would acknowledge that constitutional politics was being conducted—messy, confusing and in many respects disagreeable, but nevertheless an organized, largely peaceful political activity addressing fundamental questions of identity and the assignment of political power, and leading, with the success of the referendum, to an authoritative outcome. The photographs of murdered legislators that were pasted up on the wall of the conference centre where the negotiations were taking place attested to the risks and the fragility of the process, but it was political negotiation and compromise that chiefly shaped the contours of the 2005 constitution.

The grand objective of the constitution is reflected in Article 1. It is the purpose of the constitution to establish "a single federal, independent and fully sovereign state in which the system of government is republican, representative, parliamentary, and democratic and this Constitution is the guarantor of the unity of Iraq" (Republic of Iraq, 2005). Since its passage, the world has witnessed a new constitutional order struggling to be born. It has not been easy. In the months following the approval of the Constitution, ordinary Iraqis were far more concerned about simple survival than about the niceties of constitutional government. Communities were terrorized by jihadists and militia, thousands of Iraqis were forced to leave their homes and neighbourhoods for safe havens elsewhere in the country or abroad, the organs of state were heavily populated by factions who used their control over ministries and public resources to protect and advance their interests, and journalists, political leaders, public officials and ordinary Iraqis were targeted with acts of violence.

Yet, amid the chaos, the false starts and the missed opportunities, there was halting progress. Political parties were formed and re-formed, elections, both national and provincial, were held, and legislation was passed. And the country's governing institutions—the political executive, police, army and the like—have gradually developed a greater capacity to act in support of a perceived national interest. Issues too dangerous to address in the short term have been temporarily set aside. Throughout, the constitution and the organs of state have been treated as rather more plastic than is the norm in more developed constitutional orders. For example, timetables for dealing with the reports of the Constitutional Review Committee, or the scheduling of elections, or the resolving of the issue of Kirkuk according to Article 140 are routinely ignored.[3]

An emergent constitutional order is discernable in Iraq, however, and is gradually accumulating authority, even if specific provisions are not always adhered to. Ultimately, one would expect that the requirements of the constitution and the obligations associated with the rule of law would impose themselves on the political actors, even when their interests counsel differently. Although this does not always happen, and there are cases where political will trumps constitutional obligation, the direction of development is largely positive. The challenges to the state as such are dwindling, and there are signs that the virulence of sectarian conflict within the Arab community is in decline. A very big question, however, is whether the reduced level of conflict will endure, now that the United States has commenced its staged withdrawal.

But consider this: there is no organized domestic political force threatening the existence of Iraq as a going concern. It would appear that the Sunni community is at last coming to terms with its fate as a powerful minority within the new Iraq; the Shi'a have not the slightest interest in fracturing a political order in which they form the majority; and, though popular sentiment in the Kurdish region may favour complete independence, the leadership has made a calculation that it is in that community's interest to remain part of the country, and they have effectively pursued their goals within that overarching framework. What is more, the failure of the regionalization movement in the south in 2009 suggests that any notion of secession on the part of that resource-rich part of Iraq is simply not in the cards at the moment. It would seem that, if there are major threats to Iraq's existence as a national political community, they come more from the neighbourhood rather than from inside the home.

The one thing that would change this picture is if the Kirkuk issue spun out of control. That area has been in dispute for years,[4] and, while the parties have managed to contain the conflict so far, they have not been able to resolve it. The issue pits Kurds against Arabs and the Kurdish Regional Government against the central government in Baghdad. Caught in the middle, and already suffering from the friction between the two main parties, are the minorities in the area, the Turkmen, the Chaldo Assyrians and others (Hiltermann, 2007).[5] In 2009, tensions have grown as each side has jockeyed for advantage. Loss of control over this issue would be fateful for Iraq, since it is aligned with the deepest cleavage in the country.

There is much that is impressive in what Iraqis have managed to do so far, and, increasingly, they will own their failures and achievements. With the gradual withdrawal of the United States, Iraqis are assuming greater responsibility for their own destiny, but what they achieve, for good or ill, will have a significant impact on a region not known for constitutionalism, democracy or the respect of human rights.

This is the context, then, in which I place the evolution of Iraqi federalism.

Iraq's Experience with Federalism So Far

The Constitution of 2005

The 2005 constitution established the provisions of a genuine, if incomplete and fragile, Iraqi federation. Consistent with the focused aspirations of the Kurds, it was a radically decentralized document, giving the Kurds the security of substantial self-determination within the framework of the Iraqi state. For most analysts, the powers vested in the regional units were breathtakingly extensive, and an examination of the powers that remained at the centre left many observers asking themselves whether the country could hold together.

The federation it sketched out was also highly asymmetrical. The Kurdish part of the country in the north was constituted as a federal region from day one, with the powers and prerogatives associated with regional status in the constitution. It was the only region so constituted, and remains the only region to this day. Not only that, it had a head start in its political and economic development, arising out of the space created by the establishment of the no-fly zone after the Gulf War, and its relative security has permitted a development of the economy and public infrastructure that has been largely absent elsewhere.

However, built into the structure of the constitution was a dynamic principle, whereby other governorates together or separately, could achieve regional status in the federation. In addition to its federal elements, there were a number of consociational features in the new arrangements, designed to ensure, for example, that members of the major communities composing Iraq enjoyed some guaranteed representation in the central institutions of the state, and some control over national policy making. Finally—and this was not surprising, given the time pressures imposed on the players—a great deal was left to be done after the ratification of the core document. The basic law contemplated a stream of consequential legislation that would flesh out the meaning of many of the provisions within it.

There was, then, in the consociational and federal dimensions of the constitution, a significant recognition of the underlying communitarian diversity of Iraqi society and the legitimacy of constitutional and political efforts to give it some expression. These, then, are the key features of Iraq's 2005 constitutional arrangements from the point of view of the story we are telling: federal; in limited degree, consociational; asymmetrical; evolutionary; and incomplete.[6]

Post-Constitutional Federal Developments in Iraq

In assessing how the federal project in Iraq is progressing, there are several trends or processes worth noting: the growing strength of central institutions; the reduction of sectarian conflict and the apparent reassertion of other forms of social and economic cleavage; popular resistance to, or lack of interest in, the "regionalization" process in the Arab parts of the country; and, despite the previous point, the growth in what might be called "federal consciousness."

Growing Strength of Central Institutions

There are some pretty clear indicators that Iraq's national institutions are becoming more professional and more capable of acting in the national interest. The gradual accumulation of power in Baghdad is something that has been frequently remarked on. Biddle, O'Hanlon and Pollack, writing in the September/October 2008 issue of *Foreign Affairs*, note the substantial growth in the size and competence of the Iraqi security forces since 2006. There have been serious efforts to weed out corrupt, incompetent and sectarian officers, and the waning of the passion for de-Baathification has meant that people with professional experience, many of them Sunnis, have been recruited. Biddle et al. state that, as of autumn 2008, 80 percent of the Iraqi army's officer corps and 50 percent of its rank and file were formerly in Saddam's army (2008). Yet the public perception of sectarianism in the force has improved: the proportion of Iraqis who believed that the army was non-sectarian increased from 39 percent in June 2007 to 54 percent in June 2008.

A similar process has been under way in the Iraqi National Police, which, under a talented commander, has retrained members of the force and recruited Kurds and Sunnis into its ranks; its greater professionalism and representativeness is reflected in shifting public attitudes. Those who believed that the Iraqi police were sectarian dropped from 64 percent in June 2007 to 52 percent in June 2008, and those who believed the police were corrupt dropped from 63 percent in June 2007 to 50 percent a year later (Biddle et al., 2008: 44–46).

Some of these developments became visible by inference when Prime Minister al-Maliki decided in 2008 to send Iraqi forces into Basra and Amara to clean out the Sadrist militia and assert the authority of the state. That he felt confident enough to do it and that it was successful are signs of a growing capacity within the organs of state to act in the national interest.

This trend is, of course, not welcomed by all. Iraqis have painful memories of the centralized power of Saddam Hussein, and many have espoused federalism particularly because of its capacity to disperse and limit political power. The Kurds are especially sensitive to this; given their historical experience, any increase in national power and capacity is alarming.[7] They successfully negotiated a federal model with a very weak centre for this reason, yet many analysts would argue that a functioning Iraqi federation requires national institutions that are capable of acting effectively on behalf of the country as a whole.

The growing strength of Baghdad, combined with the continued failure to resolve the conflicting claims over disputed, oil-rich territories in the border region between the Kurdish Regional Government (KRG) and the rest of Iraq, has set the stage for increased conflict (Hiltermann, 2009). The political leadership in the KRG may be less and less willing to let the unresolved issue of Kirkuk drag on while they watch the federal government slowly getting its act together. The apparent effort in the summer of 2009 to settle the issue unilaterally by approving a KRG Constitution that lays claim to the disputed territory and the oil and gas reserves that lie underneath suggests a Kurdish intention to force the issue.

Reduction of Sectarian Conflict and the Emergence of Other Cleavages

Since 2007, not only has there been a significant reduction in the level of violence in Iraq, but the sectarian flavour of the turmoil has greatly diminished as well. Perhaps echoing the apparent judgment of the Sunni community that it had no choice but to participate in the political life of the country, the Sunni insurgents in large numbers turned on al-Qaeda in Iraq and worked out with the Americans arrangements that gave them responsibility for local security. Muqtada al-Sadr's militia have lost strength and credibility, and their defeat in Basra has greatly reduced their clout.

As violent conflict has ceased to be the main means of political expression, interest has grown in electoral politics, and the results of the recent provincial elections reflects the shifting tides described above. Perhaps most striking about the provincial election results, described and analyzed by Raider Visser in a series of notes on his website (http://historiae.org/), are the weakening of the sectarian political parties that have been so powerful in Iraq until recently and the rise of parties representing more secular interests and more national perspectives.

While it is impossible to dispute the decline in violence in Iraq, explaining why this has happened and forecasting whether it will endure is a difficult matter. Clearly, an alteration in American military strategy and the strategic realignment of the Sunni community were an important part of the story. The gradual strengthening of the state has also clearly played a role. It is possible, too, sadly, that the violence itself may have been a factor; by forcing a physical separation among Iraq's communities, it may have rendered its further use less necessary in the eyes of its domestic perpetrators. A final possibility points us toward the future. It has been argued that those who have caused the violence and fed the sectarian conflict may just be waiting the Americans out; lie low until they leave and then get back to business after they are gone. While such factors as the Sunni repositioning and the growing strength of the state might suggest that Iraq is moving beyond its hideous phase of self-destructive chaos, the notion of waiting out the Americans leads to the fear that the warring communities, inflamed by outside agitation, might rise again.

The 2010 general election will offer some clear indications of which way the wind is blowing. If there is vigorous Sunni electoral participation, and if the trend away from sectarian partisanship reflected in the January 2009 provincial election results continues, a new government based on these realities may be formed. In that case, the capacity of Iraq to stand on its own two feet—to moderate its sectarian impulses and to suppress violence—may continue and even grow.

No Strong Desire to Create New Regions

The third feature of interest in assessing what is happening to federal Iraq is the apparent popular reluctance to establish new federal regions, which would give their inhabitants collectively distinctive powers not dissimilar to those enjoyed by the Kurds. This reluctance may be explained in part by reference to the political and attitudinal fluidity within which Iraqis are currently living. They are, after all, accustomed to the system of governorates.[8] One can understand citizens wanting to let the dust settle before deciding what enduring alteration in arrangements they would like to support. Once the main political configurations in the country have been stabilized, it will be easier for a political community in a governorate to see where their best interest lie, and how their aspirations can most effectively be achieved. In addition, despite the incalculable human costs of the conflict since 2003 and the hateful things members of one community have done to members of another, there remains a vigorous commitment to Iraq on the part of a great many Iraqis and, it appears, a consequent reluctance to push further down the road of federalism-as-division. Reidar Visser, writing in *Middle East Report Online*, refers to a poll done by the Iraq Center for Research and Strategic Studies in October 2008, which found that 69.8 percent of respondents identified themselves as "Iraqis," 10.8 percent identified themselves in ethnic terms, and 6.2 percent referred to sects (2009). This national view, it seems, is beginning to be reflected in electoral outcomes.

This national identification was apparently also reflected in the failure of a prominent Basra politician, Abd al-Latif, to secure enough names on a petition to force a referendum on the transformation of Basra into a federal region. In a campaign begun at the end of 2008, the proponents of turning Basra into a region were unable to reach the 10 percent threshold of support required, though they had managed to secure the 30,000 signatures (2 percent) of the electorate that were necessary to get the initiative started. This seems to indicate a lack of popular support for the proposal, although it must be admitted that securing that large a number of signatures would be a challenge under almost any circumstances. In addition, it might be easier for the governorate councils elected in the January 31, 2009, vote to launch regionalization initiatives on the basis of the required one-third support of the council members in the relevant governorates.[9]

Growth in Federal Consciousness

This may seem at odds with the previous point, but I do not think it is. A great many Iraqis are still coming to terms with this new system of decentralized political authority and what it implies. The Kurds are what one might call "federalists by fate." Given their historical experience and their geopolitical circumstances, a broad understanding among the Kurds of the merits of federalism, particularly understood as regional self-determination (self rule, more than shared rule) is not surprising.

For the other members of the Iraqi political community, the question is more perplexing. The Sunnis are currently making the adjustment from psychologically being the dominant group in the country to being a significant minority; the Awakening, or Sons of Iraq movement, in which elements of the Sunni leadership turned against al-Qaeda in Iraq, is a sign of that, as are the growing levels of Sunni electoral participation. It is, however, another big step to reach the point at which there can be serious community reflection on the role the federal system might play in advancing Sunni interests. That conversation will start in time, but it does not appear to be going on seriously just now. And for the Shi'a, federalism is a puzzle, and a consideration of the alternatives for regionalizing the Shi'a areas of the country raises significant questions of identity and direction:

- The Shi'a are in a clear majority position nationally: does that mean that it is in their interests to oppose the creation of regions in their part of the country and rather seek to control the central state?
- Shi'a form a distinct religious community: does that mean that a super region in the southern half of the country, gathering together the believers in a powerful super-region is the best course of action to follow?
- Shi'a are distributed in governorates throughout the Iraqi south: does that mean that the distinguishable political economies of the various governorates should receive political expression in the formation of a number of different regions?

This last point suggests a further complication, reflected in the provincial election results: non-sectarian definitions of identity and interest in Arab Iraq raise questions about whether the Sunni/Shi'a characterization of that population is appropriate and whether it should be the basis on which federal developments in Iraq are considered. There has been an inclination among some commentators in the West to view Iraq through a sectarian lens, but, as the country develops, that may become a less useful framework for understanding and analysis and a less appealing construct for Iraqis as they build their federal future.[10]

These questions, touching on sensitive questions of identity and interest, are fraught and do not yield easy answers, and they pit the interests of political parties and leaders against one another. From this perspective, it is not surprising that there have not been any successful regional or federalizing moves in the last months. But this does not mean that the ongoing political process over the next several years will not begin to provide answers. It is in this context that I suggest that there is a growing federal consciousness, even if it has not emanated in significant initiatives to determine the ultimate configuration of the regional units in the Iraqi federation. A debate about the form of federalism is an indicator of federal consciousness.

Anecdotally, I had occasion to gain a powerful sense of just how dynamic public opinion on federalism in Iraq is while working on a project that delivered training courses on democratic federalism to academics and government officials.[11] I went to Baghdad in August 2006 to begin the process; team members and I organized a project planning session with government and university administrators in Amman in November 2007; and then we offered three training workshops of two to three weeks in duration to about 25 participants each time. These took place in Amman in June/July 2007, August 2007 and February 2008. There was a concluding session in Erbil in November 2008. The participants were largely from faculties of law and departments of political science from universities all over Iraq. There was a mix of Shi'a, Sunnis and Kurds, plus some members of minority groups.

The evolution in attitude and outlook from one workshop to the next was fascinating. In the first workshop (June and July of 2007), there was deep skepticism about federalism among some participants, tension and sometimes heated exchanges (especially between the Kurdish participants and the others), a tendency to make speeches and defend political positions rather than engage in academic discussion and a striking degree of ignorance about the provisions of the 2005 Federal Constitution. By the time the third workshop was held nine months later in February 2008, the speech making and tension had gone, the fact that Iraq was, and was going to remain, federal was taken pretty much as a given, and the understanding of the federal provisions of the Iraqi Constitution was detailed and thorough. I do not say that everyone at the last workshop was keen on the idea of Iraq as a federation, but the federal reality of the country seemed to have become accepted as a durable fact, or assumption, when considering the country's future.

Looking Ahead

In 2006, when thinking about the possible future evolution of Iraq's new federal system, I used three scenarios to help with these reflections. Assuming that the country did not collapse into civil war or revert to authoritarian rule of some kind, it seemed to me that there were three broad possibilities. Iraq might move in the direction of what could be called *partial federalism*, composed of a highly autonomous Kurdish region, with no regions elsewhere, relatively weak governorates and a central government in Baghdad continuing to be the focal point for most Arab Iraqis. Alternatively, one might imagine the emergence of a *highly decentralized federation*, grounded in the weakness of the federal power in the 2005 Constitution; learning from the Kurds, other sub-national political communities, sectarian or not, could create powerful regional governments that would limit and control the federal government in Baghdad. The third possible future was the gradual appearance of a *balanced federation*, in which the national government asserts itself and is able to hold its ground vis-à-vis the powerful regional governments that would gradually be formed.

How does it look now? In terms of these three scenarios, one can see elements of the first and third—but not much of the second—in the present situation. The Kurds continue to strengthen the political and economic institutions required to support a strong regional community, and the national government in Baghdad is strengthening itself as well. What has not happened, or at least not yet, is the assertion of coherent regional power elsewhere in the land. But there still remain several possible futures embedded in Iraq's current reality.

Let me conclude by sketching one out, based on my understanding of the current political situation in Iraq. Again, this assumes that Iraq does not lapse into civil disorder or authoritarianism, but continues to inch forward on the path of constitutionalism. It has two components: asymmetry and what I call "federalism at variable speeds." I will discuss each briefly below.

The asymmetry is obvious. One of the most stable and most predictable elements in the equation is the Kurdish region. It will continue to be a well-organized, highly autonomous part of federal Iraq with a strong and distinct identity based on language, ethnicity and historical experience. The Iraqi federation, for as long as it endures, will necessarily be constructed around that existential reality. It seems unlikely that Kurdish aspirations for self government will generate a significant secessionist movement so long as the Kurds are allowed the space they require within Iraq. This, then, defines what will be a continuing asymmetry in Iraq's federal arrangements: the presence of a distinctive national community within the larger framework of Iraq. Federal policy will always have to take this into account. Indeed, even if the rest of the country were to be formed into regions, endowed with powers similar to those enjoyed by Kurdistan, its situation would still be asymmetrical because of the distinctive identity of the Kurds in Iraq and the national sentiments they share.

The second component of this scenario is "federalism at variable speeds." If it is true that the federal penny has dropped and there is a widespread and growing consciousness in Arab Iraq of the implications and possibilities of decentralizing power in a federation, it is reasonable to expect further developments on the decentralization front. But they will obviously happen at a different speed than what is happening in the Kurdish region, and, indeed, they will probably occur at different speeds in different parts of the rest of Iraq. The failure so far to mount successful regionalization movements, together with the passage of the law relating to governorates and the largely successful provincial elections of January 2009, suggest that the federalization of Iraq may proceed down two somewhat different paths.

The link between the governorates and the centre is very strong, and their dependence on Baghdad is considerable. This may mean that for a time, Baghdad may be able to manage the political evolution of the provinces with some success. However, over time, given the popular base that political leaders in the governorates will enjoy, there may well be increasingly assertive moves on the part of some governorates and a local desire for greater autonomy and self control.

Should that happen, one possibility is that some provincial councils will vote to hold referendums in their jurisdiction on the creation of a region, thus creating, if successful, a new federal unit or units in the federation. A second possibility—and one that would be easier to put into effect—is for governorates simply to begin acting like regions. There are plenty of resources in the constitution to assist governorates in pursuing this end. For many international analysts, one of the notable and unfortunate elements of the 2005 Constitution is the confusion and lack of clear differentiation between regions and governorates; the distinction between the two is blurred, and often the constitution assigns authorities and responsibilities to region and governorate alike. The division of powers section of the constitution (Section 4, Articles 109–115) virtually conflates governorates and regions, speaking again and again of the two as enjoying the same constitutional rights. The Iraqi Constitutional Review Committee was vigorously advised by the United Nations Assistance Mission in Iraq (UNAMI) and others to remove this ambiguity, but it explicitly chose not to do so in its report.

This ambiguity, I believe, embeds major "federal potential" in the governorates; that is to say, I think that there is constitutional scope for governorates over time to grow into significant federal units, endowed with powers not too dissimilar from full-fledged regions. On the basis of the present situation in Iraq, that seems a more likely occurrence in the short term than a rash of successful movements to create regions.

This, then, raises the possibility that over time one might see the emergence of a federal system in which there are two formally distinct types of subnational units: a Kurdish region (and possibly one or two other regions) on the one hand, and multiple Arab governorates on the other, with both playing a valid and authentic role in the ongoing functioning of the federation.

What will actually happen in the future to federal Iraq is anybody's guess, but these thoughts are offered in the spirit of sensing what may be intimated by the present situation, and therefore what might possibly occur. It seems clear that Iraq, with its new constitutional regime and its untried federal system, will experience significant and no doubt unpredictable change in the next while, and that its actual experience will probably prove the best forecasters wrong. That we can be speculating at all, however, about the federal and constitutional future of Iraq is a wonderful thing, and not something many of us would have been able to indulge in back in 2005 or 2006.

Conclusion

In this chapter, I have focused chiefly on constitutional developments in Iraq and the slow emergence of a federal system. If one pulls back further and surveys the prospects for the country as a whole, two broad possibilities seem to lie ahead for Iraqis: either their indigenous institutions and political leaders will be strong and creative enough to cope with whatever challenges the insurgents and the internal conflicts and cleavages present, or they will be too weak and fail, in which case Iraq will face acute civil conflict between Kurds and Arabs or a downward spiral into the kind of hell it experienced in 2006 and 2007.

If it is the former, then a future—something like what was sketched out in the previous section of this chapter—might lie ahead, and the US withdrawal will be able to continue. This future would not necessarily be pretty to watch. It would probably fall into the category of *muddling through*, but then, that is what most political societies do most of the time. If it is the latter, Iraqis will experience again something like the suffering they have known all too well in the recent past, and President Barack Obama will have yet another dreadful challenge to add to the tangle of issues he is grappling with in the Middle East.

If some approximation of constitutional government emerges in Iraq, the puzzle with which I began this chapter will need to be addressed, because it will mean that President George W. Bush's ill-conceived and ill-executed intervention—even if it did not produce this good result—at least unleashed a train of events that led ultimately to this outcome. Having worked in Iraq since 2004, I offer the following thought: should that happen, the Iraqis themselves will be largely responsible. Inevitably, the outside world has viewed them chiefly as victims—first of Saddam Hussein, then of American policy failures, finally of the insurgents. But they are actors as well as victims. Despite their lack of political experience, their deep mistrust of one another, their understandable thirst for vengeance and the settling of scores, Iraqis, in my experience, display a loyalty to their country and a desire to set things right not readily apparent from a distance. May those positive impulses prevail.

Notes

1 Real life is, of course, rather more complicated than this paragraph would suggest. What about, for example, Nigeria, or Pakistan or the United Arab Emirates (UAE)? The UAE's provisional constitution of 1971 declares it to be a federal state, but it is as much confederal as federal in its structure and operation, and it is not democratic. The leaders of the seven constituent emirates compose the Supreme Council of Rulers, which holds both executive and legislative authority. Nigeria and Pakistan, both federations, have moved in and out of authoritarian rule over the last several decades. Their political experience exemplifies the point, since they have found it difficult to combine federalism and a respect

for constitutionalism with the seizure of political power, usually by the military, and the centralization of authority that usually goes with it.
2 Iraq also became a magnet for terrorists from across the region, who acted as a kind of conflict accelerant.
3 Article 140 requires the holding of a census and a referendum in Kirkuk and other disputed territories to determine the will of their citizens by "a date not to exceed the 31st of December 2007."
4 The issue is reflected in the "Law of Administration for the State of Iraq for the Transitional Period" of March 8, 2004 (the TAL). Article 53 (c) excludes Kirkuk from any process of multi-governorate region formation.
5 For an examination of the plight of minorities in Iraq, see "Minorities in Iraq: The Other Victims" (Lamani, 2009). See also "Iraq's Minority Crisis and U.S. National Security: Protecting Minority Rights in Iraq" (Youash, 2008).
6 See a fuller discussion of the constitution in Cameron, "Making Federalism Work" (2007).
7 *The Future of Kurdistan in Iraq* offers a helpful view of the large issues Kurds are confronting in Iraq (O'Leary, McGarry and Salih, 2005).
8 And one could argue that, with the overlapping authorities for regions and governorates provided for in the constitution, reluctant regionalists could pretty much have their cake and eat it too by staying with their governorates.
9 However, it must be remembered that, while it may be easier for political leaders to launch a regionalization process, the proposal to create a region still has to be approved by the people of the governorate(s) in a referendum.
10 Reidar Visser provides a thoughtful background analysis of this issue focusing on the south of Iraq (2007).
11 This was a Forum of Federations project, financially supported by the Canadian International Development Agency (CIDA).

Works Cited

Biddle, Stephen, Michael E. O'Hanlon and Kenneth Pollack (2008). "How to Leave a Stable Iraq." *Foreign Affairs*. Vol. 87, No. 5 (September/October): 40–58.

Cameron, David. 2007. "Making Federalism Work," in *Iraq: Preventing a New Generation of Conflict*, edited by Markus E. Bouillon, David M. Malone and Ben Rowswell. Pages 153–68. Boulder and London: Lynne Rienner.

Hiltermann, Joost (2007). "Kirkuk as a Peacebuilding Test Case," in *Iraq: Preventing a New Generation of Conflict*, edited by Markus E. Bouillon, David M. Malone and Ben Rowswell. Pages 125–40. Boulder and London: Lynne Rienner.

―――― (2009). "Everyone Wants a Piece of Kirkuk, the Golden Prize." *International Crisis Group*. February 26. Available at http://www.crisisgroup.org/home/index.cfm?id=5950.

Lamani, Mokhtar (2009). "Minorities in Iraq: The Other Victims." Waterloo, ON: The Centre for International Governance Innovation, Special Report. January.

O'Leary, Brendan, John McGarry and Khaled Salih (eds.) (2005). *The Future of Kurdistan in Iraq*. Philadelphia: University of Pennsylvania Press.

Republic of Iraq (2004). "Law of Administration for the State of Iraq for the Transitional Period (TAL)." Baghdad, March 8.

——— (2005). "Iraqi Constitution" (Unofficial translation). Baghdad.

Visser, Reidar (2007). "Suffering, Oil, and Ideals of Coexistence: Non-Sectarian Federal Trends in the Far South of Iraq." Paper presented at the MESA Annual Meeting, Montreal, November 17–20. Available at http://historiae.org/south.asp.

——— (2009). "A Litmus Test for Iraq." *Middle East Report Online*. January 30. Available at http://www.merip.org/mero/mero013009.html.

Youash, Michael (2008). "Iraq's Minority Crisis and U.S. National Security: Protecting Minority Rights in Iraq." *American University International Law Review*. Vol. 24, No. 2: 341–76.

4

The Struggle for Autonomy and Decentralization
Iraqi Kurdistan

David Romano

Since 2003, the United States (US) has focused a large proportion of its efforts in Iraq on post-Saddam state building and regime consolidation. The deteriorating security situation in the Arab parts of Iraq, and the new Iraqi governments' difficulties in managing the situation, caused severe problems for reconstruction, humanitarian aid efforts, the return of displaced Iraqis and even the provision of basic services to the Iraqi population. An improved security situation after 2006, however, led to a more confident prime minister in Baghdad trying to assert central Iraqi government power and centralize some of the powers denied to Baghdad in the 2005 Iraqi Constitution.

The effort to build a strong Iraqi state, however, magnifies a traditional Iraqi problem of sectarian mistrust, particularly if this effort is rushed or pursued carelessly. Historically, nationally oppressed Kurds in Iraq looked for any opportunity or allies to distance themselves from Baghdad's control. In turn, governments in Baghdad (Baathist and non-Baathist) have at times of weakness pronounced themselves amenable to Kurdish autonomy and a vision of Iraq as a binational state of Arabs and Kurds. Abd al-Karim's 1958 rapprochement with Mullah Mustafa Barzani, the 1966 Bazaaz Declaration and the 1970 Autonomy Accords offer prime examples of such "moderate moments" for Baghdad. As soon as the various Iraqi central governments consolidated themselves and grew stronger vis-à-vis the disaffected Iraqi Kurdish minority, however, moderation and compromise were replaced with pacification campaigns and the iron fist of military force and tight central government control.

Politics among various groups in Arab parts of Iraq does not always deserve a sectarian label, as a number of observers have pointed out (see, for example, Visser, 2009). The enduring dynamic between Kurds and Arabs in Iraq, however, does display a largely sectarian logic. A history of Kurdish uprisings against Sunni Arab rule from Baghdad, starting even before the Iraqi state achieved independence, as well as a number of Baghdad-directed massacres, ethnic cleansing campaigns, harsh authoritarian rule and human rights abuses specifically targeted against Iraq's Kurdish minority helped to ensure that Iraqi Kurds would view politics through a sectarian lens for a long time to come. Their history in Iraq has caused Kurds to identify as Kurds first and Iraqis second, if at all. In turn, Iraqi Arabs have largely failed to appreciate the Kurdish experience in the country, which exacerbates Kurdish alienation and the need for real security guarantees in any post-Saddam national compact. Even today, as most Arab Iraqi political parties insist that they are Iraqi nationalist, they also commonly refer to themselves in sectarian terms. In a recent interview with *Asharq alAwsat*, for instance, Sheikh Ali Hatim, the leader of the National Front for the Salvation of Iraq, stated that his party was not sectarian and was "open to all Iraqi nationalists who want to join it," and then in the same interview stated, "Neither Al-Tawafuq nor any other group represents the Sunnis. We are Iraqi Arab Muslim clans and tribes" (Faya, 2008). Ethnic cleansing that occurred in Baghdad and the Iraqi governments' reluctance to incorporate Sunni Awakening Councils into the army and police likewise suggest that many Shi'a leaders may "speak Iraqi" but act sectarian. A good number of Iraqi and foreign observers who fervently yearn for a united, peaceful Iraq tend to hear the "we are not sectarian" portion of many Iraqis' discourse and then systematically discount clear evidence, actions and statements to the contrary.

The analysis presented here begins with an overview of Kurdish–Arab relations in Iraq, including the unprecedented de facto autonomy achieved by Iraqi Kurds in the wake of the 1990–91 Gulf War. Re-engagement of Iraqi Kurds and Baghdad in the wake of the 2003 US invasion and official recognition of federalism and Kurdish autonomy in the 2005 Permanent Iraqi Constitution are subsequently examined. The increased tensions between Baghdad and the Kurdistan Regional Government of Iraq (KRG) after 2006 then takes the analysis into a discussion of the still prevalent political conflict between Iraqi Kurds and Arabs. This includes an overview of the factors that impede or encourage coexistence and cooperation between Baghdad and the KRG, particularly in light of the omnibalancing and multiple-level games that Iraqi political actors must pay close attention to. The chapter concludes by assessing how Kurdish alienation from the Iraqi state, and the Kurds' resulting struggle to safeguard their autonomy, plays a central role in these ongoing Baghdad–KRG relations, with a host of implications for the future.

Arab–Kurdish Relations in Iraq: The Forced Marriage

Although Arabs and Kurds in Iraq do not constitute monolithic, unitary entities, successive Sunni Arab rulers of the Iraqi state, the Arab nationalist ideologies they brandish and the reactions engendered among the large majority of Iraqi Kurds make it reasonable to generalize about "Arab-Kurdish" relations in Iraq. While personal relations between ethnic Arabs and Kurds have often been, and continue to be, remarkably good, political relations suffer from a very negative, painful history. A creation of British colonial policy after World War I, the Iraqi state lacked Iraqis for much of its history. Although an Iraqi identity eventually began to take hold among Arabs in the state, the same could hardly be said of Kurds. Recurring Kurdish revolts against Arab authorities in Baghdad from the 1920s through to the 1990s all point to an enduring problem rather than just alienation from Saddam Hussein's Baathist regime between 1968 and 2003.[1] Iraqi history consists of an almost continuous stream of broken promises from Baghdad to the Kurds from the moment the Joint Anglo–Iraqi Statement of Intent Regarding the Kurds was pronounced in 1922. The Statement of Intent assured Kurds that:

> His Britannic Majesty's Government and the Government of Iraq recognize the right of the Kurds living within the boundaries of Iraq to set up a Kurdish Government within those boundaries and hope that the different Kurdish elements will, as soon as possible, arrive at an agreement between themselves as to the form which they wish that Government should take and the boundaries within which they wish it to extend and will send responsible delegates to Baghdad to discuss their economic and political relations with His Britannic Majesty's Government and the Government of Iraq. (cited in McDowall, 1997: 169)

Subsequent to this broken promise, the League of Nations Commission that attached the Mosul Villayet (territory that comprised almost all of Iraqi Kurdistan) to the new Iraq promised that: "The desire of the Kurds that the administrators, magistrates and teachers in their country be drawn from their own ranks, and adopt Kurdish as the official language in all their activities, will be taken into account" (Vanly, 1970: 148). Not only were such promises ignored, but resulting Kurdish agitation was met by extreme coercion and repression. At times when the Iraqi army fared poorly against Kurdish rebels (up until the 1940s, frequent intervention from British military units were required to suppress Kurdish revolts), Baghdad pronounced itself amenable to various degrees of Kurdish autonomy within Iraq. Abd al-Karim's 1958 rapprochement with Mullah Mustafa Barzani, the 1966 Bazaaz Declaration and the 1970 Autonomy Accords serve as prime examples of such accommodating moments. The first two attempts at accommodation failed as soon as forces in Baghdad became stronger and more confident in their ability to suppress the Kurds, while the 1970 Autonomy Accord failed due to a combination of factors: the failure to delineate the boundaries of a Kurdish autonomous region, tension over whether or not Kirkuk would be included within the Kurdish region, and encouragement from foreign powers (the United States, Britain, Iran and Israel) for the Kurds to forsake the agreement and militarily force more concessions from Baghdad. Ethnic cleansing policies, begun in the 1960s, also pushed Kurds and Turkmen out of oil-rich regions around Kirkuk, Mosul, Khanequin, Kalar and other parts of northern Iraq, replacing them with Arab settlers from southern Iraq. The Iraqi Kurdish litany of suffering culminated with the chemical weapons massacres and *Anfal* campaigns of 1987–88, killing between one and two hundred thousand civilians. The international community remained largely silent during the Baghdad regime's genocidal campaigns of the 1980s, and only branded Iraq a rogue state after it invaded Kuwait in 1990.

De Facto Kurdish Autonomy: 1991–2003

As a result of the 1990–91 Gulf War, Iraqi Kurds gained unprecedented autonomy in a Switzerland-sized de facto state in northern Iraq. Although the two hegemonic Kurdish political movements, the Kurdistan Democratic Party (KDP) and Patriotic Union of Kurdistan (PUK), fought a limited civil war over control of the autonomous region between 1994 and 1998, they also achieved significant successes once free of Baghdad's control. Free elections were held in 1992, most of the villages destroyed in the *Anfal* campaigns were rebuilt, the economy grew to levels surpassing pre-1991 indicators (despite the international sanctions on Iraq and Iraqi sanctions on the Kurdish region), a nascent civil society emerged and degrees of liberalization and political freedoms unheard of in the rest of Iraq took hold.[2] These 12 years of autonomous rule provided Iraqi Kurds with crucial experience in self-government and time to build functioning political institutions. Iraqi Kurdistan thus enjoyed relative stability as the rest of Iraq descended into chaos after 2003.

Kurdish autonomy remained fragile from 1991 to 2003, however, due to competition between the KDP and PUK and the unwillingness of any member of the international community, much less neighbouring states, to accept an independent Kurdish state. Saddam Hussein's army and Republican Guard forces lay poised just south of the autonomous region, and were always ready to make a play to retake the territory at a moment's notice.

Kurdish Re-engagement with Iraq: De Jure Autonomy and the 2005 Constitution

The 2003 US invasion of Iraq and the subsequent removal of Saddam's regime brought opportunities and risks for Iraqi Kurds. Sensing both, the KDP and PUK moved to bury their differences and unite their political forces vis-à-vis outside actors (at the time of this writing, they have also united their administrations in the Kurdish Autonomous Region, with the still to be addressed exceptions of the Ministries of Defense, Finance and Interior). The Kurds cooperated with Coalition Forces against Saddam's regime, and rather than holding onto territories they captured in the process (especially Kirkuk and Mosul), they turned them over to US forces and withdrew their *Peshmerga* (Kurdish fighters). Rather than expel Arab settlers from Kirkuk and other regions that had experienced ethnic cleansing in the past, Kurdish parties agreed to a managed return process that would arbitrate competing claims of expelled Kurds and Arab settlers.[3] The Kurds then went on to play a key role in setting up the post-Saddam Iraqi political structure. In 2005, in tandem with the Shi'a Islamic Supreme Council of Iraq (ISCI, known as the Supreme Council for the Islamic Revolution in Iraq at the time), they succeeded in drafting a decentralized federal constitution that was ratified by the vast majority of Iraqi voters that year. The Autonomous Kurdistan Regional Government of Iraq (KRG) received official recognition from the new federal Iraqi government, and Kurdish Peshmerga were recognized as a national guard for the region rather than a militia. Although disputes about extending the borders of the KRG region and returning ethnically cleansed Kurds to their homes remained, these were supposed to be dealt with in Article 140 of the 2005 Permanent Iraqi Constitution.

Article 140 promised a census of territories under dispute, normalization (meaning a return of forcibly displaced Kurds and Turkmen) and a referendum to determine the final status of Kirkuk and other contested regions (essentially, whether or not these areas would become part of the KRG, their own region or continue under administration from Baghdad). Article 140 was to be implemented by December 31, 2007. After a number of postponements, it seems apparent that Nouri al-Maliki's government and other Arab political actors do not intend to allow implementation of this article of the 2005 Constitution. As part of a strategy to make non-implementation an unacceptable status quo, Kurdish parties have in turn blocked a number of legislative agendas, the most important being a hydrocarbons law to manage Iraq's oil production and revenues.

A Return to Arab–Kurdish Conflict? Signs from the 2009 Provincial Elections[4]

The January 31 provincial elections in Iraq produced some ominous signs for the Kurdistan Regional Government. Although provincial elections do little to change the balance of power in the country's central government, they can offer an indicator of the national mood of Iraq. In this case, Arab Iraqis seemed to show a growing preference for Iraqi Arab nationalist political parties and a strong central government.

The biggest loser in the provincial elections was the Shi'a religious Islamic Supreme Council of Iraq party. The ISCI went from being the hegemonic party in Iraq's southern provinces to an embarrassing second- or even third-place showing in most southern provinces. In Basra, where the ISCI advocated centring a Shi'a autonomous region comparable to the Kurdistan Region in the north, preliminary results suggest that the ISCI netted around 11.6 percent of the vote, compared to Nouri al-Maliki's "State of Law" party, which garnered 37 percent (*New York Times*, 2009). In Najaf, the ISCI took around 14.8 percent of the vote compared to al-Maliki's 16.2 percent and the Sadrists' 12.2 percent. Baghdad (a province unto itself in the Iraqi system of governorates) displayed the most embarrassing showing for the ISCI, however, with only 5.4 percent of the vote compared to al-Maliki's 38 percent and the Sadrists' 9 percent.

Nouri al-Maliki, in turn, emerged as the elections' biggest winner, greatly improving on the weak followings his Dawa party had attracted in previous elections. Al-Maliki even seemed to attract significant numbers of votes from outside his Shi'a sectarian base, downplaying religious themes in favour of Iraqi nationalist slogans and the promise of security and strong government—ideas that can appeal to Sunni Arabs, secular voters and even Christian Iraqis. Especially in Baghdad and Basra, where al-Maliki enjoyed the most significant electoral gains, voters seemed to express support for the major Iraqi army operations he launched in early 2008. These operations regained government control of Basra and major parts of Baghdad from Moqtada al-Sadr's Mahdi Army militia and criminal gangs in some neighbourhoods. Nouri al-Maliki managed to take credit not only for these successes but also for the overall security gains in central Iraq and Baghdad derived from the US military surge and the recruitment of Sunni tribal Awakening Councils. Where he once appeared to many as an ineffective and compromised choice for Iraqi Prime Minister, al-Maliki thus managed to turn his image into that of the strong leader that many Iraqis believed they needed.

Iraqi Kurds view these results with concern. At Iraq's federal level of government, the ISCI has generally worked closely with the Kurdish parties and shared their goal of decentralized Iraqi federalism, with a weak central government in Baghdad. If the provincial elections indicate what the national-level parliamentary elections will look like when they are held in early 2010, Iraqi Kurdish parties will need more political allies to compensate for the ISCI's decline.[5] If Arab Iraqi leaders think that they can get more votes and support with a platform of Iraqi nationalism and strong central government, as al-Maliki seems to have done, such political allies may become increasingly hard to find.

Part of Nouri al-Maliki's ascendance seems to be occurring at the expense of the Kurdistan Regional Government. Kurdish relations with al-Maliki went from reasonably good in 2006 (when Kurdish parties saved al-Maliki's government from collapse as Shi'a and Sunni parties withdrew support from him) to increasingly tense in 2008 and the beginning of 2009. Much of the Iraqi Arab electorate appears resentful of Kurdish gains since 2003 and displays little patience or understanding for Kurdish demands. Politicians like al-Maliki have moved to capitalize on this resentment and burnish their Iraqi nationalist credentials. Al-Maliki and his ministers now increasingly criticize the KRG. At a press conference on November 20, 2008, al-Maliki "accused Kurds in Iraq of pursuing several unconstitutional policies, including the development of an oil business independent of Baghdad and the opening of representative offices in foreign countries. He...also criticized the activities of Kurdish defense forces, known as *Peshmerga*, outside the region" (Aslan, 2008).

The KRG responded with a statement:

> It is unfortunate and deeply regrettable that the press conference of Iraq's Prime Minister [of November 20] illustrates efforts being made to take the people of Iraq back to a period we are desperately trying to get beyond. It was a period where the excessive concentration, or centralization, of economic and political power condemned all Iraqi peoples to unimaginable suffering... Though the Prime Minister has taken the oath to promote and protect the Constitution of Iraq—as it currently exists—it is, indeed, disconcerting when he cites the Constitution in attacking others while apparently violating it when taking unilateral decisions. The Prime Minister is obligated to act within the limits of the current constitution and not in accordance with a future constitution he may prefer. (KRG, 2008)

KRG leaders also harshly condemned al-Maliki's move to recruit and arm "support councils" in their region and the disputed territories south of it. In an apparent effort to create a militia directly loyal to him, al-Maliki has approached tribal leaders in northern Iraq, including those who had collaborated with Saddam in his military campaigns against Kurdish rebels (KRG, 2008). In the 1980s, Kurdish tribes, such as the Harki, Surchi and Zebari, which are traditional opponents of leading Kurdish tribes of the KRG (such as the Barzanis), assisted Baghdad in its massacres of Kurds in Iraqi Kurdistan.[6] For al-Maliki's government and Sunni Arab parties in northern Iraq to now form alliances with such tribes poses an existential threat in the minds of most Kurds in the Kurdish Autonomous Region. KRG President Masoud Barzani also accused al-Maliki of marginalizing Kurds in the Iraqi army and appointing his own people to head each of Iraq's 16 army divisions rather than following the legal parliamentary procedures of choosing commanders by consensus (Parker, 2009).

In addition, al-Maliki has deployed Iraqi army units northward, to areas the Kurds want to incorporate into their autonomous region. The Kurdish Autonomous Region of today merely consists of the areas from which Saddam Hussein withdrew his forces in 1991 and does not include many predominantly Kurdish areas just south of 1991's "Green Line." One such mostly Kurdish town south of the autonomous region is Khanequin, where in August of 2008, al-Maliki suddenly sent an Iraqi army brigade to "help with security." The Arab Iraqi army unit nearly traded fire with Kurdish Peshmerga sent to intercept them, until mediation led both forces to agree that neither would enter the town.

For towns just south of the current Kurdish autonomous region's accidental borders, like Khanequin, Makhmour, Kalar, Kirkuk and

Chamchamal, the significant oil resources around them only add to the determination of both Baghdad and the KRG to control them. The multi-ethnic demography of towns like Kirkuk and Mosul, with Kurdish, Arab, Turkmen and Christian populations, further complicates the issue. Although the aforementioned Article 140 of the 2005 Iraqi Constitution stipulates that, among other things, these areas must have a referendum to decide whether or not to join the KRG region, several deadlines for the referendum (the first of which was in December 2007) have already come and gone. Residents of Kirkuk were not able to vote in the 2009 provincial elections, as disagreements over who is eligible to vote in such a referendum still await resolution (the three KRG provinces of Dohuk, Erbil and Suleimaniya did not have provincial elections either since they are functioning under a separate KRG electoral calendar). A deadline of March 31, 2009 for a special parliamentary committee to table a new Kirkuk election law was also missed. In Diyala and Nineweh provinces just south of the KRG, Kurds largely controlled the provincial councils (as they do in Kirkuk) due to a 2005 electoral boycott by Arab Sunnis. Electoral results from January 2009 mean they will be expected to relinquish control of Nineweh (Mosul) to the Sunni Arab Hadba party (which garnered 48.4 percent of the vote to the Kurdish Alliance's 25.5 percent) and control of Diyala to the Tawafuq Sunni Arab Iraqi Islamic Party, which garnered 21.1 percent of the vote to the Kurdish Alliance's 17.2 percent (at the time of this writing, several predominantly Kurdish municipalities in Nineweh still refused to recognize the authority of the new Hadba Mosul governor, who in turn refused to incorporate pro-KRG political leaders into his new cabinet).

All of these developments, and especially Prime Minister al-Maliki's apparent ascendance and increasingly tense relations with Kurdish leaders, indicate a growing risk of renewed Arab–Kurdish conflict in Iraq. Given some common interests between Kurds and Arab parties such as Tawafuq and the ISCI, such a conflict would probably not initially pit Kurds against all the Arab political blocs. Should Arab-Kurdish violence break out, however, ethnic identities could quickly polarize and end the shared interests of Kurds and some Arab parties. In general, as the security situation in the centre and south of Iraq improves, an increasingly confident al-Maliki-led government appears less conciliatory and more aggressive toward Iraqi Kurdistan. According to *The Economist*, "Mr Barzani is said to have recently told Mr Maliki to his face: 'You smell like a dictator'" (*The Economist*, 2008). Arab Iraqi voters in turn appear to be either rewarding al-Maliki for his assertiveness or for his improved security record in central Iraq, or both. Voters may also be upset with the ISCI's failure to provide services and development in line with their expectations.

Preventing Another Failed Iraqi State: Making the Arranged Marriage Consensual

Both Iraqis and outside observers clearly fear what appears to be a brewing showdown between the KRG and ascendant Arab political groups in Baghdad. Violence from such a conflict could prove worse than the darkest moments of insurgent bombings and death squads that plagued central Iraq in 2006. It would also signal a far more significant breakdown in the post-Saddam Iraqi state.

Many reasons exist for growing Arab–Kurdish tensions. Both Kurdish political actors and Arab parties, whether Sunni, Shi'a or secular, are struggling to maximize their power in the new and unsettled Iraqi political arena. If the growing conflict between Erbil and Baghdad were just a competition for political and economic power, however, a settlement might appear more readily obvious. Under such circumstances, obvious solutions would entail Iraqi Kurds foregoing additional territorial aspirations and conceding more power to Iraq's central government in return for a host of promises: a guaranteed share of all Iraqi oil revenues, official recognition of the Kurdish region's borders (in the territory that emerged from 1991 to 2003) and a role in the central governing institutions of the correspondingly stronger Iraqi state. Proponents of a stronger Iraqi central government advocate this kind of "solution." The Washington Institute for Near East Policy, for instance, encourages a plan in which concessions made by the KRG should include:

- "The gradual establishment of Iraqi federal government authority over *peshmerga* units should be promoted as a confidence-building measure between Baghdad and Irbil."
- Accepting the creation of awakening councils "in areas such as Kirkuk and Ninawa."
- New provincial elections in disputed territories, wherein "the number of Kurdish-backed governors and police chiefs would be reduced" [due to a Sunni Arab boycott of elections in 2005, and their resulting under-representation]—this was accomplished in January 2009 everywhere except in Kirkuk province, with the expected decline in the Kurdish preponderance of votes for most areas.

- The greater incorporation of non-Kurds into security forces in the disputed territories (especially Kirkuk).
- No significant territorial adjustments in favour of the KRG. (Knights, 2008: 28–29)

In return, the Kurds would receive additional "counterterrorism equipment and training," more Peshmerga pensions paid from Baghdad, "explosives scanning and disposal equipment" and other equipment such as "body armour, weapons, vehicles and radios" for security forces in the Kurdish provinces (Knights, 2008: 28–29).

Even if such an unbalanced "solution" to the tensions between Baghdad and Erbil were fathomable for Kurdish leaders, they would never be able to convince their constituencies to accept the arrangement. The Iraqi Kurdish position does not stem solely from a desire to maximize Kurdish economic and political power, or even to prepare the field for eventual secession. Given their history in Iraq, Kurds are a traumatized people. In light of their minority status in Iraq, Kurds also have an existential fear of a necessarily Arab-dominated federal government in Baghdad, and "solutions" without real security and autonomy guarantees (as opposed to promises and agreements on paper) mean little to them. A suggestion by Nouri al-Maliki (or an American think tank like the Washington Institute for Near East Policy) of a scenario in which the Peshmerga fall under Baghdad's direction would never be accepted by Kurds. The 2005 Constitution was intended to address such Kurdish fears. It provides Kurds with some important guarantees in addition to recognition of a KRG-controlled Peshmerga (as the Kurdistan National Guard), the supremacy of regional law over central government edicts (in most cases), the KRG's right to veto central government military deployments into the Kurdish Autonomous Region, the right to develop their own as yet undiscovered oil resources and a broad array of additional autonomous rights.[7] For some of the Arab political parties (in fact, most, with the exception of the ISCI) to demand a revision of the 2005 Constitution thus provokes extreme anxiety for Kurds and calls into question the entire basis of the voluntary post-2003 inclusion in the Iraqi state. US officials' implicit or explicit encouragement to revise the 2005 Constitution—part of a short term strategy to garner more support from Sunni Arab political actors—may thus set the stage for a serious Arab–Kurdish rupture.

Because they are a minority nation within the Iraqi state, the Kurdish leadership, and most average Kurds, desire to include all majority

Kurdish-inhabited areas within the Kurdish Autonomous Region, rather than adhering to the "accidental" demarcation line to which Saddam withdrew his forces in early 1992. The KRG's attempt to incorporate Kirkuk, with its 13 percent of producing oil fields in Iraq, does not constitute an attempt to maximize KRG revenues, given that Kurdish leaders agree that revenues from all existing oil fields should be divided proportionally among all Iraqis. Rather, much of Kirkuk has a Kurdish majority. Physical control of the oil fields also provides Kurds with another tangible guarantee that Baghdad will deliver their share of the revenues. Given Iraqi Kurdistan's landlocked geography, control of the oil fields does not even set the stage for secession, since all pipelines run through Arab Iraq, Turkey and Syria. In short, Iraqi Kurds suffer from a security dilemma—both the Kurdish leadership and vast majority of the population do not trust Baghdad or Arab Iraqi political actors. In the words of one high ranking KRG official: "Americans in Baghdad seem to have a strange faith in promises, institutions and agreements on paper" (author's personal interview, November 23, 2008). Any proposed and enduring political arrangement that fails to pay sufficient attention to these real fears (perhaps justified, given Iraq's history) cannot lead to voluntary Kurdish inclusion within the Iraqi state.

At the same time, non-Kurds on the edges of Iraqi Kurdistan (Arabs, Turkmen and Christians) fear that their rights and prospects will fare poorly should they be incorporated into a Kurdish nationalist autonomous region. Political leaders in Baghdad, in turn, feel pressure to protect such communities, maximize their own power and obstruct any potential Kurdish bid to secede from Iraq. Most Arab political leaders, whether Sunni, Shi'a, Christian or secular, would face a political maelstrom among their constituents if they failed to pay heed to these issues. Even actors such as the ISCI would prefer not to see an expansion of KRG territory or Kurdish absorption of Kirkuk.

Iraqi Kurds and various Arab Iraqi political actors thus need to find a compromise that satisfies enough of each actor's needs. They need to do so privately, since the maximalist demands of their respective constituencies and the risk of being "out hawked" by political rivals in their own communities will otherwise destroy any existing zone of agreement.[8] Neighbouring states need to be consulted before and after such negotiations but should not be an official part of them, given the added difficulties and possible perverse effects of directly including their influence in the process. Once an agreement has been reached between KRG leaders and enough important non-Kurdish political actors (Nouri al-Maliki, ISCI, elements of the Turkmen community, a number of Sunni parties and tribes, for instance), each party to the bargain must then sell the agreement to their respective communities, and the Iraqi government would then convince neighbouring countries to accept the compact. This process and the bargain that is reached would need the vigorous backing of the American and United Nations' (UN) representatives in Iraq from the instant it is made public.

The International Crisis Group (ICG) in its October 2008 report suggests a "grand bargain" to resolve the growing Arab–Kurdish tensions in Iraq. The compromises envisioned by the ICG come much closer to fulfilling the basic needs of both the Kurdish and Arab communities, in contrast to the Washington Institute for Near East Policy's proposals and others like it. The ICG "Oil for Soil" report states:

> Claims to Kirkuk notwithstanding, what the Kurds arguably need most is protection for the Kurdistan region from a potentially powerful central state and surrounding countries, as well as a chance for the region to flourish by trading freely with the outside world. The KRG could meet these objectives by pursuing the following policy objectives: delineation of its internal boundary with the rest of Iraq, an advanced degree of political autonomy, significant economic leverage *vis-à-vis* the federal government, a decentralised Iraq to prevent the re-emergence of a powerful central state and peaceful relations with Syria, Turkey and Iran. (2008: 27)

More specifically, the proposal would see the KRG defer claims to the city of Kirkuk and nearby oil fields, if not all the territory in Kirkuk (Ta'amim) province, for a period of ten years. Such a postponement (perhaps to a future time when the issue can be settled more easily) would spare Kurdish leaders from an unacceptable loss on this issue. US security guarantees for the KRG, including the possibility of a US base in the KRG region, would further alleviate Kurdish security fears. Finally, Iraqi and international actors (mainly the UN) would provide assurances that "the constitutionally mandated decentralisation [of the 2005 Constitution] will not be reversed should a powerful central government rise again" (ICG, 2008: 27). The KRG would also play a role in managing and operating oil fields in the area in cooperation with the central government. This would provide a physical guarantee regarding any hydrocarbons law—should Baghdad fail to deliver the KRG's agreed upon proportion of oil revenues, the Kurds could stop production at fields they control. Along the lines of the United Nations Assistance Mission for Iraq (UNAMI) Phase One recommendations (2008), such a negotiated settlement would attach many majority Kurdish inhabited districts just south of current KRG borders to the KRG, while leaving Arab (and Turkmen) districts such as Hawija and Tuz Khurmatu a part of Iraq proper or part of a Kirkuk "stand alone" region.

Such a "grand bargain" would thus involve a linkage of various outstanding issues of contention in order to create an acceptable enough deal for all relevant political actors. Although Kurdish leaders will face a difficult task convincing their constituents that deferring claims to Kirkuk for ten years constitutes a victory, the other Kurdish gains and guarantees in the deal would soften such a bitter pill. Especially given the continuing non-implementation of Article 140 of the 2005 Constitution and the shifting winds in the rest of Iraq, KRG leaders would have to accept that they now have less room to manoeuvre on Kirkuk. Although grand bargains are generally risky for the weaker negotiating partner (as evidenced by the Palestinians' hesitancy in negotiating a final settlement with Israelis, for instance), Iraqi Kurds probably have a stronger negotiating position vis-à-vis Arab Iraq today than they will in the future. With most American forces set to withdraw from Iraq in the next few years, Iraqi Kurds face an uncertain future. The desire to settle as many issues of contention between Baghdad and the KRG as possible, sooner rather than later, points to the pressing need for a grand bargain.

Such a grand bargain would also allow Arab and Turkmen political leaders to go back to their communities and claim a limited (but hopefully sufficient) victory, wherein Mosul, Arab and Turkmen districts near the KRG and Kirkuk City and its oil fields remain under Baghdad's control. To improve these leaders' chances of selling such a grand bargain to their constituents, the KRG could also simultaneously announce its intention to coordinate more "low politics" issues with Baghdad—basic law enforcement protocols, natural disaster coordination and relief, health policy, air traffic control and other such matters. In addition to avoiding a logistical nightmare concerning such matters, allowing Baghdad to provide central coordination on these things would help assure Iraqis that the KRG region does not plan to secede from the country.[9] Additionally, KRG leaders might even consider a public relations campaign aimed at the rest of Iraq (perhaps even in the guise of tourism promotion) in order to make it easier for Arab and Turkmen leaders to sell their constituents any concessions they make to the Kurds.

Such a grand bargain seems unattainable without significant and well-executed UN and US assistance. Different frames of reference hinder the way Arab and Kurdish political actors view negotiations. Arabs feel that they have already conceded a great deal to the Kurds with the Kurdistan Region's extensive autonomy and the incorporation of Kurds into top central government posts. Many even feel that the 2005 Constitution gave the Kurds too much autonomy and was forced upon Iraq in a pact by KRG leaders and ISCI politicians. Kurds, in turn, feel that they have made great concessions by not attempting to secede from Iraq, cooperating with and contributing to the post-Saddam Iraqi state and not retaining territories they took control of in 2003. They also feel that the constitution "was not a document imposed upon Iraq by them and does not satisfy all of the Kurds' demands… Rather, they see it as a compromise by them undertaken for the interests of the 'new Iraq' and evidence of their commitment to the integrity of the state" (Stansfield and Anderson, 2009: 142). Hence each actor appears loath to make further concessions.

War weariness among all Iraqi communal groups is probably the factor that will assist most in the negotiating of such a grand bargain. Given that the assurances they negotiated in the 2005 Constitution serve as the basis upon which Iraqi Kurds agreed to forego secession, however, international actors, the United States in particular, would be well advised to immediately cease expressing support for a substantial revision of this constitution. The new and fragile Iraqi state would probably fracture should such constitutional negotiations be reopened at this time, before the country's various communities have learned to work together and trust each other more. If Arabs decide to forego the 2005 Constitution and its provisions for robust Kurdish autonomy, the Kurds' willing marriage to the rest of Iraq will end. Kurds will feel as though they have precious little to lose by attempting to secede: "Ironically, then, the resurgence of Arab/Iraqi nationalist political sentiment premised on the preservation of a unified, centralized Iraq is the one thing most likely to shatter the unity it seeks to preserve" (Stansfield and Anderson, 2009: 144).

Although a Kurdish bid for statehood would involve severe risks for KRG leaders, the defeat of such a gambit would not be a foregone conclusion. Kurdish objectives would be limited to fighting hard enough and long enough, and inflicting enough casualties on their opponents (Iraqis or the forces of neighbouring states or both), to force a withdrawal and recognition of Kurdish independence and/or international mediation. As the United States has learned in its various "low intensity" conflicts, the will to fight can prove at least as important as the strength of the combatant. Kurdish populations in neighbouring Turkey, Syria and Iran would most likely be galvanized by such a conflict, threatening the stability of these states as well. Naturally, Iraqi Kurds, other Iraqis, neighbouring states and international actors would all prefer to avoid such a risky, bitter and costly conflict, which makes finding a way to avoid it that much more pressing. A grand bargain that can see a voluntary incorporation of Kurds within Iraq, settling all outstanding major points of contention and delaying a resolution of Kirkuk's status therefore appears more crucial than ever. Such a bargain must be something Arab and Kurdish leaders can, with the support of the US, the UN and international community, sell to their constituencies. Most importantly, any agreement must pay close attention to real and tangible security guarantees for Iraqi Kurds. Simply put, Iraqi Kurds face an existential threat that Iraqi Arabs do not.

Kurdish Autonomy and Its Implications for the Future

Ethnic nationalism is often viewed as a potential source of conflict to be managed, rather than a human value to be actualized (in a way that does not impinge on the rights of others. See, for example Horowitz [1985] and Hechter [2004]). Such reasoning leads them to advocate a "civic nationalism" for Iraq that eschews "ethnic federalism" and focuses instead on human rights and equal citizenship for all Iraqis. A stronger Iraqi central government, in such a scenario, would unite all Iraqis irrespective of their sectarian differences.

Such views employ a double standard, however, in which an Iraqi state centred on an Arab ethnic identity and maintaining its membership in the Arab League can offer a civic identity to all its people, while an Iraqi Kurdish autonomous region based on a Kurdish ethnic identity is somehow more exclusionary or racist. The Kurdistan Regional Government has never indicated that non-Kurds in the region it controls would enjoy lesser rights than Kurds—indeed, minorities in the KRG have fared much better than minorities in the rest of Iraq, as evidenced by the mass exodus of Christians from cities such as Baghdad and Mosul to the KRG region since 2003. Kurds residing in places like Baghdad do not vote in KRG elections. KRG authorities also increasingly promote a civic identity of Kurdistani (rather than Kurdi), wherein all the residents of Iraqi Kurdistan—including Arabs, Turkmen, Assyrians, Chaldeans and Yezidis—share a common experience, culture and belonging within the autonomous Kurdish region. Additionally, the 2005 Iraqi Constitution permits other provinces to form autonomous regions as well, if at least three provinces express a desire to amalgamate in this way.

The vision of an Iraq based on human rights and civic identities, instead of well-designed checks and balances on the exercise of political power (decentralized federalism in particular) also places unwarranted faith in Iraqi leaders and the political institutions of the country. Iraqi history, including the era before Saddam Hussein's rise to power, offers no reason for anyone to expect an Iraqi political system that respects human rights and eschews sectarian politics and conflict, although a more benign Iraqi political arena may one day emerge, with checks and balances in place. Identities and resultant identity-based conflict in Iraq are not static, and a virtuous cycle of politics functioning within established institutional frameworks may help develop an Iraqi identity for all Iraqis. As time passes within a functioning and balanced Iraqi political system, sectarian divides may recede—including Arab–Kurdish distrust. To assume these divisions away and base current policy on a shared Iraqi identity and a Baghdad government that will respect human rights and not fall prey to sectarian politics, however, places the cart before the horse. The way to increase the likelihood of a healthy political dynamic taking hold in Iraq lies in the removal of a "race to control the centre" by diffusing political power away from Baghdad. Iraqi Kurds demanded such a diffusion of power as a condition for supporting the 2005 Constitution and remaining in the country. They also seem reasonably well positioned to safeguard these demands or throw Iraq into bloody civil war should Baghdad try to emaciate the KRG's autonomy. It therefore seems reasonable to assume that Kurdish autonomy, whatever the precise borders of Iraqi Kurdistan, will remain essential for Iraq's future success. The medium- and long-term implications of such autonomy, however, merit careful consideration.

In the medium term, KRG leaders will either show that they can govern effectively or face a number of increasingly serious problems. Effective governance will necessitate reigning in rampant corruption within the KRG's two hegemonic parties. The Kurdistan Democratic Party and Patriotic Union of Kurdistan currently divide the 17 percent of Iraqi oil revenues allotted to the KRG on a 52 percent–48 percent basis, respectively. Only when corruption is brought under control, and KRG finances are made more transparent, will development efforts start to show more results for all of the KRG's inhabitants. Additionally, effective governance in the KRG will necessitate a good human rights record, particularly vis-à-vis minorities. Any perceived abuses toward especially Arab, Shi'a or Turkmen minorities will put pressure on Iraqi leaders south of the KRG and neighbouring countries to take action. Turkish leaders, for instance, have already turned the fate of Iraqi Turkmen into a central issue for the Turkish state—whether or not this represents an excuse to justify Turkish meddling in Iraqi Kurdistan, any KRG abuses of the Turkmen community may trigger a serious response from Ankara.

If Iraqi Kurdistan in the medium term succeeds in demonstrating effective governance, stable politics and avoidance of provocative meddling toward the Kurdish minorities of neighbouring Turkey, Iran and Syria, the region may well come to accept a de facto Kurdish state within Iraq. Turkey and Iran have already invested in the KRG, and in May 2009, KRG oil exports via Turkey began. Neighbouring states might even relax their policies toward their own Kurdish minorities if the Iraqi Kurdish experiment in self-rule within Iraq succeeds. A thriving KRG will in turn have very little incentive to risk everything with a bid to secede from Iraq, even in the longer term. Much will depend, of course, on how Iraqis resolve current tensions between Baghdad and Erbil.

If tensions between Baghdadi Arab leaders intent on centralizing Iraqi state power and KRG leaders intent on maintaining real Kurdish autonomy boil over into violent conflict, however, the resulting instability could lead to a number of outcomes. A Kurdish state, albeit a poor, isolated and insecure one in the medium term, is one such possibility. Renewed authoritarian control and oppression from Baghdad, as well as intervention by neighbouring states, could also result from such a breakdown. Prudent leaders in both Baghdad and the KRG thus have strong incentives to avoid a real rupture. Should KRG leaders fail to govern their region effectively, however, especially by managing corruption and respecting minority and human rights, instability or outside pressure on the KRG could also lead to serious problems. Especially if KRG leaders develop an incentive to engage in more risky foreign policies in order to deflect domestic criticism, the results could put Kurdish autonomy within Iraq at risk. Political elites in Arab Iraq might also perceive a potential for increased popularity by "acting tough" toward the KRG, unless the risks inherent in such an approach continue to outweigh the potential gains.

The incentive for KRG leaders to remain active in Iraqi national politics, to share KRG oil revenues with the rest of Iraq and to maintain alliances with non-Kurdish Iraqi political groups will thus remain strong for the foreseeable future. Especially Sunni Arabs, with little resources of their own and sandwiched between the Kurdish region and majority Shi'a areas to the south, would need to see that Kurdish autonomy need not be inimical to their interests. With the right policies, federal institutions and incentives, as well as some measure of luck, Arab–Kurdish relations could thus enter a virtuous cycle. In the long term, the trust and stable institutions created from such a virtuous cycle could then allow for the creation of an Iraqi political system less reliant on security guarantees, checks and balances and extreme decentralization. In the short term, however, Iraqi Kurds will remain vigilant against threats and promises alike.

Notes

1. For an overview of the Kurdish experience in modern Iraq, see "Kurdish nationalist challenges to the Iraqi state" in Romano, 2006, Pages 183–222.
2. For more on the 1991–2003 Iraqi Kurdish *de facto* state, see Romano, 2004.
3. For more on this, see Romano, 2005.
4. Portions of this section are from the previously published Romano, 2009.
5. ISCI's poor showing in the 2009 provincial polls is not necessarily an indication of southern Iraqis' disdain for regionalism, of course. Stansfield and Anderson, for instance, offer the following observation: "For ISCI and other Shi'a parties, including those most prominent in Basra (namely Hizb al-Fadilah), al-Maliki's constitutional visions are also received with concern. They would be diametrically opposed to plans of these parties to develop their own regions (as in the case of al-Fadilah and prominent politicians such as the governor of Basra, Mohammed al-Wailil). These are not just pipe-dreams of local political leaders keen to make Basra into a northern Persian Gulf version of Dubai (as is often mentioned). They are plans with real popular appeal, grounded in a sense of being increasingly disconnected from Baghdad and dismissed by many Western academics as nonsensical and 'historically illiterate.' The pressure to regionalise in the south is coming from very real economic drivers that those academics would be well advised to take seriously rather than pointing to historical patterns that are at best debatable" (2009: 143).
6. For more on tribal rivalries and Iraqi Kurdish politics, see chapters 8 and 14–18 in McDowall, 1997.
7. For more on the Kurdish view of the importance of the 2005 Constitution, see pages 107–40 in O'Leary, 2009.
8. For more on negotiating strategies that might be applicable to the Kurdish–Arab case, see Putnam, 1998.
9. The author would like to thank Jason Gluck for his comments on this matter.

Works Cited

Aslan, Azad (2008). "Kurds Have No Place in Iraq." *Kurdish Globe*, December 4. Available at: http://www.kurdishglobe.net/displayArticle.jsp?id=340F20BB3B1E1AACF2D4B512B54E343E.

The Economist (2008). "Is It Really Coming Right?" *The Economist*. November 27.

Faya, Ma'ad (2008). "Iraq: National Front for the Salvation of Iraq Leader Vows to Fight Islamic Party," *Asharq alAwsat*. September 25.

Hechter, Michael (2004). "Containing Ethnonationalist Violence," in *Facing Ethnic Conflicts*, edited by Andreas Wimmer, Donald L. Horowitz and Richard J. Goldstone. Lanham, Maryland: Rowman & Littlefield. Pages 283–300.

Horowitz, Donald (1985). *Ethnic Groups in Conflict*. Berkeley: University of California Press.

International Crisis Group (2008). "Oil for Soil: Toward a Grand Bargain on Iraq and the Kurds." *Middle East Report #80*. October 28.

Knights, Michael (2008). "Guiding the Kurdish Role in Securing Northern Iraq," in *The Future of the Iraqi Kurds*, edited by Soner Cagaptay. Washington: The Washington Institute for Near East Policy, Policy Focus #85. July. Pages 21–30.

Kurdistan Regional Government (KRG) (2008). "Full Text of KRG Response to Iraqi Prime Minister's Accusations." Kurdistan. December 1. Available at: http://www.krg.org/articles/detail.asp?smap=02010100&lngnr=12&anr=26811&rnr=223.

McDowall, David (1997). *A Modern History of the Kurds*. London and New York: I.B. Taurus.

New York Times (2009). "Election: Preliminary Results," *New York Times*, Baghdad Bureau, February 5.

O'Leary, Brendan (2009). *How to Get Out of Iraq with Integrity*. Philadelphia: University of Pennsylvania Press.

Parker, Ned (2009). "Interview with Kurdistan President Massoud Barzani." *Los Angeles Times*. January 12.

Putnam, Robert (1998). "Diplomacy and Domestic Politics: The Logic of Two-Level Games." *International Organization*. Vol. 42, No. 3 (Summer): 427–60.

Romano, David (2004). "Safe Havens as Political Projects: The Case of Iraqi Kurdistan," in *De Facto States*, edited by Paul Kingston and Ian Spears. Pages 153–66. New York: Palgrave Macmillan.

——— (2005). "Whose House Is This Anyway? IDP and Refugee Return Policies in Post-Saddam Iraq." *Oxford Journal of Refugee Studies*. Vol. 18, No. 4: 430–53.

——— (2006). *The Kurdish Nationalist Movement: Opportunity, Mobilization and Identity*. Cambridge: Cambridge University Press.

——— (2009). "In the Aftermath of Iraq's Provincial Elections, Part One: A Dangerous Year Ahead for Iraqi Kurds." *Terrorism Focus*. Vol. 6, No. 5. Jamestown Foundation, February 19.

Stansfield, Gareth and Liam Anderson (2009). "Kurds in Iraq: The Struggle between Baghdad and Erbil." *Middle East Policy*. Vol. XVI, No. 1 (Spring): 134–45.

United Nations Assistance Mission to Iraq (2008). *UNAMI Presents First Analysis to GOI to Help Resolve on Disputed Internal Boundaries*. June 5. Available at: http://www.uniraq.org/newsroom/getarticle.asp?ArticleID=702.

Vanly, Ismet Chériff (1970). *Le Kurdistan Irakien: Entité Nationale*. Neuchatel: Les Editions de la Baconnière.
Visser, Reider (2009). "Post-Sectarian Strategies for Iraq." *Historiae.org*. March 18. Available at: http://historiae.org/post-sectarian.asp.

5
Armed Forces Based in Iraqi Kurdistan
A Lens to Understand the Post-Saddam Era[1]

Maria Fantappié

The dialectic between centripetal and centrifugal forces is a main dynamic in the state formation process,[2] and this tension has been remarkably visible in two crucial moments of Iraqi state formation: throughout the 1920s—at the very end of the British mandate—and in the aftermath of the American invasion of 2003.[3]

Since the time of the Hashemite Monarchy, the central authority has attempted to contain the centrifugal forces, which had come mainly from the Kurdish and Shi'a peripheries (Batatu, 1978). The main strategy focused on trying to integrate these communities into the framework of the central institutions (the public service, the bureaucracy and the national army).[4] In the last two decades of the Saddam Hussein era, the central institutions ceased to function as a means of integration and increasingly became repressive instruments in the hands of Saddam Hussein's clan (Parasiliti, 2000).

Despite the centrifugal forces co-opted by the central power, therefore, the peripheries continued to resist the dictatorial policy of the central government. The 1991 uprising in the southern and northern governorates is a prime example of the centrifugal forces working against the Iraqi central authority. The establishment of an autonomous region in the Kurdish governorates demonstrated the deterioration of the Iraqi central government faced with the increasing power of its Kurdish outskirts.

State rebuilding in the post-Saddam era is developing along a similar line. Today, the emerging central Iraqi government is confronted daily by the most powerful centrifugal force in Iraq, notably the Kurdish Regional Government (KRG). The relationship between the Iraqi central government and the KRG lies at the core of the political difficulties facing present-day Iraq. Among them are the choice between a centralized or decentralized system of sharing power, the question of disputed territories and, in particular, the status of Kirkuk, the distribution of natural resources and the *Peshmerga* integration into the new Iraqi army.[5]

In this light, the army represents an important lens through which to understand the Kurdish centrifugal tendencies in relation to the Iraqi central government (Owen, 2001: 198–217). Also, at the heart of the definition of state capacity is the state's ability to monopolize the means of collective violence across the whole of its territory. Accordingly, the army must factor significantly into an analysis of the state formation process (Dodge, 2005). Initially, the Iraqi army functioned as the engine of the Iraqi state formation process, but later it became an instrument of repression. The deterioration of the Iraqi army has also corresponded with the emergence of a Kurdish armed forces—the Peshmerga movement, which aims to erode the power of the central government.

The Iraqi state was consolidated by senior army officers under the republican regime of Qassem and Aref (1958–68). Throughout the 1950s and the 1960s, the Iraqi army served as an instrument of Iraqi state building as well as a vehicle for the national integration of different communities. In contrast, during the last decades of the Saddam Hussein era, recruitment occurred on the basis of political, ethnic and religious affiliation. The Baathification of the Iraqi army eventually led to the emergence of the Peshmerga resistance movement, which contested the exclusive policy adopted by the central power. The consolidation of the autonomy of the KRG occurred alongside a consolidation of the armed forces during the sanctions period and after the American invasion.

In the aftermath of the Baathist state collapse, centrifugal forces operated not only on the periphery of the borders but also in the framework of the new central institutions. Paradoxically, in the aftermath of the American invasion, the former dissenting factions of the central Iraqi state were charged with rebuilding a new political centre and its institutions. Since 2003, Kurdish leadership has actively participated in the state rebuilding process and contributed to the establishment of the new Iraqi army. As a result, two of the four military academies of the new Iraqi army are currently based in Kurdistan.

This chapter analyzes the interdependence between the progressive deterioration of the Iraqi army and the rise of a centrifugal military power—the Peshmerga movement. From this perspective, I aim to depict a broader perspective of the Peshmerga integration into the new Iraqi army. I will also describe the centrifugal forces that are operating in the new central institutions, with a focus on their role in undermining the rise of a new, strong central state, and outline the main characteristics of the Kurdish participation in the rebuilding of the army.

Today in Iraq, the relationship between the Kurdish region and the central State is characterized by the presence of two different military forces on Kurdish soil: the Peshmerga Security Forces and the two Iraqi national military academies—Zakho and Sulaymaniyah. The analysis of the Erbil-Baghdad relation will be based on two case studies—the Erbil-based Peshmerga Security Forces currently seeking to be legitimized as "the Kurdistan Army" and the Iraqi Zakho Military Academy, based on Kurdish soil in the Dohuk governorate. While the former provides insight into Kurdistan's increasing autonomy, the latter allows us to understand the region's role in Iraq's reconstruction after the fall of Saddam Hussein.

Finally, an analysis of the armed forces based in the Kurdish territory gives considerable insight into the interdependence between the Kurdish periphery and the Iraqi centre. As I will show in the following pages, a proper analysis of the increasing autonomy of the Kurdistan Region requires a more nuanced understanding of Kurdistan. In other words, Kurdistan must be understood from within, including the terms of its relationship with Baghdad, the process of increased independence from the former Iraqi state and its politics proper in the post-Saddam era.[6]

The Peshmerga Security Forces: Autonomy through the Centre, Autonomy from the Centre

The integration of Peshmerga forces into the new Iraqi army is one of the principle sources of tension between Baghdad and Erbil. The Iraqi Constitution, approved by referendum in October 2005, stipulates that all secondary armed militia forces be integrated into a singular national army.[7] In spite of this, the KRG persists in refusing to disband its Peshmerga units and, above all, to label them "militia." The Kurdish authorities maintain that the Peshmergas are "regular forces" with a specific function: securing the borders of regional Kurdistan. The KRG's refusal is principally based on their wish to maintain a regional defence force independent from Baghdad.

It is difficult to accurately define the Peshmerga armed forces today for two reasons: first, because of the role they have played in the process of Kurdish national construction, and second, because of their current degree of military organization. If the Kurdish nationalist militants do not hesitate to refer to it as a regular army of the Kurdistan region, the political leaders of the Kurdish Democratic Party (KDP) officially define it as a "force for the securitization of the region" (Interview with M., Erbil, April 2009). Although former high-ranking officials in the Iraqi army consider it "an insult to the military tradition of Iraq,"[8] officers of the new Iraqi army define it as a "national police force in charge of border control" that will soon become part of the New Iraqi army (Interview with B. Zeibari, Dohuk, April 2009).

Considered from a purely technical angle, the Peshmerga security forces of today display all of the characteristics of a regular army. They have a well-defined internal hierarchy, all of the requisite symbolic and ceremonial systems, training camps where different programs are offered for regular soldiers and specialized forces, a complete and complex set of uniforms, and so on. Even though the Peshmergas were originally an armed resistance movement,[9] they currently exhibit many key characteristics of regular armed forces. So how did the resistance movement become a structured, armed corps? What model was assumed for the current military and corresponding training structures?

To answer these questions, we need to highlight the key phases in the history of the Peshmerga Security Forces and acknowledge the contribution of the Peshmerga's interaction with the former Iraqi army and the United States (US) army in its transformation from a guerrilla movement into a structured armed corps.

The Peshmerga security corps is the end result of the tensions between the rising powers of the Kurdish nationalist movement and the former Iraqi state. The organizational level of this centrifugal armed force indirectly benefited from the failure of the centripetal efforts of the Iraqi state. Moreover, the former Iraqi army provided the Peshmerga movement a military model of organization.

Since the 1940s, the relationship between the Iraqi army and the Peshmergas has not simply been one of antagonism. On the contrary, the Peshmergas inherited a considerable number of combat techniques, organizational models and modes of operation that defined the former Iraqi army. After deserting the Iraqi army and returning to the Peshmerga movement, Kurdish officers trained at Rustamiyah Military Academy in Baghdad imported these elements of military organization into the Kurdish resistance movement.[10] From the Iraqi state's very inception, Kurds and other communities participated in the state's central institutions, particularly in the army. Their presence grew considerably under the Republican regimes (1958–68), especially in the lower to middle ranks of the army (Marr, 1985: 282). Nonetheless, following Saddam Hussein's rise to power, opportunities for social mobility within the army were greatly curbed.[11] This encouraged deserting and subsequent reintegration into the Peshmerga movement, a development that often opened the door for higher army ranks to enter the Kurdish Nationalist Resistance.[12] Such desertions of Kurdish officers from the Iraqi army occurred at four principle junctures: on the occasion of the Barzani revolt that preceded the Algiers Accord (1974–75); during the Iran–Iraq war (1980–88); after the 1991 uprising throughout the sanctions period (1991–2003); and after the 2003 fall of Saddam Hussein's regime (Lortz, 2005).

Of these, the most significant "migration" took place during the sanctions. Attracted by generous salaries from Erbil, many Kurdish officers "returned to the mountains."[13] A turning point in the history of Kurdistan was reached in 1991 when the region attained a certain degree of autonomy from Baghdad.

During this decade, the Peshmergas' status shifted from Kurdish tribal militia to armed corps aspiring to become "Kurdistan's Army." Nevertheless, the movement's internal divisions continued to see Peshmergas loyal to Massoud Barzani, and the KDP oppose those loyal to Jalal Talabani and the Patriotic Union of Kurdistan (PUK). The differences between the two parties in the Kurdish political arena have been apparent since the 1970s,[14] and they have continued beyond 1991. While the KDP Peshmergas took control of the governorates of Dohuk and the northern part of the governorate of Erbil, the PUK Peshmergas established their authority at Sulaymaniyah (Tripp, 2007: 278). These divisions undermined attempts to construct a unified Kurdish army.

Throughout the 1990s, each of the two Peshmerga factions sought first to legitimize itself and become "an army" and second, to organize itself and become "the Kurdistan army." They did this by reproducing their long-standing enemy's organizational model. Each faction attempted to hone its forces' organization at the training centres based in Erbil, Dohuk, Sulaymaniyah and Kirkuk. Those Kurdish officers formerly of the Iraqi army were co-opted by both sides—they were put in charge of Peshmerga training with the intention to "transform them into officers" on the basis of programs used at the Rustamiyah Military

Academy in Baghdad where officers were trained in "special training programs" (*daurat khassa*) within each of the training centres. Yet leaders of both factions wasted no time in founding "military academies" that were veritable "machines to produce officers":

> At this point [in the 1990s], the military academies of Zakho and Sulaymaniyah were founded. They needed "a machine to produce officers." These academies served to train and graduate officers but also to recognize former Peshmerga fighters as officers, giving them a military rank. The Peshmerga didn't really have military studies so what they did was to take up the systems in place at Baghdad. It was really the same academy as in Baghdad in terms of the training structure and organization. (Interview with a high-rank Peshmerga of the Zerevani Corps trained in Zakho Academy during the 1990s. Erbil, April 2009)

As many Peshmerga officers report, the "Academy" institutions became doubly useful to Peshmerga on both sides. Not only did they serve to legitimize promotions given to soldiers within the training centres, but they also helped to train young Peshmergas to become officers. The PUK was the first to found a military academy near Sulaymaniyah in 1993. The founding of the Zakho academy by the KDP followed shortly thereafter in 1994–95 (Fantappié, 2009: 47–57). Kurdish officers of the Iraqi army were charged with the training programs and the management of the academies. Those affiliated with the PUK taught at Sulaymaniyah, while those affiliated with Barzani and the KPD were responsible for training at Zakho. Within these institutions, the Peshmergas organized themselves on the basis of the British military system, which was also the organizational system of the former Iraqi army.[15] At Zakho and Sulaymaniyah, the programs for training recruits and for teaching military science were based on those used in Baghdad.[16] In addition, military intelligence personnel (*asaysh*) were also organized and affiliated, respectively, with both parties.

Tensions between the factions did not take long to spill over, erupting halfway through the 1990s (1994–98). At one point during the conflict, Massoud Barzani called on the Iraqi army to intervene in order to regain control of the governorate of Erbil. Saddam's Republican Guards provided a decisive contribution to the defeat of J. Talabani's Peshmerga.[17] Conflict between the KDP and PUK lasted until September 1998, when the two sides agreed on a US-backed ceasefire. Over the course of the following years, both parties continued to share control of Kurdistan's territories. The project to train a unified military corps resurfaced with the

American invasion of Iraq, when the Peshmerga formed a common front for the securitization of the northern governorates and also managed to control certain territories outside of Kurdistan's traditional borders.

The American army also contributed to the increase of the organizational level of the Peshmerga forces, giving them the legitimacy of regular armed forces during "Operation Iraqi Freedom" in 2003. Also, the American invasion gave the Peshmerga the opportunity to deploy beyond traditional areas into the governorates of Ninewah (Mosul, Sijar, Makhmour and Sheikhan), Diyala and Kirkuk (Asaad, 2008). The collaboration with special American forces in Mosul led to the creation of a Peshmerga corps called the "Kurdish special forces," which brought together the best fighters of the region.

This collaboration and the securitization of the northern governorates represented another important step in the Peshmerga forces' organization process. For the first time, the soldiers of these special units confronted guerrillas and fought Islamist and nationalist insurgency groups,[18] even though, traditionally, their training had focused almost exclusively on altitude and alpine warfare. Collaboration with the American forces allowed them to refine their combat techniques and provided them the legitimacy necessary to be considered regular military forces in charge of national securitization. Upon the arrival of the US Special Forces Group in January 2003, the Peshmerga were assigned by the US army to destroy Ansar al-Islam, based on the Iraqi side of the Iran–Iraq border, and to contain the revolt organized by the Republican Guard units in Kirkuk and Mosul.

In April 2003, Paul Bremer's Coalition Provisional Authority (CPA) announced the disbanding of the Iraqi army, which allowed the Peshmerga to integrate unemployed, specialized Kurdish officers of the former Iraqi army.[19] The disbanding also set the conditions for a "security vacuum" that made the Peshmergas the only autonomous armed forces in charge of maintaining security (International Crisis Group, 2003). Similarly, in the first phase of the "political reconstruction" of Iraq, the Kurds helped to fill the political void of post-Saddam Iraq. Kurdish participation in the "centre," from which they were traditionally excluded, had major consequences for domestic politics in Kurdistan. While Talabani became the Iraqi president in 2005, Barzani consolidated his power within the KRG as President of the Iraqi Kurdistan Region. Barzani's Peshmergas (Zerevani Peshmerga Security Forces) progressively sought legitimization as soldiers of the "Army of Kurdistan," while part of Talabani's Peshmerga became integrated into the New Iraqi Army.

The Zerevani Peshmerga Security Forces are the end product of this long transformation. They are based in Erbil at the Zerevani training camp, which includes the offices of the high ranking military officials as well as the specific training facilities.[20] The camp houses five divisions for a total of over 100,000 men, who are assigned different roles (securitization of a particular part of the city, bodyguards for consulates and embassies, etc.).[21] Today, the majority of Peshmergas are in charge of border control—particularly "borders with Iraq"—and securing internal roadways.

The training camps are the result of a patchwork of different models: they draw principally on the training that was offered in Iraqi academies, complemented by techniques typical of the Peshmerga movement (mountain-based training, navigation, Kalashnikov assembly and disassembly) and anti-terrorist techniques learned from the US Army. The mixture of these different models allows the Peshmerga forces to maintain a high level of military efficiency. This military efficiency is also the outcome of a strategic internal equilibrium between the KDP political leadership and the military political branch. Civilian leadership maintains control over the military by bestowing high ranking positions to the Kurdish officers who had experience in the Peshmerga resistance prior to the 1990s. In contrast, officers of the former Iraqi army who have only recently shifted to the Peshmerga movement are primarily in charge of entertainment and technical advising. In this way, the KDP has managed to secure control over its security forces without undermining technical efficiency. As a result, it benefits from the loyalty and obedience of past Peshmerga fighters and from the military knowledge of the officers of the former Iraqi army.

Despite the technical similarities with other national armies, the members of the Peshmerga security forces originate mainly from two governorates—Erbil and Dohuk—although some are also from Ninewa. Furthermore, the territories over which the security forces hold jurisdiction are limited to those under Barzani's and KDP control. Currently, the Zerevani Peshmergas are in charge of security in the governorates of Erbil and Dohuk, with partial representation in Mosul. Conversely, the Sulaymaniyah governorate is under the control of the PUK Peshmergas. Although Erbil's Peshmerga Ministry finances the Zerevani forces, the Sulaymaniyah Ministry finances its own Peshmergas, and their respective military intelligence services are also separate.

The first agreement regarding the unification of the Peshmerga Ministries was signed in January 2006, but it has yet to be applied.[22] More recently, in April 2009, both leaders announced that the ministries would indeed be combined and a unified commando unit established. The integration of the two Peshmerga ministries into one organization, however, and even the creation of a unified commando unit across both factions, does not necessarily equate to the establishment of a truly unified military force or a "United Army of Kurdistan." Indeed, it is unlikely that such an announced integration would be successfully implemented, for while administratively unified, each will continue to maintain control over its "portion of Kurdistan" and recruit on the basis of birth origins. Also, given that the KDP won the July 2009 elections, senior positions in the Peshmerga ministries and the military information services might be given to Barzani, which could lead to the progressive absorption of PUK Peshmergas into the Zerevani and Erbil forces.

The relationship between Kurdistan and the central Iraqi power in Baghdad strongly influences such a united army project. It is highly unlikely that the latter would accept two active armies in Iraq. A compromise between the Kurdish periphery and Baghdad may therefore see the progressive integration of Peshmerga units into the Iraqi army. Regardless, it is probable that, at such a time, the KRG would seek to maintain control over these units at all costs. Such a strategy would have Peshmerga officials agree to the formal integration of their units into a central army while maintaining control over them, thus ensuring they remain loyal to the KDP and the PUK respectively. The central Iraqi government could employ the "old technique" of divide and rule. Conversely, Baghdad could put pressure on the division between the two parties in an attempt to absorb the centrifugal trend of the Kurdish region, a strategy that was employed several times during the Saddam Hussein era. The Nouri al-Maliki government could try to co-opt Talabani forces for the central government against his adversary Massoud Barzani. However, this hypothesis seems more unlikely than the progressive integration of the PUK Peshmerga into the KDP forces. Kurdish national solidarity seems to trump competition between the traditional two parties in times of increased power at the centre. Following another traditional alliance-path, the joining of the two parties against a common enemy is ensured, especially in cases where the centre is perceived to be an "Arab centre" that threatens Kurdish autonomy.

The New Iraqi Army and Its Dependence on the Periphery

The increasing autonomy of the Kurdish Regional Government and the organization of its armed forces were achieved with the help of the technical and human resources of the former centre. Paradoxically, the former Iraqi army and its officers played a crucial role in inspiring and helping to transform the Peshmergas into an armed corps.

After the state's collapse the centrifugal forces, traditionally excluded by the central power, were charged with the reconstruction of a new Iraqi political centre and its institutional apparatus. Until 2003, the Kurdish periphery fought the central government in order to achieve and ensure its own autonomy, but the rebuilding of the Iraqi state required the participation of each of the previous centrifugal forces. Once the Kurdish leadership had infiltrated the central institution apparatus, its strategy consisted of ensuring Kurdish participation in the centre in order to consolidate its own autonomy. In spite of this development, the new Iraqi institutions and army have become increasingly independent from the different political forces that had helped to create them.

Currently, the relationship between Kurdistan and Baghdad remains a key issue in the process of Kurdistan's regional construction and that of Iraq. The political centre's dissolution in 2003 and the subsequent disbanding of its institutions heralded the arrival of the Kurds in Baghdad, which ultimately saw Kurds placed at the very centre of Iraqi politics. Playing an active role in the centre's reconstruction has allowed Kurdish politicians to participate in a number of key government institutions and obtain leverage from the regions under control of these institutions. Since 2005, the Kurdish Front (Democratic-Patriotic Alliance) led by the KDP has come to realize that its presence in Baghdad is necessary in order to consolidate Kurdistan's autonomy.[23] If the central Iraqi state previously imposed its politics on the Kurdish periphery, the latter is now an integral part of the former and thus can play this card to its advantage. Increasingly, Kurdistan's relationship with the government in Baghdad has been framed as Erbil "invading" the centre and "Kurdifying it." Such discourse has come to colour the Erbil/Baghdad relationship.

This strategy becomes more apparent when analyzing the case of the reconstruction of the Iraqi army. From 2005 onward, four military academies took charge of training the officers of the new Iraqi army: the Nasiriyah Academy, in a nearly exclusive Shi'a region; the Ar-Rustamiyah Academy in Baghdad, which has reopened its doors; and finally the two

Kurdish military academies of Zakho and Sulaymaniyah, which are to be "transformed" into Iraqi military academies. Although the officer training centres were previously in Baghdad, the capital's academy is now but one of four institutions in charge of providing the Iraqi army with new officers. This fragmentation of officer training centres means that most are now located in regional centres that are seeking ever greater autonomy, as evidenced by the case of the Zakho Military Academy.

The Zakho Military Academy

Since 2004, the Zakho Military Academy has officially been one of four Iraqi military academies dependent upon Baghdad's Defense Ministry. How did this "transformation" occur, and to what extent has the former Kurdish KDP-affiliated academy been transformed into a national Iraqi academy? Clearly, the Zakho Military Academy has profited from central government financing. Prior to 2004, it depended essentially on financing from the KRG (and more specifically financing reserved for Barzani's KDP Peshmerga Ministry), but since the transfer of responsibility, both officers and regular soldiers have received pay raises (regular soldiers saw a salary increase of around 200 dollars—from 500 to 700 dollars, or 787,000 dinars) (Interview with T., Kurdish soldier of the New Iraqi army, Zakho Military Academy, April 2009). The academy improved its facilities (refectory, dormitories, etc.) and expanded them to be able to cater to an increasing number of students. The academy was also able to finance the construction of new training structures (training arena, professional 500m running track, swimming pool, etc.) and tend to the general maintenance of all of the buildings (the facility is particularly clean, and the edifices are gilded with decorative floral bands) (Interview with M., Lieutenant Colonel in Zakho, April 2009).[24] Furthermore, before 2004, lessons were given half in Kurdish and half in Arabic, but today the official language of instruction is Arabic. The Baghdad Ministry of Defense now officially oversees recruitment, whereas before, recruitment was managed by the Erbil Peshmerga Ministry.

If the transition has led to structural renovations and better infrastructure and financing in general, the academy's transformations appear to be far less consequential in human terms—officers employed, recruits trained and regular soldiers enrolled at Zakho. Since its establishment in the mid-1990s, the Zakho academy had been run by Kurdish officers from the former Iraqi army. They were employed by the academy with the understanding that they would use military knowledge gathered in

Baghdad to train the officers of the Kurdistan Democratic Party. In 2005, 10 officers from the former Iraqi army joined the 27 that were already running the academy (Interview with C., Brigadier in Zakho, April 2009). Nonetheless, the majority currently have a broadly similar profile: almost all of the upper ranking members of the academy (from Captain to General) are Kurdish and are originally from the Dohuk region (principally the cities of Aqrah and Zakho). Some of them graduated at the end of the 1980s from the Baghdad Academy, ultimately returning to the Zakho Academy during the 1990s, while others joined the academy after the army was disbanded in 2003.

Overall, there has been limited change in personnel since the Zakho academy became a part of the Iraqi army academies. One marked change is the presence of a lone Sunni Arab officer among the upper ranking members. He entered the academy in 2006 and is part of the correspondence sector between the Baghdad Academy and the Zakho Academy.

Similarly, there are very few Arabs among the recruits currently in training to become officers. An agreement, stipulated between the Ministry of Defense and the Kurdistan government, cites equal representation for Arab students and Kurdish students, but the latter seem to make up a majority of the academy's enrolment. A visit to the academy's dormitories is sufficient to observe that not only are the majority of students Kurdish, but also that Arabs and Kurds have difficulties sharing the same quarters.[25] Relationships between young Kurdish recruits and young Arab recruits are clearly precarious, and not least for linguistic reasons. Since 1991, the curriculum of regular Kurdish schools all but did away with Arab language teaching, a policy that has clearly compromised the possibility of subsequent integration between young Kurds and Arabs. Although the academy's official language is Arabic, it appears that the preferred language for communication on all levels is still Kurdish.[26]

This discrepancy can be seen most among regular soldiers, all of whom are Kurdish and originally from the governorates of Dohuk, Erbil and Mosul. Even though the Ministry of Defense should have formally taken over the recruitment process, Baghdad's first list of candidates is subsequently examined by the Zakho academy's administration, giving them the last word in the choice of new recruits (Interview with Major M., Zakho, April 2009). As a result, the Zakho Academy's internal composition has not really changed since 2005, but a change of labels grants it access to increased financing and more sophisticated weaponry. A soldier who witnessed the transition of Zakho Academy affirms:

In 2003 I was recruited by the Zakho Academy when it was still a Kurdish Academy. Afterwards, it became an Iraqi Academy ... [B]ut, quite frankly I haven't noticed any relevant differences between now and then. Before, the Academy was dependent from the Peshmerga Ministry and since 2005 it depends from [sic] the Ministry of Defense in Baghdad. Moreover, the number of officers increased as well as our salary... that's all. (Interview with C., a Kurdish soldier in Zakhu, April 2009)

Ultimately, the KRG benefited from the transformation of the Zakho Academy into an Iraqi military academy to the extent that it was able to access the centre's resources and still maintain autonomy in the training of its own officers. The decision to transform the Kurdish academy into an Iraqi academy is a strategy aimed at "installing" Kurdish security forces in a central institution in formal terms, which effectively allows them to retain strong affiliations with the government of Kurdistan and notably the KDP.

When visiting the Zakho academy, it is hard to believe that it is a military academy for the new Iraqi army. The academy's symbol is stitched around the right arm of every uniform. The flag is emblazoned with the academy's symbol and dominates the esplanade where daily training takes place. The Iraqi flag is all but lost among the images and symbols of Kurdistan.

The control of the KDP over the academy's internal functioning fuels feelings of frustration among the mid-ranking cadres; it also acts to undermine the young recruits' and soldiers' motivation as they tire of defining the new Iraqi army's identity. The promotion of loyalty to the KDP further acts to undermine the technical efficiency of the new Iraqi army. Unsatisfied and frustrated, the middle ranking officers and soldiers tend to evaluate the former Iraqi army and the Peshmerga security corps as a more efficient armed force in terms of military technique and training. For some, the former Iraqi army seems to have represented a "role model" in terms of military technique and military formation, while others cite the Peshmerga security corps as a training program role model.

In contemporary times, the new Iraqi army does not function as a space for the inclusion of the many communities that make up Iraq, nor does it act as an instrument of coercion for a lone dictator, as it was under Saddam Hussein's regime. The new Iraqi army rather appears to be a field of competition for the country's dominant political forces, which employ central financial resources to increase their respective military capabilities. Instead of being reconstructed, the centre of Iraq has become recomposed of the political parties of the post-Saddam era and functions in defence of the ethnic and confessional communities that they represent. Given that both the opponents and centres of power are multiplying, each seeks greater military resource allocations to ensure their own security.

This rivalry began within Kurdistan at a time when both predominant political factions had control over their own Iraqi academy. Although the KDP controls the Zakho Academy, the PUK maintains control over the Sualymanyah Academy. The competition has taken on the form of an Arab–Kurdish confrontation, such as when the Iraqi battalions of the KDP sought to maintain their presence within the "borderline" territories between Kurdistan and Iraq.

Mosul

The case of Mosul shows the extent to which the Kurdish battalions of the Iraqi army, which previously followed the orders of Nouri al-Maliki, now follow the head of the KDP, Massoud Barzani. In 2003, Barzani's Peshmerga were charged with the task of securing Mosul in collaboration with the 101st division led by General Petraeus. But since 2005, the Peshmerga forces have been gradually replaced with the first divisions of the New Iraqi Army (Iraqi Civil Defense Corps [ICDC]). Yet the result of the 2005 elections allowed the KDP to maintain its control over the ICDC forces, which are led mainly by Kurdish officers. By the end of 2008, Nouri al-Maliki had decided to progressively replace Kurdish officers with Sunni and Shi'a Arab officers from Baghdad. In one particular case, Kurdish officers of the Iraqi army even refused to obey their transfer from the Ninewah governorate.[27] In this context, the loyalty of the Kurdish officers of the New Iraqi Army to the central government remains uncertain, given their devotion to the KDP's agenda.

Kurdish officers are mainly recruited and trained in the military academies based in the Kurdistan territory. While they have also maintained their presence in the central academy of Rustamiyah, they are probably not trained in the southern academy of Nasiriyah. The academy system in present-day Iraq reflects the fragmentation of a central power faced with pressure from the centrifugal forces. The al-Maliki administration's effort to reorganize the military formation around the Iraqi capital of Baghdad, in the Rustamiyah Academy, will encounter strong opposition from the Kurdish academies and from some of the officers strongly affiliated with the Kurdish political leadership.

Beyond the political affiliation of the high-ranking Kurdish senior officers, many of the middle-ranking officers of the northern academies were also previously part of the former Iraqi army. According to several interviews conducted by the author, these middle-ranking officers also show an attachment to the idea of a central Iraqi state that does not monopolize power in the hands of an Arab government. Given such circumstances, Baghdad is aiming to re-establish its grip over the whole of the Iraqi army and should thus try to put targeted pressure on these Kurdish military officers.

Conclusion

This chapter has aimed to highlight the interdependence between the Kurdistan region and the central government in Baghdad, by analyzing Kurdish political and security autonomy as an expression of the centrifugal forces within the Iraqi state formation.

Profound societal linkages connect the past, present and future of Iraqi Kurdistan to the Iraqi state. While claiming to be an autonomous region, contemporary Kurdistan and its future form remain undeniably linked to Iraq. In this chapter, Iraqi Kurdistan has been treated as a "territory" of Iraq rather than as an "autonomous region," although in reality, this territory was effectively incorporated into Iraq for 50 years, having been governed by the central administration and populated by people that commuted from Baghdad or to Mosul for studies or work. The "channels" that have enabled communication between Iraq and Kurdistan are numerous, and they traverse the administrative structures and the life stories of three generations. Similarly, even today, the links between the new Iraq are many; Kurdistan is an "autonomous region," but it still retains its status as a "territory" and is therefore part of the contemporary Iraqi state. Thus, even though the Kurdish periphery obtained autonomy in 1991, historical dynamics continue to define its relationship with the Iraqi centre. Kurdistan constructed a number of its institutions, and drew partial inspiration from, the model that has been closest to it—the Iraqi state. The progressive transition of the Peshmerga movement toward an armed corps was based on the organizational paradigm of the Iraqi army.

The interactions between Kurdistan and Iraq intensified when the Iraqi state was collapsing in March 2003. The dissolution of its central institutions—most notably the army—provided an opportunity to appropriate the centre and strongly influence the reconstruction process. The

Kurdish Zakho Military Academy's transition to an Iraqi Zakho Military Academy illustrates the increasing predominance of the Kurdish security forces within the Iraqi army, particularly those affiliated with the KDP.

In consideration of this interdependence, a Kurdish–Arab military clash between Peshmerga, in alliance with the Kurdish officers of the Iraqi military academies, and the Arab leadership of new Iraqi army is hardly possible. Some of the Peshmerga officers and Kurdish officers of the new Iraqi army still share a common attachment to the idea of a central Iraqi state. This hypothesis becomes more probable if the central government becomes increasingly perceived as a monotonic Arab power, similar to how it was perceived during the last decades of the Saddam Hussein era.

Instead of being expressed in a direct military clash, the Kurdish–Arab competition will probably be played out as a political struggle in the central institutions of government. Within this context, the daily political compromise between the Arab and Kurdish political forces will determine the equilibrium of power-sharing between both polities.

Iraqi Kurdistan, given its special status, is most often "dissociated" from the Iraqi context. In this chapter, I have proposed to "resituate Kurdistan within Iraq" to show the interdependence between the "centre" (the central Iraqi state) and one of its peripheries (Iraqi Kurdistan) throughout the history of Iraq. It is crucial that we consider this interdependence today, at a time when such definitions are becoming increasingly relevant.

Notes

1 This chapter is based on research conducted in Iraqi Kurdistan in April 2009. The fieldwork has been carried out in the main cities of Kurdistan (Erbil, Sualymanyah, Dohuk and Zakho). The author conducted 15 interviews within the Peshmerga Security Corps (Zerevani) with high rank officials from the former Iraqi army, the new "Peshmerga officers" and the "Peshmerga soldiers." Moreover, the author had the opportunity to visit the Zakho Military Academy where 18 interviews were held with officers and soldiers who had witnessed the transition from the Kurdish Academy to the Iraqi Academy.
2 For broader analyses of the centrifugal and centripetal forces in the state-building process see Elias, 1980 and Badie, 1988.
3 For a comparative analysis of the British mandate period and the American administration in Iraq since 2003, see Luizard, 2004.
4 See Marr, 1985: 288.
5 For an analysis of the recent developments in the KRG–Baghdad relationship, see International Crisis Group, 2009b.

6 The relationship between the Kurds and the central state in Iraq, Iran and Turkey has been analyzed in Bozarslan, 1997.
7 In 2004, the Transitional Autonomy Law (TAL) avoided directly addressing the militia problem. A second attempt to deal with the problem culminated in Allawi announcing a deal on June 2004, which committed all of the parties to the demobilization of their militias. However, A. Mirad, a senior Patriotic Union of Kurdistan (PUK) leader, claimed that: "The Peshmerga are not included in the agreement" (Dodge, 2005: 20). Article 9.B of the Iraqi Constitution approved October 15, 2005 states, "The formation of military militias outside the framework of the armed forces is prohibited."
8 It is nonetheless revealing to recite the opinion of a privileged witness, one of the rare high-ranking Kurdish officials of the former Iraqi army to have left the military world for the business world: "People from these Peshmerga training camps don't even know how to read and write, some of them became battalion commander or even general without any preparation. In terms of 'military science' they're truly impious" (or *Kuffar*, in Arabic).
9 The confrontations between the first Peshmerga fighters and the Iraqi army began in the 1930s. The Peshmerga movement expanded in the 1940s when Mustafa Barzani organized his Peshmergas through the "Republic of Mahabad" experiment (1945–46). The Peshmergas began to train themselves as a resistance movement throughout the 1960s under the Republican regimes of Abdel al-Karim Qassem and Aref (1958–68). For a historical and military overview of the Peshmerga movement, see Lortz, 2005.
10 The Rustamiyah Military Academy, based in the east of Baghdad, was one of the best military academies of the Middle East. The height of its influence was in the 1970s. For more information, see: http://www.patriotfiles.com/index.php?name=Sections&req=viewarticle&artid=8076&page=1.
11 Once in power in 1978, Saddam Hussein implemented a veritable "Baathification" of the army. Recruitment was progressively done on the basis of political, ethnic and religious belonging (Picard, 1990; Parasiliti, 2000: 130–40).
12 Beyond purely nationalist motivations, social mobility as a factor must be taken into account. The majority of officers within the Iraqi army were Lieutenants or Captains. Once "returned to the mountain," they reached the rank of Sergeant or Battalion Commander. The passage from one armed corps to the next, particularly in the 1970s and 1990s, allowed the officers a degree of social mobility that they never would have had within the Iraqi army (Fantappié, 2009).
13 For an analysis of the economic situation in Kurdistan during the embargo, see Natali, 2007.
14 Although dissent within the KDP had begun during the 1960s, the PUK was officially only formed in Damascus in 1975 and was headed by J. Talabani and others ex-KDP followers. The PUK was formally organized in 1977 following Talabani's return to Iraq from his exile in Damascus. He divided his Peshmerga organization into regiments and stationed one regiment in each district of Iraqi Kurdistan. The growing Peshmerga organization caused tension with the KDP throughout the late 1970s (1976, 1977 and into 1978). During the Iran–Iraq War, Talabani and the PUK politically and militarily opposed Barzani and the KDP: first, in 1980, when he supported the Iranian Kurdish Democratic Party (KDPI)

against Barzani's forces that allied with Tehran; second, in 1984, when he negotiated a ceasefire with Saddam Hussein. With the creation of the Kurdistan National Front in 1987, the two parties organized a joint Peshmerga force. See McDowall, 2004: 352–66.
15 The military structure of the former Iraqi army has been analyzed by I. Al Marashi (2008).
16 One Kurdish officer who deserted the former Iraqi army and became an officer in the Zakho Academy confirmed: "At the Zakho Academy, I proposed to the young Peshmergas the same formation of the Rustamiyah Academy, I just translated it from (*sic*) Arab language to Kurdish language" (Interview, Erbil, April 2009).
17 Since 1996, the KDP has received help from the Iraqi army. The heaviest Iraqi attack occurred in Erbil in August 1996 when the Iraqi military seized Erbil and helped the KDP Peshmerga to push the PUK frontline closer to the Iranian border. As a result of the failed coup and the KDP–Iraqi alliance, numerous PUK leaders were captured (Lortz, 2005: 63–64).
18 In 2001, the PUK Peshmerga faced the Ansar al-Islam and al-Qaeda guerrilla fighters that were established on the Iraq–Iran border. Later in 2003, they began their collaboration with the US army to destroy the Islamist militants.
19 Order No.2, *Dissolution of the Entities*, proclaimed by the Coalition Provisional Authority (CPA) on April 23, 2003, prescribed the disbanding of Iraq armed forces, information services and the Ministry of Defense (Tripp, 2007: 282).
20 The "Zerevani" camp was constructed in part by the "Multinational Force" (MNF), based in Erbil after June 2004, to follow the peacekeeping process after the American invasion. This multinational force was made up of about 3,600 Korean troops, including engineers who helped construct the camp. The retreat of the "Zaytun Division" was announced in April 2007, see: http://www.unhcr.org/cgibin/texis/vtx/home/opendoc.pdf?tbl=SUBSITES&id=471efc6d16.
21 Although the number of Peshmergas has not been officially confirmed, some believe the number to be around 100, 000 fighters (Asaad, 2008).
22 "The Kurdistan Government Unification Agreement" anticipates the unification of the Ministries that were separated into two parts in 1991: the Ministry of Finance, Justice and of Peshmergas. See http://www.unhcr.org/refworld/country,,NATLEGBOD,,IRQ,,469cdd7a2,0.html.
23 The Democratic Patriotic Alliance of Kurdistan is the name of the electoral coalition first presented as a united Kurdish list in the January 2005 elections in Iraq. The alliance represents a coalition of the KDP and PUK and other smaller Kurdish parties (Tripp, 2007: 290).
24 During my visit to Zakho, M. showed me all of the training spaces and told me about the changes that had taken place inside the academy since 2005. As well, in certain interviews, the officers employed at Zakho since the 1990s made multiple mentions of the improved infrastructure and services at the Academy since 2005.
25 During my stay at Zakho, I had the occasion to visit the dormitories of students from the academy of the first and second battalion. The Arab students, though present, were but a minority. As such, it is difficult to find mixed rooms (Kurdish and Arab students).

26 During my stay at Zakho, I had the opportunity to dine with the upper-ranking officers of the academy who communicated in Kurdish with one another.
27 For more information about the Arab-Kurd clash in Mosul after 2003, see International Crisis Group, 2009a: 7–8; Dagher, 2007; Kamal, 2009.

Works Cited

Al Marashi, I. (2008). *Iraq's Armed Forces: An Analytical History*. New York, NY: Routledge.
Asaad, Dana (2008). "The Pershmerga: Militia or Regular Army?" *Niqash*. Vol. 21 (May). Available at: http://www.niqash.org/content.php?contentTypeID=75&id=2205&lang=0.
Badie, B. (1998). *Le développement politique*. Paris: Economica.
Batatu, Hanna (1978). *The Old Social Classes and the Revolutionary Movements of Iraq's Old Landed and Commercial Classes and its Communists, Ba'athists, and Free Officers*. Princeton, NJ: Princeton University Press.
Bozarslan, H. (1997). *La question kurde. Etats et minorités au Moyen Orient*. Paris: Presses de Sciences.
Dagher, S. (2007). "Fractures in Iraq City as Kurds and Baghdad Vie." *The New York Times*. October 27.
Dodge, T. (2005). "Order and Violence in Post-Saddam Iraq," in *Iraq's Future: The aftermath of regime change*. Adelphi Papers. Issue 372: 9–23. New York, NY: Routledge,
Elias, N. (1982). *The Civilizing Process: State Formation and Civilization*. Oxford: Blackwell.
Fantappié, M. (2009). *Armée Irakienne: histoire d'un" tour de passe-passe" entre Bagdad et Irakien*. Paris: Mémoire pour l'IEP (Institut d'Etudes Politiques).
International Crisis Group (2003). *Iraq Building a New Security Structure*. Middle East Report, No. 20. December 23.
——— (2009a). *Iraq's Provincial Elections: The Stakes*. Middle East Report. January 27.
——— (2009b). *Iraq and the Kurds, Trouble along the Trigger Line*. Middle East Report. July 8.
Kamal. Adel (2009). "New Ninawa Governor Rejects Kurdish Alliance." *Niqash*. February 26. Available at: http://www.niqash.org/content.php?contentTypeID=75&id=2393&lang=0.
Lortz, M.G. (2005). *Willing to Face Death: A History of Military Forces—The Peshmergas—From the Ottoman Period to Present-Day Iraq*. Master of Arts thesis in international affairs, Florida State University, US. Available at: http://etd.lib.fsu.edu/theses/available/etd-11142005-144616/.
Luizard, J.P. (2004). *La question irakienne*. Paris: Fayard.
Marr, P. (1985). *The Modern History of Iraq*. New York, NY: Westview Press.
McDowall, D. (2004). *A Modern History of the Kurds*. London, UK: I.B. Tauris.

Natali, D. (2007). "The Spoil of Peace in Iraqi Kurdistan." *Third World Quarterly.* Vol. 28, No. 6: 1111–29.

Owen, R. (2001). *State, Power and Politics in the Making of the Modern Middle East.* New York: Routledge.

Parasiliti, A. (2000). "Friends in Need, Foes to Heed: The Iraqi Military in Politics (1)." *Middle East Policy.* Vol. VII, No. 4 (October): 130–40.

Picard, E. (1990). "Arab Military in Politics: From the Revolutionary Plot to the Authoritarian Regime," in *The Arab State,* edited by Giacomo Luciani. Pages 189–219. London: Routledge.

Tripp, C. (2007). *A History of Iraq,* rev. ed. Cambridge: Cambridge University Press.

Interviewees

M., Peshmerga soldier at Zerevani, Erbil, April 2009

K., Peshmerga Capitain at Zerevani, camp, April 2009

A.W., General of Peshmerga at Zerevani camp, April 2009

M., Head of the Military Intelligence, (KDP), Massif (Erbil), April 2009

C., Head of the training center of Zerevani Camp, ex-Kurdish officer of the former Iraqi Army, Erbil, April, 2009

C., a Kurdish soldier in Zakhu, April 2009

C., Capitan in Zakho, April 2009

M., Lieutenant Colonel in Zakho, April 2009

C., Brigadier in Zakho, April 2009

Major M., Zakho, April 2009

B. Zeibari, "Chief of Staff" of the Iraqi army, Dohuk, April 2009

An ex-officer of the former Iraqi army, Erbil, April 2009

T., Kurdish soldier of the New Iraqi army; visit at the Zakho Military Academy, April 2009

Interview with a high-rank Peshmerga of the Zerevani Corps trained in Zakho Academy during the 1990s. Erbil, April 2009

6
The Extinction of Iraqi Minorities
Challenge or Catastrophe?

Mokhtar Lamani

As former Arab League Ambassador and Special Envoy to Iraq (2006–2007), I witnessed Iraqis from various ethnic, religious and sectarian backgrounds suffering as their societal foundations collapsed—foundations that had been historically rooted in a Mesopotamian heritage. The current Iraqi crisis has become a question of life or death for hundreds of thousands of its citizens and this chapter aims to shed light on the dire situation that has unravelled on the ground in Iraq, particularly after 2003.

The Mesopotamian region, most of which corresponds to modern-day Iraq, has been home to two of humankind's greatest achievements: agriculture and urban civilization. The culmination of these two achievements resulted in the formation of Sumer, a collective of city-states. The region has been the birthplace and, for millennia, the home to dozens of ethnicities and religions that together formed a unique but delicate cultural, religious and social mosaic. This mosaic has persisted for centuries through various empires such as the Akkadian, Babylonian, the Kassite and the Assyrian and through the Islamic empires, up to the Ottoman Empire. This mosaic later became an important aspect of modern Iraq's state identity. For thousands of years, under countless regimes and through successive conflicts, these minority groups have persisted and enriched Iraq's social mosaic. The ongoing sectarian violence and the inability of the current Iraqi leadership to achieve national reconciliation and to establish a secure social environment has threatened to destroy the country's unique historical properties. Iraqi minorities are experiencing a disproportionate amount of violence and social instability that offers permanent exodus as the only escape. Although Iraq's minorities make up only 5 percent of the total population, after the 2003 United States (US) invasion of Iraq, they comprised more than 20 percent of the displaced population (Westcott, 2003).

Mesopotamia and the broader Middle East are composed of a myriad of different religious, ethnic and tribal minorities, all of which have coexisted throughout history and preserved their rich identities and traditions over the centuries. Despite their significant cultural and intellectual contributions to the diversity and prosperity of the communities in which they have resided, minority groups are often thrown into the vortex of contemporary conflicts throughout the Middle East. In some countries, many Middle Eastern minorities are subject to increasing hostility at the hands of extremist groups and governmental bodies. Ironically, some groups that are demographic majorities in their countries are minorities with respect to their political representation in the government, and consequently, they are subject to the tribulations that minorities experience.[1]

A constitution based on equal citizenship is still absent in the Middle East. One element of such a constitution would include the abolition of citizens needing to declare their ethnic and/or religious denominations on official government identification papers—a fact of life for people in most Middle East countries today. In certain cases, citizens are left with no choice but to affiliate themselves with denominations other than their own in order to be recognized by their government and officially represented denominations.

Modern Iraq has crystallized strong geopolitical and geostrategic tensions that are marked by three layers of complexity. The first is the unfolding situation of Iraq's internal socio-political crisis and its varying effects; the second has at its root the extremely complex nature of the region's political dimension, in particular with Iran and other neighbours, and its interplay with the internal aspects of the Iraqi crisis; and the third is the international pressures that are inherent to Iraq's position in the region, compounded by its geopolitical importance to the international economy as a potentially major oil producer and its strategic location on the Arab-Persian Gulf. These geopolitical and geostrategic tensions cannot be divorced from the tensions and threats that Iraq's minorities face on a daily basis. Minorities are used as pawns by all parties on the chessboard—i.e., the new Iraq—as the internal, regional and international struggle for Iraqi allies intensifies. Little if any attention is paid to minorities' genuine needs; rather, their suffering is used to advance the agenda of others.

In 2008, the original objective of this study involved conducting field research on Iraqi minorities and any diasporas that may have relocated to Syria, Jordan or Egypt (where Syria hosts the most Iraqi refugees of any country at 1.2 million; Jordan follows next with 500,000) (Costantini, 2009). Unfortunately, this study did not cover Syria, as studying the situation of its displaced Iraqi minorities was unwelcome at the time. Indeed, throughout the entire Middle East, academic and non-governmental investigations surrounding minority issues have always been a sensitive topic.[2]

If there were ever a need for dynamic new thinking to address governance challenges in Iraq, it is now. By sounding the alarm over the desperate plight of Iraq's minorities, it is hoped that this chapter can begin to stimulate much-needed dialogue that can advance positive change and the protection of Iraq's threatened minorities.

Where the term "minorities" is used in this chapter, it refers to the many ethnic and religious groups that have historically existed in Iraq; "minorities" as a term is not a simplistic typology used by occupying forces to explain Iraq's ethnic makeup. There is great diversity beyond the artificial divisions (between Shi'a, Sunni and Kurd) that have become common-speak in Western media. In many ways, the contemporary Iraqi political system that has divided Iraqi people into three ethnic groups has actually emphasized minorities' vulnerabilities to the dangers that have persisted since 2003.

The purpose of this chapter is to illuminate, as best as possible, the suffering that Iraqi minorities are currently enduring—although the individuals of each group suffer in their own unique and particular way. The subject of this chapter is one that is constantly evolving; the situation on the ground in Iraq and its implications for all Iraqis is a rapidly changing dynamic. In order to update various conclusions and assess the current direction of events, the intention is to present as accurate a portrait as possible. Also offered in this chapter are suggestions that may help to alleviate the very difficult circumstances in which Iraqi minorities are finding themselves.

The Situation of Iraq's Minorities since 2003

It is useful to begin by noting that all Iraqis are suffering and that this chapter is not meant to devalue the suffering of any group or individual.

However, there are specificities to the case of minorities that places them under particularly exceptional threat. With the post-2003 rise of sectarianism in Iraqi society, it has been estimated that as many as 25 to 30 percent of the general population have been forced to leave their homes—leaving them either internally or externally displaced. According to the United Nations High Commissioner for Refugees (UNHCR), there were 4.5 million Iraqi refugees at the beginning of 2008, and 2.3 million and 2.2 million were internally and externally displaced, respectively (Costantini, 2009). In such an existence, one of every seven Iraqis is likely to be subject to some type of displacement. In the case of Iraq's minorities, however, the percentage of those displaced is much higher. Specifically, for example, more than 80 percent of the Mandaean population has been forced to flee. Among Iraqi Christians and other ethnic or religious groups, nearly 60 percent of their populations have been displaced (Taneja, 2007).

Many Iraqi minorities are at a real risk of extinction. As one interfaith expert consulted by the author stated, "When a Muslim is driven from his home, he usually plans on returning once the situation has stabilized; when a Christian or other minority leaves, they never want to come back"(Lamani, 2009). Sadly, the evidence collected to date seems to support this view; the UNHCR reported that 30 percent of the 1.8 million Iraqi refugees that are currently seeking asylum are of a minority. In 2007 however, the UNHCR reported that less than 1 percent of displaced Iraqi refugees returned; even among this small number of returnees, not a single Christian, Mandaean or Yezidi person was reported (UNHCR, 2008: 13).

Another example of expulsion was the Faili Kurds from Iraq during the Iran–Iraq war. For approximately 40 years, campaigns against minorities were carried out by successive Baghdad governments—essentially systematic campaigns of expulsion and/or assimilation (Fawcett and Tanner, 2002). Kurds, Turkmen and Assyrians—among other minorities—were targeted and forced from their homes. If violence was not a feasible means of driving forth these campaigns, institutionalized discrimination was utilized; governments implemented restrictions on access to education and property ownership depending on varying discriminating characteristics. Commonly, Arabs from the other Iraqi regions were imported to replace those minorities forced to leave. The Kirkuk region served as a large incentive for such campaigns due to its rich wealth in precious resources of oil and arable land. As one Iraqi Kurd's story revealed,

Any non-Arab who needs to have any official dealings with the Iraqi Government—whether property conveyance, vehicle registration or enrolling children in schools—has to fill in a form that says: "I wish to correct my ethnic origin into Arabic." Those who refuse to sign the form are automatically expelled to the Kurdish-controlled area. Those who "correct" their ethnic identity are told that "since they are Arabs," they should move to the south of Iraq. (BBC, 2001)

In the 1990s, during the United Nations' Oil-for-Food program, Assyrians were prohibited from using their ration cards, as only "Arab Christians" were allowed (Lewis, 2003). It was during this time that many Assyrians, to escape assimilation, fled to Lebanon and Syria from Iraq's Baath dominance and its discriminating policies. Similarly, many other groups followed these exoduses: in 1991 approximately 50 percent of Iraq's Christian population had left for primary destinations such as Australia, Europe and North America. In 2001, among all Iraqis fleeing the country, 30 percent of them were Christians. This minority group has essentially suffered from a mass exodus, as they compose only 3 percent of Iraq's total population (Petrosian, 2006). Table 6.1 identifies the number of Iraqi individuals involved in various events and the results these events had on refugee and returnee numbers.

It is important to point out that the 2003 US invasion and subsequent occupation further exacerbated the vulnerable situation of Iraq's minorities. The persistent climate of fear and insecurity, as well as the entrenchment of sectarianism in the emerging Iraqi political system, spurred massive population displacement, sectarian strife and far-reaching instability. The situation in the country has devolved to such a fragile state of affairs that it threatens to spiral out of control and engulf the entire region.

Violence and displacement have been ongoing incessantly in Iraq since 2003, but two significant peaks should be mentioned; these are peaks characterized by large waves of people suffering multiple acts of violence and forced displacement. In 2006, the first wave of Sunni–Shi'a violence reached its peak and caused thousands of minority families to flee from the ethnic cleansing that was taking place to create homogeneous Sunni and Shi'a neighbourhoods (predominantly in and around Baghdad). During this time, most minorities across Iraq were being forced to flee abroad or to the northern parts of the country. In 2008, a second wave of violence against Christians in Mosul caused thousands of Christian families to flee the city and go to Iraqi-Kurdistan. During these periods, Iraq witnessed extensive displacements of people that

Table 6.1 Displaced Persons

Reason	Number of Displaced Persons
Expelled in the 70s and 80s	372,347
Victims of 1988 Anfal campaign	222,839
Victims of ethnic cleansing	58,706
Victims of the in-fighting	77,004
Returnees from Iran	40,145
Refugees from Iran	491
Refugees from Turkey	2,552
Victims of conflicts with PKK	15,335
Others	16,086
Total	**805,505**

Source: UNCHS-Habitat, IDP Site and Family Survey, January 2001.

fundamentally altered parts of its demographic composition. It is important to contextualize that these two highlighted cases are the peaks in an ebb and flow of a constant state of violence and displacement.

The flight of minorities that could not escape the country to Iraqi-Kurdistan has created enormous pressure on the governing institutions within the Kurdish region. In particular, the region's government struggles to provide protection and basic services to the large number of displaced individuals who flee to its territory. One example is the provision of basic education; an already burdened education system is unable to provide spaces to incoming minority groups. Kurdish officials have reported that it already has over ten thousand Kurdish students awaiting school placements. Finding more space for internally displaced refugees is an added burden. The lack of government capacity to provide basic services to local residents, let alone tens of thousands of displaced people, exacerbates an already challenging political and socioeconomic environment.

To gauge people's views on the conditions needed to reintegrate minorities into Iraqi society, we asked minority group leaders and other members if they would stay or return to Iraq if its constitution offered equal citizenship to all Iraqis (irrespective of their ethnic or religious affiliation). Unanimously, all minorities interviewed, of all ethnic and religious backgrounds, pessimistically stated that such rights would be impossible in the "new Iraq." While many indicated that they indeed wanted to stay in or return to Iraq, the situation was described as being too dangerous. For many, the only solution was to leave the country and settle abroad. In addition to this general despair and fear felt by minorities, there were several specific problems that they all shared regardless of whether they were displaced internally in Iraq or externally in Jordan or elsewhere. These included the lack of access to basic education for their children and the lack of access to local universities. Compounding their already vulnerable socioeconomic and sociopolitical situation, they often lacked access to employment opportunities. Restrictions placed by local professional associations have made life difficult for educated Iraqis. Minorities also complain of a dearth of policies that could better integrate them into their new communities. Finally, for many Iraqis there is a sense that the international community is not concerned with their particularly vulnerable situations.

A Focus on Iraq's Minorities: The Yezidis, Mandaeans, Christians and Turkmen

What follows are synopses on four selected Iraqi minority groups. These examinations present the current situation on the Yezidis, Mandaeans, Christians and the Turkmen. Following these more detailed cases, a brief illustration is presented on other minority groups. The focus in all of these case studies is the specific concerns of each minority within Iraq's current sociopolitical situation.

The Yezidis

The first minority group of focus, the Yezidis, provides an excellent example of a minority group with very specific concerns. Almost all Yezidis live together in and around the so-called "disputed territories." Even though they are minorities at the regional and national levels, they are often majorities inside their own villages. Consequently, they have not been forced to leave their homes to the same degree as other groups that are more thinly spread and exposed across Iraq, such as the Mandaeans or the Christians. This does not mean, however, that the Yezidis have escaped persecution. During research undertaken in 2008, it was reported that there have been no Yezidis in Mosul since 2007 due to their violent targeting by extremist groups. Unlike Christians, who have the option of paying a tax to radical Islamic groups in order to stay in their homes, the Yezidis can only choose between conversion, expulsion or execution. In April 2006, alleged Sunni al-Qaeda militants targeted Yezidi individuals, commandeering a bus carrying 23 Yezidi men and executing them (Minority Rights Group International, 2008). One year later, the affiliates of the same extremist group attacked a Yezidi community, which would turn out to be "the single most devastating terrorist attack of the Iraq war" (Minority Rights Group International, 2008). Among two villages in the Nineveh Plains, 250 to 500 Yezidis were murdered by a series of truck bombs.

Many Islamic extremists consider the Yezidi to be "devil worshippers," and extremist leaders have openly called for their killing should they refuse to convert. Research conducted in 2008 revealed a recording of Imam Mullah Farzanda, who preaches in the Dohuk Governorate of Iraq's Kurdistan region. In this recording, Imam Mullah Farzanda made statements during one of his Friday sermons that declared it the duty of all "good Muslims to kill any Yezidis in Iraq" if they refused to convert to Islam. Extremists have made the Yezidis a direct target, despite their relative isolation and small population numbers.

The Yezidi are of Kurdish lingual and ethnic descent (Minority Rights Group International, 2008); their religion has been traced back to elements from 4,000 years ago, where the religion appears "to be a synthesis of pagan, Zoroastrian, Manichaean, Jewish, Nestorian Christian and Muslim elements" (Minority Rights Group International, 2008). It is based mainly on the teachings of Shaykh 'Adī (Açıkyıldız, 2009). In addition to being religiously dualist, they uniquely deny any descendence from Eve and believe their origins to be only from Adam. Thus, intermarriage with non-Yezidis is prohibited and conversion is impossible. According to Yezidi beliefs, they can only be baptized at the sanctuary of Shaykh 'Adī in Lalish, found in the region of Sheykhan in Iraqi Kurdistan (Açıkyıldız, 2009). This sanctuary is the centre of their faith and is critical as a site to perform their religious rites. This explains the extreme attachment that they have to their land, temple and community. The social chaos that has spread throughout Iraq since 2003 has threatened to undermine this community's ability to practice their religious beliefs. In the Iraqi village of Qal'at Shihan, for example, Yezidis have traditionally been the majority; in recent years they have moved toward becoming a minority in their own village because of the influx of displaced peoples fleeing sectarian violence in other parts of the country. This demographic transition has been difficult for the Yezidis, who have expressed anxiety about their new exposure to potentially hostile groups.

In addition, the Yezidi communities have socio-religious constraints that make their demographic situation susceptible to further disruption. As previously mentioned, their religion does not permit intermarriage with non-Yezidis, and, moreover, there is a caste system within the Yezidi faith that discourages marriage between the varying castes. These strict social rules surrounding marriage, combined with the Yezidis' already small population, make their forced displacement very harmful to their populations' demographic viability.

Thus, the violence and dispersal that they are enduring could lead to the extinction of this millennia-old group. Consequently, the Yezidis interviewed stated the need for their unique cultural identity to be recognized and protected by regional and national governments. In particular, they want their religious places in Lalish and their villages to be protected. Many have expressed that the best solution would be a secular Iraqi government—one that will protect their rights in a manner equal to the rights of other groups.

The Mandaeans

The second minority group of focus, the Mandaeans, has not historically been geographically concentrated. They are pacifists of Gnostic faith, and their ancestry has been traced as far back as the third century CE (Reinke, 2006). The Mandaeans of Iraq's marshlands had inhabited the area since the fifth century, but after Saddam Hussein expelled them from the area, the local marshland population dropped from approximately 6,000 individuals to 1,500. With the outbreak of sectarian violence in 2006, the Mandaeans became further spread across several urban centers in Iraq, particularly Baghdad, Basra, Amara and Nasiriya, as well as in southern Iran. Their thin distribution has made them especially vulnerable to sectarian violence between Sunnis and Shi'as, and, consequently, they have fled Iraq by the tens of thousands. Those who could not escape Iraq fled north and took refuge in the city of Erbil in Kurdistan. Prior to the US invasion of Iraq in 2003, it was estimated that there were as many as 60,000 Mandaeans worldwide and many of those lived in Iraq (Reinke, 2006); by 2007, 80 percent had been forced to leave the country and it had been estimated that less than 5,000 remain (Crawford, 2007).

Similar to the Yezidis, Mandaeans do not intermarry and their beliefs are considered heretical by the extremist groups that target them. However, it is not only extremists who target Mandaeans. Criminal gangs have also targeted them because there is a perception that this minority group is wealthier than ordinary Iraqis, as many of them formerly traded in alcohol, jewellery and other lucrative businesses. According to the Sabian Mandaean Association of Australia (SMAA) in 2004, approximately,

"35 Mandaean families underwent forced conversion in Fallujah alone." Targeted kidnappings of Mandaeans for ransom have also been observed (Taneja, 2007).

The Mandaeans face systematic discrimination in Iraq (Reinke, 2006). Individuals have been denied rights to work their jobs, have faced unjustified arrests and have been subject to forced military conscription, despite their religious beliefs prohibiting any type of violence against others.

All of the Mandaean families interviewed for this study noted that it was their strong desire to remain in Iraq, but their security was too threatened to stay. They did not believe that a constitution based on equal citizenship would ever materialize or that their security needs could be met in the short or medium term. Instead, many only wanted help to leave Iraq and settle in a safer country, such as Australia or the United States. Although Mandaean religious beliefs require them to live near running water for their baptisms, the location or particulars of the river itself is not crucial. Emphatically, security was their primary concern.

In discussion with Mandaean refugee groups in Jordan, it was disclosed that approximately 650 Mandaean families had been forced to flee to Jordan and a further 2,100 families escaped to Syria. Among the 650 families that fled to Jordan, only 202 of them remain—the rest have already relocated to the US and Australia. Among the 202 remaining, 172 have already received approval for transfer to other countries and the remaining 30 are awaiting their transfer approvals.

Mandaeans are constantly under the threat of not meeting a population level sufficient enough to secure the future of their religious identity. Bashar al-Sabti, a spokesman for the Iraqi Minorities Council stated that, "For Mandaeans, the biggest threat is extinction. [Their] killing is equal to three deaths for every one person left alive. This is accelerating [their] fear of extinction. Everyone is living in a state of general fear" (Taneja, 2007). As a closed religious group, they fear being spread too thinly across the world, resulting in their religion disappearing over time. They consider dispersion to be a threat to their existence and are trying to facilitate their entire group's emigration to a single country in order to prevent terminal separation. Their preference has been to stay in Iraq, but failing that possibility, they are attempting to flee as a group to a safer place of residence where they can practice their religion in security and maintain their identity.

The Christians

The third minority group of focus, the Christians, numbered approximately 1.4 million people in Iraq during the early 1980s (Marr, 1985); today there are less than 700,000, and they comprise only 3 percent of Iraq's population (Marr, 2008). Rough estimates show that one-third of all Christians left Iraq in the 1990s. Since the 2003 US invasion of Iraq, Iraqi Christians have faced ongoing violence with two peaks of large significance. In 2006, sectarian violence was rampant throughout the country and Iraqi Christians were often perceived, and therefore targeted, as a "fifth column" and in the service of American occupiers. Again, in 2008, many Iraqi Christians were driven out of Mosul and into Ankawa and other parts of Iraqi-Kurdistan. Like the Mandaeans, Christians were dispersed across Iraq and have been caught between larger extremist groups from leading sects as they fought one another. Businesses and their owners have been targeted because they sell alcohol, as this indicates that they are either Christian or Yezidi—the only groups that openly trade in alcohol (Taneja, 2007). Their shops have been bombed, looted and defaced; owners have been assassinated. Many Christians, like those in Mosul, reside within the so-called "disputed territories," and this has added an internal political dimension to their persecution. In several interviews with a number of Christian groups, witnesses spoke of how their people had been assaulted, killed or forced to pay the Jizyah tax. In some cases, Christians continued to be threatened even after paying the tax. Most Iraqi Christians have tried to leave the country and those unable have, along with many others, taken refuge in Iraqi-Kurdistan.

The Christian identity is not as homogeneous as some of the other Iraqi minorities. Many Christians consider themselves not only as part of a particular faith, but also as part of one of four distinct ethnicities that are present in Iraq; Chaldeans, Assyrians, Armenians and Syriacs have distinct languages, cultures and identities that help to distinguish Iraq's Christian communities. Chaldeans, the largest of the Christian sects and founded in the fifth century, follow an eastern rite of the Catholic Church; Assyrians, the second largest of the Christian sects, are part of the Church of the East or Nestorian; Armenians are part of either the Roman Catholic or Eastern Orthodox Churches; and Syriacs consider themselves Eastern Orthodox. Furthermore, some other Christians consider themselves Arab-Christians—a religious minority but not a separate ethnicity. The Christian community is one of the largest minority communities in Iraq, and their ethnic and cultural divisions have made it more difficult for them to achieve any type of consensus approach to their vulnerable situation.

Beyond the internal complexities of the Iraqi Christian identity, there is a strong external component in the powerful Christian diaspora found in other countries, especially the United States (Analeed Marcus, 2007). These groups have helped to raise awareness about the circumstances of Christians in Iraq; however, they have also added an international layer of complexity to the internal problems that Iraqis face. One particular example involves foreign Christian groups aggravating an already politically contentious situation—i.e., their support for the Nineveh plains proposal that would create a separate autonomous region that would cater to and be administered by minorities. Certain groups in the US, such as the Assyrian American National Federation, the Chaldean Federation of America, the Chaldean American Chamber of Commerce and the Assyrian National Council of Illinois have showed support for such a plan, which culminated in the 2007 US House Appropriations Committee committing $10 million to the Nineveh Plains proposal. The proposal would help create an autonomous safe haven for Christians in Iraq facing persecution (Analeed Marcus, 2007). Certain Christian groups, particularly those located in Iraq, oppose the proposal, as they see it "demanding the creation of a ghetto [which] is especially against the Christian message which sees [Christians] as the salt and yeast in the dough of humanity" (Sako, 2009). They believe such a plan would only serve to support the segregation of peoples based on ethno-religious grounds and project the image that cooperation and peace among diverse neighbours is impossible or unlikely.

The Turkmen

The fourth minority group of focus, the Turkmen, is a distinct ethnic group whose ancestors are probably from the Turkmen tribal dynasties of the fourteenth and fifteenth centuries. Mostly middle class, and comprising 2–3 percent of Iraq's population (Marr, 1985), approximately 60 percent are Sunni and just fewer than 40 percent are Shi'a (with the remainder being Christian). Like the Christians of Mosul, the Turkmen also reside within the so-called "disputed territories" and have been put under pressure from several groups that are trying to gain political advantage over one another. Approximately 85 percent of Iraqi Turkmen live in the regions surrounding Mosul, Kirkuk, Erbil and Tel Afar; the rest are in Baghdad and smaller villages, such as Tuz Khurmato (Munier, 2007).

The unique culture of the Turkmen, like that of other ethnic minorities, was not recognized by past Iraqi regimes. "Arabization" and "correction" campaigns refused to acknowledge the Turkmen's distinctiveness and tried to extinguish their populations, particularly in Kirkuk city (Iraqi Turkmen Human Rights Research Foundation, 2003). The "Arabization" process consisted in part of administrative boundaries being constantly modified in order to decrease the representative power of the Turkmen. Forced removal and deportation of Turkmen followed, with resettlement by imported Arab individuals; discrimination through employment opportunities and appointments, and unjustified job firings, was common.

Presently, the Turkmen community finds itself at the centre of one of Iraq's most contentious political questions—the fate of the oil-rich northern province of Kirkuk. The Kurds claim that in the 1970s, over 220,000 of their people were exiled from their land by Saddam Hussein during the "Arabization" process, and some also fought in the Gulf War (Cordesman, 2006). It was during this time, and shortly after, that the Kurds further claimed that over 120,000 Arabs were imported into their lands. Regarding the Turkmen and how they surround this issue, there exist two factions. The first faction supports the Kurdish claim to the Kirkuk region and would like to become a part of the region. The second faction, however, strongly opposes the Kurdish claim for fear of being assimilated into the Kurdish identity. Today, the Kurdistan Regional Government consists of three former Iraqi provinces and the politicians of this federal region are looking to lay claim to oil resources within the so-called "disputed territories," particularly in and around Kirkuk. This claim has been rejected by many of the local Arab and Turkmen groups (Cole, 2009). They oppose the creation of an autonomous region and favour a strong central government that would respect their sensitive status as minorities in the region. As the major parties position themselves to seek maximum advantage against the other in this debate, the Turkmen community is often used by various internal and external parties without any regard to their true cultural or ethnic wellbeing. Violence toward the Turkmen has sparked recently with the terrorist bomb attack in June 2009, which claimed the lives of at least 80 people in the town of Taza Khurmatu in the Kirkuk region—a town composed mostly of Turkmen (*Iraq Slogger*, 2009). Currently, the Turkmen comprise 26 percent of the Kirkuk region's population, while Kurds and Arabs comprise 35 percent each; other minorities make up the remaining 4 percent of the region's population (Cordesman, 2006).

Other Minority Groups

The four minority groups focused on above are just some of the many groups that contribute to Iraq's ethnic and cultural mosaic. Some others, not specifically explicated upon, include the Shabaks, Bahá'is, Faili Kurds and Kaka'is (Yaresan). These minorities do, however, share many of the same vulnerabilities as the other minority groups discussed; they have an equal stake in the evolution of a national Iraqi identity that is based on equal citizenship and void of sectarian bias.

Similar to the groups focused on above, other minority groups have been forced to leave their homes as majority groups attempt to create religiously and ethnically homogeneous enclaves within their communities (see Table 6.2). The Shabaks are mostly located within the so-called "disputed territories" of Mosul and the Nineveh plains; like the Christians and Turkmens that also reside there, Shabaks have been caught in the violent political gamesmanship between majority parties over territory. In the areas around Mosul, the Shi'a Shabak and the Shi'a Turkmen endured a great amount of suffering from the hands of al-Qaeda between 2006 and 2008.

The Jewish history of the region extends as far back as 2,600 years, where their origins extend to Babylonian captivity in the sixth century BCE. A 1947 census indicated there were approximately 118,000 Jewish individuals in Iraq. Post-creation of the Israeli state, a mass exodus ensued in 1951. Today, the Jewish population that once exceeded 150,000 individuals has dwindled down to a mere 10 to 15, solely in Baghdad.

Other minority groups include Faili Kurds and those of the Bahá'i religion. The Faili Kurds experienced expulsion during the Anfal campaign and have been exiled from their home territories for almost 30 years. This group struggles to return to their expropriated homes, however, many of their homes no longer exist. One of the culminating effects of this diaspora's expulsion is their offspring's missing knowledge regarding their ancestry. Today, the Faili Kurds are somewhere between Iraq and Iran; the fate of their return home is solely dependent on the political relations between the two countries. Another minority example, those of the Bahá'i religion, are still not recognized by the majority of Middle Eastern governments, and they have been denied any right to express their identity. In 1970, the notorious Law 105 was passed that prohibited Bahá'i followers from practicing their religion. The consequence was imprisonment until said individuals officially denounced their religious beliefs (Taneja, 2007).

Table 6.2 Estimates of Iraq's pre- and post-2003 ethnic/religious composition

Minority group	Pre-2003	2008
Christians	1,000,000–1,400,000	600,000–800,000
Jews	a few hundreds	10–15
Mandaeans	30,000	13,000
Palestinians	35,000	15,000
Turkmen	800,000	200,000
Yezidis	Unknown	550,000

Source: Taneja (2007).

All of these problems have at their root an absence of a common Iraqi identity. A governance approach that emphasizes equal citizenship based on respect for human rights and not sectarian affiliation is desperately needed in Iraq. Ultimately, a national identity rooted in equality is the only long-term solution that can address all of the problems experienced by Iraq's minority groups. Unfortunately, Iraq's major political and religious parties have not adopted or advocated the principles needed to promote a common Iraqi identity and governance challenges have consequently worsened.

Socio-Political Challenges

The relationships between the various Iraqi political and religious groups are marred by a high level of mistrust. As many groups try to capitalize on uncertainty in Iraq, they maximize their demands as a way of achieving their minimum objectives. However, this approach causes more problems than it solves for all of those concerned. Numerous interviews with politicians confirmed the highly politicized nature of the issues surrounding minorities and the problems created or exacerbated with each group maximizing their demands.

Each sectarian group, and for some, their associated political party, is trying to use these maximizing tactics to criticize other parties. Sectarian-based political parties' competing demands make the situation even worse for minorities who live in the "disputed territories." Minority groups in Iraq are the victims not only of intra-sectarian and extremist violence but also of competing political agendas; their displacement is a consequence of both.

All parties are essentially reacting instead of acting and this has had profoundly negative consequences on the country and its people. There is little regard for the deep level of suffering that minority communities have endured. Rather than seeking to address the root causes of their misery, major political parties are using this suffering to advance their own political agendas.

Minorities have often received limited or conditional recognition of their identity, as they are often told that they are in fact Arab or Kurd; or that they must change their religion depending on the political demands of the majority group at that given time. The rising influence of religious political parties does not make Iraq's minority groups any more optimistic that the country's future will recognize and fully respect their identities while treating them as equal to majority communities.

The situation in Iraq stands in stark contrast to the United Nations' Universal Declaration of Human Rights. Two clauses stand out in particular: Article 3 stating that "Everyone has the right to life, liberty and security of person," and Article 18 stating that "Everyone has the right to freedom of thought, conscience and religion" (United Nations, 1948).

Furthermore, the United Nations' Declaration on the Rights of Indigenous Peoples, adopted by the United Nations (UN) General Assembly in September 2007, clearly lays out numerous protections for indigenous cultures in Article 8 that include their protection from "assimilation or destruction" (United Nations, 2007). The article also presents the state's responsibilities in bringing about the aforementioned provision through its supposed role in combating and/or preventing propaganda; dispossession of lands, territories or resources; and "forced population transfer[s]," among various other responsibilities.

It is clear that none of these conventions are being respected in Iraq today. Minorities in particular are constantly under threat, and while violence may have hit a relative low in late 2008 and early 2009, the central government has thus far proved incapable of dealing with the root causes of this discrimination. This translates into a significant likelihood of recurring violence in the not too distant future, particularly as contentious questions are addressed, such as the fate of regional boundaries and the future return of displaced groups. No solution can provide lasting security if it does not strive for the protection of human rights as mandated by UN conventions.

Iraq has had a history of denying voting rights to minorities. In this context, the debate that surrounded Article 50 of the Iraqi Constitution in 2008 has been a flashpoint for anxieties relating to the place of minorities in the Iraqi political system and society. Article 50 guarantees minimum representation for minorities to elected positions in their region's provincial governments: "In the first version ... 15 seats were set aside in six provinces for minorities, 13 for Christians and one each for Shabaks and Yazidis" (AsiaNews.it, 2008). The passing of the election law would have been a strong indication that the Iraqi government was taking a strong step in the direction of enabling its minorities' democratic rights, especially in what had been the upcoming regional elections in January 2009. Article 50, however, was annulled from the provincial election law draft in September 2008 by the Iraqi parliament in the lead-up to the referendum for its ratification. This course of action had been chosen due to the inability to reach a consensus on the number of minority representatives per province. This abrogation of the article from the draft, followed by the drafts ratification, prompted a huge backlash from minority groups and their international supporters. Ultimately, the president of Iraq intervened personally to ensure its reinstatement into the election law. The fact that this controversy occurred in the midst of ongoing violence against religious and ethnic minorities sent a powerful signal to those groups that the majority parties were not interested in their wellbeing. This election law crisis risked pushing minorities out of the political process and leaving them with only limited or symbolic representation at a time when they were experiencing serious threats of extinction.

The debate surrounding Article 50 should at best be a temporary one. The best protection for these minority groups is equal and non-sectarian citizenship. Legislation that provides quotas for each minority's representation should only serve as a temporary measure until equality is established. This is to say that every Iraqi, regardless of their religious or ethnic background, should eventually be free to strive for any position within the political process and not be limited to or excluded from seats set aside for certain groups.

Conclusion

All Iraqis are caught in multiple and contradictory narratives about violence and victimhood. The US invasion (and occupation) and its mistakes have led to the destruction of Iraq's tender social tissue, and the new political class in Iraq is not yet in a conciliatory state. The individuals at decision-making tables are still reacting in an atmosphere of mistrust that persists among them. This atmosphere is further complicated by two emerging trends. The first is the ongoing, unsustainable fragmentation within the political and social arena that has reached a point where it is now impossible to identify all participating actors. The second is the ongoing narrow focus of the major parties in consolidating their power bases rather than adhering to a truly national process of reconciliation—the only real peaceful guarantee for Iraq's long-term future.

If nothing is done or changed, the extremism that has developed within certain groups will threaten various minorities to the point of extermination, as well as create the potential for the destruction of many millennia-old Mesopotamian cultures. The current emergence of religious parties as the main political actors in the new Iraq has left minorities in an extremely insecure position and has cast doubt on the current government's ability or willingness to address any of these new challenges.

The solution cannot be partial. One cannot seek to address the concerns of minorities without putting the issues into a broader framework that recognizes the Iraqi national crisis, the historically fragile position of minorities in Iraq, the catastrophic consequences of the US invasion and the resulting damage to Iraq's social tissue. The way forward must take into account the dangers inherent in the present situation as well as the conflicting agendas of both internal and external actors.

The new administration in the US under President Obama has promised change, and this may offer a possibility of some sober reflection on previous US foreign policy toward Iraq. This change in administration may present a tangible opportunity to implement much-needed corrections that can more effectively address the whole Iraqi crisis, including a real effort toward national reconciliation.

For all of these reasons, the establishment of an independent international monitoring committee would be a helpful first step in addressing these issues and in bringing forward practical and constructive proposals. A committee composed of only Iraqi actors would be fundamentally limited by the conflicting agendas and mistrust that permeate the present atmosphere between them. This international monitoring committee would need to be composed of senior figures known for their professionalism and credibility; in addition, they should possess easy access to key decision makers locally, regionally and internationally.

The complexities associated with the Iraqi crisis continue to multiply at drastic rates. The current coping mechanisms are proving to be inadequate to address the crisis in a fashion that leads to a durable, long-term solution—a solution that would correct the current situation, as well as be acceptable to all actors involved. It goes without saying that the extinction of Iraqi minorities would be a tragedy not only to them and to Iraq as a whole, but for all of humanity.

Appendix 6.1

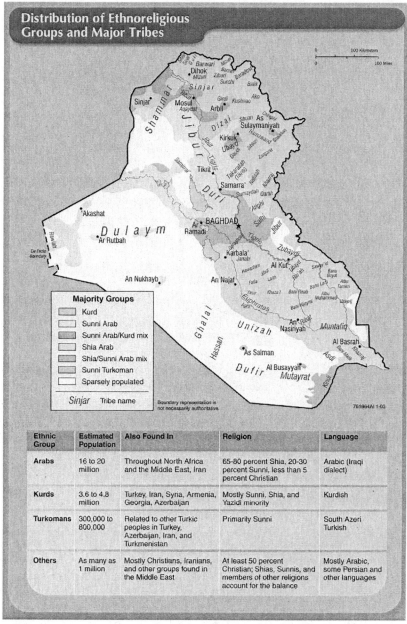

Source: Iraq: Country Profile, CIA, January 2003. Perry-Castañeda Map Collection, University of Texas at Austin.

Notes

1 See as well the case of Shi'a Muslims in Sunni-ruled Bahrain and the case of Sunni Muslims and Christians in Alawite-ruled Syria.
2 In addition, one of this chapter's Canadian research members was unable to obtain a Syrian visa for entrance into the country. The research team, however, was able to meet with leaders and other important individuals in the remaining countries that the investigation was to include.

Works Cited

Açıkyıldız, Birgül (2009). "The Sanctuary of Shaykh 'Adī at Lalish: Centre of Pilgrimage of the Yezidis." *Bulletin of the School of Oriental and African Studies.* Volume 72: 301–33.

Analeed Marcus, Ashtar (2007). "US House Approves $10M for the Nineveh Plains in Iraq." *Assyrian International News Agency.* June 25. Available at: http://www.aina.org/news/20070625182902.htm.

AsiaNews.it (2008). "UN Criticizes Iraq's New Election Law." *Asian News*, October 6. Available at: http://www.asianews.it/index.php?l=en&art=13405.

BBC (2001). "Iraqi Kurds' Story of Expulsion." *BBC News*, November 3. Quoted in Fawcett and Tanner, 2002: 12.

Cole, Juan (2009). "Death Toll in Kirkuk Rises to 33; Growing Arab–Kurdish Violence Threatens Stability of Iraq; 4 US Troops Killed." July 1. Available at: http://www.juancole.com/2009/07/death-toll-in-kirkuk-rises-to-33.html.

Cordesman, Anthony H. (2006). "The Kurds and Other Minorities." Washington, DC: Center for Strategic and International Studies (CSIS). June 23.

Costantini, Peter (2009). "Iraqi Refugees in the U.S.: Strangers in Paradise." *Assyrian International News Agency.* June 29. Available at: http://www.aina.org/news/2009062900549.htm.

Crawford, Angus (2007). "Iraq's Mandaeans Face Extinction." *BBC News.* March 4. Available at: http://news.bbc.co.uk/2/hi/middle_east/6412453.stm.

Fawcett, John, and Victor Tanner (2002). "The Internally Displaced People of Iraq." Washington: The Brookings-SAIS Project on Internal Displacement. Occasional Paper. October. Available at: http://www.brookings.edu/~/media/Files/rc/papers/2002/10iraq_fawcett/iraqreport.pdf.

Iraqi Turkmen Human Rights Research Foundation (2003). "The Summary of Violation of the Human Rights of the Iraqi Turkmen and Attempts to Assimilate Them during the Dictatorial Baath Period." Iraqi Turkmen Human Rights Research Foundation (SOITM). December 13. Available at: http://members.lycos.nl/soitum/GR.pdf.

Iraq Slogger (2009). "Kirkuk: Sadrists Demand Protection for Turkmen." June. Available at: http://www.iraqslogger.com/index.php/post/7823/Kirkuk_Sadrists_Demand_Protection_for_Turkmen.

Lamani, Mokhtar (2009). *CIGI Special Report—Minorities in Iraq: The Other Victims*. January. Available at: http://www.cigionline.org/sites/default/files/Minorities%20in%20Iraq%20final.pdf

Lewis, J. E. (2003). "Iraqi Assyrians: Barometer of Pluralism." *Middle East Quarterly*. Vol. 10, No. 3. Available at: http://www.meforum.org/558/iraqi-assyrians-barometer-of-pluralism.

Marr, Phebe (1985). "The Land and People of Modern Iraq," in *The Modern History of Iraq*. Pages 9–15. Colorado: Westview Press.

———(2008). "Introduction," in *Iraq's Refugee and IDP Crisis: Human Toll and Implications*. Pages 9–13. Washington, DC: Viewpoints Special Edition, Middle East Institute.

Minority Rights Group International (2008). *World Directory of Minorities and Indigenous Peoples—Iraq: Yezidis*. April. Available at: http://www.unhcr.org/refworld/docid/49749d0641.html.

Munier, Gilles (2007). "Les Turcomans Irakiens: un people oublié ou marginalise." Le blog de France-Irak Actualité, May 31.

Petrosian, Vahram (2006). "Assyrians in Iraq." *Iran and the Caucasus*. Vol. 10, No. 1: 113–48.

Reinke, Sarah (2006). "Mandaeans in Iraq: After Centuries of Persecution—Today Their Very Survival Is Threatened." Society for Threatened Peoples. Available at: http://www.gfbv.de/reedit/openObjects/openObjects/show_file.php?type=inhaltsDok&property=download&id=694.

Sako, Louis (2009). "Nineveh Plain: A Ghetto for Iraqi Christians Is an Illusion." *Asian News*. April 20. Available at: http://www.asianews.it/index.php?l=en&art=15025&geo=23&size=.

Taneja, Preti (2007). *Assimilation, Exodus, Eradication: Iraq's Minority Communities since 2003*. Minority Rights Group International. February 11. Available at: http://www.minorityrights.org/?lid=2805.

United Nations (1948). *Universal Declaration of Human Rights*. New York. December. Available at: http://www.un.org/en/documents/udhr/.

——— (2007). *Declaration on the Rights of Indigenous Peoples*. New York. September. Available at: http://www.un.org/esa/socdev/unpfii/en/drip.html.

United Nations High Commissioner for Refugees (UNHCR) (2008). *Second Rapid Assessment of Return of Iraqis from Displacement Locations in Iraq and from Neighboring Countries*. Geneva. Available at: http://www.reliefweb.int/rw/RWFiles2008.nsf/FilesByRWDocUnidFilename/SHIG-7CEDPJ-full_report.pdf/$File/full_report.pdf.

United Nations Centre for Human Settlements—Habitat (UNCHS) (2001). *IDP Site and Family Survey*. Geneva. Available at: http://www.unhabitat.org/downloads/docs/3410_15997_IDP%20survey%20Tables.doc.

Westcott, Kathryn (2003). "Iraq's Rich Mosaic of People." *BBC News*. February 27. Available at: http://news.bbc.co.uk/2/hi/middle_east/2783989.stm.

7
Iraq's Economy and Its Brain Drain after the 2003 Invasion

Joseph Sassoon

One of the most important consequences of the internal and external displacement of the Iraqi population that took place as a result of the 2003 United States–led invasion was the exodus of a high percentage of well-educated professionals.[1] This chapter will analyze Iraq's brain drain within the historical context before 2003 and the economic conditions that prevailed post-2003.

The brain drain that occurred after the 2003 invasion was not the first occurrence of such a phenomenon for Iraq. In the aftermath of the 1968 coup d'état that brought Saddam Hussein and the Baath party to power, an initial exodus began. However, during the 1970s and 1980s, the government began focusing on attracting Iraqis back, and incentives were introduced to revive the private sector of the economy. Emphasis was placed on improving education, and laws were passed to enhance women's rights and encourage education. As a result, the urban middle class of professionals expanded. But after the 1991 Gulf War, which had come so soon after the 1980–88 Iran–Iraq war, a second wave of Iraqis began to leave as they realized that with two wars almost back-to-back, the opportunities for professional careers would dwindle dramatically. The fabric of Iraq's society seriously began to unravel during the 1990s, aggravated by hyperinflation and the collapse of the Iraqi dinar. This was truly the beginning of the demise of the middle class.

By the time of the 2003 invasion, estimates of Iraqi exiles ranged from two to four million people. Whatever the statistics are, there is no doubt that Iraq under Saddam Hussein had suffered an enormous brain drain, with many well-educated professionals settling in other Arab countries and in the West.

In 2003, after two wars, many years of sanctions and the increasing economic autonomy of Kurdistan, Iraq's economy was highly fragmented and there was little in the way of a national macroeconomic policy. Since 1980, Iraq had faced one economic and political crisis after another and "normal" circumstances did not exist. The country's dependence on its relatively huge oil revenues since the early 1950s, culminating in the late 1970s and early 1980s, turned Iraq into a classic case of rentierism.[2] Thus, Iraq's economy was severely weakened in every area: foreign reserves were depleted, development planning had virtually ceased, infrastructure was severely damaged and a vast majority of the population was impoverished.[3] Yet, in spite of the shattered economy and weak institutional organization, the Iraqi state functioned and essential services were provided to the population. However, with the fall of Baghdad, the state collapsed and there was nothing to take its place. All of the government's ministers, deputy ministers and thousands of top Baathists had fled the country. The US Office of Reconstruction and Humanitarian Assistance (ORHA), which had been set up only seven weeks prior to the invasion under General Jay Garner to "manage" Iraq after the war, did not fill the gap; its involvement in running the country and economy was rudimentary, since its emphasis was to be on refugee work and oil field repair. As it happened, there was neither a refugee problem nor oil field fires. In other words, ORHA's planning for the post-war period was based on assumptions that proved to be wrong (Phillips, 2005: 131). Garner himself admitted to Congress that, "this is an ad hoc operation, glued together over about four or five weeks' time." and added that his team "didn't really have enough time to plan" (Schmidt and Sanger, 2003). By May 2003, Garner was replaced by Ambassador L. Paul Bremer as the new civilian administrator to oversee the Coalition Provisional Authority (CPA), the body responsible for the reconstruction of Iraq.

The massive looting that took place throughout the country further exacerbated the dire economic situation; 17 out of 23 ministry buildings were destroyed, and looters dismantled the electricity grid creating power shortages (Phillips, 2005: 134–35). For example, the headquarters of the Ministry of Higher Education and Scientific Research in Baghdad, which oversees the administration of all universities and technical institutes in the country, was burned and looted repeatedly between April and July 2003. There is no doubt that the looting also had a devastating effect on the post-war administration. American officials estimated the cost of looting in the early weeks following the end of the war to be around $12 billion (Packer 2005, 139). Within a week of his arrival, Bremer issued the decree of de-Baathification. Overnight, almost 30,000 Iraqis—including middle management in economic ministries, teachers and doctors—were dismissed from their jobs.[4] Needless to say, this only exacerbated the shortage of competent managers of the economy at all levels. At the same time, the CPA was finding it hard to recruit the right people for the right jobs. It never had enough translators and interpreters and few of the recruits had regional knowledge or expertise in the fields they were overseeing (SIGIR, 2005: 78–80).

One of the main hurdles in managing the Iraqi economy was the US attempt to impose ambitious and almost unrealistic plans. Bremer was convinced that Iraq needed "a vibrant private sector to succeed" (Bremer, 2006: 200). That might have been true, but given that Iraq was emerging from almost 50 years of socialism, plans of privatization on such a scale were like applying shock therapy to an already feeble patient. Bremer imagined Iraq as a post-war Germany or post-Communist Russia, and believed that things could be turned around fast (Packer, 2005: 196). He frequently lamented to his colleagues that "there's no Ludwig Erhard in Iraq—or at least we haven't found him yet" (Bremer, 2006: 201).[5]

It is important to emphasize that Iraq was in non-stop crisis mode. The CPA was essentially extinguishing fires—mostly political—and did not have the luxury of focusing only on the economy. It was trying to cope with a crippled economy, plagued by distortions and inefficiencies, and a sub-standard infrastructure. The CPA also spent money on numerous small but vital projects—sewers, bridges, schools and so on, that affected the day-to-day quality of life (Packer, 2005: 241).

Unfortunately, the amount spent was not enough and was sometimes too late. In September 2003, Congress passed an $87 billion appropriation bill that included $18.4 billion for Iraq's reconstruction. In addition to this vast sum, the CPA was able to use oil proceeds, frozen assets and transfers from the Oil-for-Food Program. By the end of 2005, the total aid that Congress had allocated to Iraq's reconstruction reached $21 billion, of which about $8 billion remained unspent a year later. The failure to spend this money, particularly in the critical first year after the war, became a major problem in light of the increased violence and very high levels of unemployment.[6] For example, by August 2004, almost 10 months after Congress had passed the bill, only $400 million (just over 2 percent) had been spent (Packer, 2005: 242–43). Some observers felt that the reconstruction project never took off because it was "heavily centralized under Bremer's office in Baghdad and the Pentagon in Washington" (Diamond, 2005: 307).

On June 28, 2004, the CPA was dissolved and sovereignty was transferred to the Iraqi government, and with it a new chapter began in Iraq's economic policy.[7] The economy was seen by the Americans as the third vital pillar of a multi-strategy approach to stabilize Iraq, alongside security and political development. In conjunction with the Iraqi government, the economic objectives were stated as follows:

1. Strengthening the foundations of economic growth;
2. Revitalizing the private sector;
3. Improving the quality of life;
4. Strengthening of governance and security. (United States Department of Defense, 2006: 12–13)

Meanwhile, as violence spread and ethnic cleansing began in earnest following the Samarra bombing of February 2006, the emigration of highly skilled Iraqis intensified. Apart from insecurity and violence, a combination of other factors led to new waves of brain drain: low levels of services (electricity, water, sewage, etc.), high levels of unemployment and inflation, and pervasive corruption (Merza, 2007: 173). The internal displacement, whereby more than 2.7 million lost their homes, created another "push" factor for the exodus.

Academics and doctors who were associated, even remotely, with the Baath party were targeted. The scope of the targeting soon expanded, and a combination of militias and criminal gangs began killing or kidnapping professionals and their families. It is important to point out that in spite of the high numbers of professionals who left Iraq, the opportunities for those who stayed behind were slim, forcing many to move to the calmer Kurdistan in search of better opportunities.

As of 2009, estimates for unemployment ranged from 23 percent to 38 percent, which even at the lower rate is socially and economically destabilizing (Brookings, 2009: 40). Unemployment, as a serious problem for Iraq, began in the late 1990s under Saddam Hussein's regime when the economy was opened to unlimited tax-exempted imports from neighbouring countries. This led to the closure of many small and family oriented enterprises (Misconi, 2008: 22). Employment was also a political tool for the Baath regime and after 2003 continued to be so, as referred to by Herring and Rangwalla as "employment brokerage" by the different political parties (2006: 131).

The dissolution of the Iraqi Army by Bremer, which had employed between 400,000 and 500,000 people (estimated at 7 percent of the labour force), together with de-Baathification, added roughly 8–10 percent to the rate of unemployment, especially among the Sunnis. The open market economic policy, coupled with an unfavourable investment climate due to violence, exacerbated the unemployment situation. This was not helped by the fact that the agricultural sector was almost crippled. High rates of unemployment tear at the fabric of society by depriving families of economic security. The unemployment crisis also threatens the gains that were made by women in Iraq during the 1960s and the following two decades. Unemployment among women was estimated at 70 percent in 2004 and has forced professional females to seek employment as housekeepers and in other domestic work (Women's International League for Peace and Freedom, 2006). By 2007, a labour survey indicated that only 17 percent of women had jobs. One factor that has aggravated the unemployment situation is the dominance of the public sector: since 2005, the public sector has doubled, and by the end of 2008 it provided 43 percent of all jobs and almost 60 percent of all full-time employment (UNOCHA, 2009).

What is important from the point of view of brain drain is the unemployment rate among the highly skilled. A survey conducted in 2004 by United Nations Development Programme (UNDP) and the Iraqi Ministry of Planning showed that unemployment reached an astonishing 37.2 percent among young men with secondary or higher education (UNDP and the Ministry of Planning and Development Cooperation, 2005: 133). Economists have been warning that "unemployment is a time bomb and could undermine long-term security and social stability" (*IRIN*, 2009).

Another economic problem contributing to the exodus of professionals was inflation. Again, this problem has been recurrent for Iraq. As a result of the invasion of Kuwait and the subsequent sanctions, hyperinflation became a structural problem (Alnasrawi, 2002a: 104). Consequently, people were forced to liquidate their assets and huge disparities in income between the rich and the poor were created (Al-Shabibi, 2002: 24–25). This weakening of the middle class in Iraq gathered momentum after the 2003 invasion.

After the collapse of Saddam Hussein's regime, inflation stabilized at around 32 percent to 34 percent per annum. However, in late 2005, inflation began to rise sharply due to increased violence, the fallout from state control, corruption, higher wages, an increase in the cost of house rentals and the rise of fuel prices (*Economist Intelligence Unit*, 2009).

Supply shortages and a poor distribution system exacerbated the problem (Merza, 2008: 8–9). By mid-2007, inflation had reached about 65 percent. However, with the drop in oil prices, inflation, according to Iraqi official statistics, hovered at the end of 2008 around 12 percent (*Reuters*, 2009).

In addition to the economic problems plaguing the country, corruption has become part and parcel of Iraq. Corruption was prevalent during Saddam Hussein's era—whose fundamentals were structured by an authoritarian system, particularly the system of resource allocations, most notably during the 13 years of sanctions that created shortages of goods and services. However, following the invasion, corruption became integral to the way the country was governed and became a method of expanding the power and base of the politicians. As a result, Nouri al-Maliki's government has been systematically dismissing oversight officials who were installed to fight corruption in Iraqi ministries (Glanz and Mohammed, 2008). The Special Inspector General for Iraqi Reconstruction (SIGIR) has criticized time and again not only the Iraqi government but also the US embassy in Baghdad for a lack of clear anti-corruption goals or specific measurable objectives targeted at achieving these goals (SIGIR, 2008). In fact, SIGIR warned that "the rising tide of corruption in Iraq" is "a second insurgency" (House of Representatives, 2007). Corruption can be identified in four major areas: oil production, public contracts, government services and employment (Merza, 2008: 22–23). The last three have a direct impact on brain drain.

Thus corruption and wasteful reconstruction efforts have dominated the management of Iraq's economy since 2003. The rebuilding effort six years after the invasion, with $117 billion spent on reconstruction, did not much more than restore what was destroyed during the invasion and the looting that followed.[8] Ali Allawi, who served in the Iraqi government from the end of 2003 to mid-2006, described "the exploitation and corruption" that took place in different ministries and the shocking methods of embezzlement by so many ministers and senior officials. He described Iraq and its bureaucracy following the invasion:

> [T]he Iraqi state combined the worst features of a centralised bureaucracy with vestiges of the occupation, and a near collapse of the information, reporting and control mechanisms that underpin any government authority. The legacy of corrupt practices, outdated management systems, incompetence and nepotism was neither seriously challenged nor bypassed. (Allawi, 2007: 349)

Six years after the war, and despite many condemning reports by American and Iraqi anti-corruption watchdogs, the cases of corruption are rife in a culture of impunity. As Rahim al-Okaili, the commissioner of the anti-corruption group, the Commission on Public Integrity, told a journalist: "The reason for the massive corruption in Iraq is the belief by the corrupt that they are shielded from prosecution by the protection afforded to them by their political parties and sects" (Dagher, 2009b).[9]

As the country plunged into a state of uncontrollable violence and economic problems mounted by the day, the targeted attacks on academics gathered momentum in 2006. The dividing line between insurgency and mafia-style gangs became blurred. Some kidnappings, for example, were connected to the sectarian strife, but others were carried out purely for ransom. The gangs believed professionals were an excellent target due to their position in society and their theoretical earning power. In January 2004, there were about two kidnappings per day in Baghdad, but by mid-2006, there were 30 daily kidnappings in the capital (al-Khalidi, Hoffman and Tanner, 2007: 7). Iraq became the "killing fields" for academics.

Although there are no accurate statistics on the number of Iraqi academics and doctors who fled the country, one rough estimate suggests that there are 1,500 Iraqi academics living in Syria, Jordan and Egypt. Presumably a number have also gone further afield. Estimates of the number of doctors who have left Iraq since 2003 vary widely from 3,000 to 17,000. What is clear, however, is that Iraq has lost a large percentage of its medical specialists (some say 70 percent) and probably 25–35 percent of its overall medical staff. These are massive numbers considering that the majority of this exodus occurred over a period of just 18 months.

Data concerning assassinated academics and professionals are relatively more accurate. *The Brussels Tribunal* compiled a list of 350 names of professionals (the vast majority being PhD holders) who were murdered (*The Brussels Tribunal*, 2008). The Iraqi Lawyers Association published a list of 210 lawyers and judges killed since the invasion and said that the number of lawyers in Iraq has decreased by 40 percent during that time (*IRIN*, 2007). Thus, hundreds of Iraq's finest minds were left with no option but to flee the engulfing flames of sectarian hatred and pervasive violence that dominated every aspect of life and threatened them and their families. It should be pointed out that another reason for the exodus of the skilled professionals is the encroachment of religion and the Shi'a militias on day-to-day academic life, which makes it impossible to write or freely express secular or opposing views.

The implications for Iraq of this brain drain are extensive and far-reaching. However, there are three significant areas where it has been felt particularly deeply: the economy, health and education. The emigration of professionals has constrained the ability of the civil service to execute and plan the policies needed to revive the Iraqi economy. In the health and educational sectors, the *crème de la crème* of their cadres have been lost, leaving a huge void.

With regard to management skills, a report by the US Government Accountability Office (GAO) concluded that "the central ministries had spent only 4.4 percent of their investment budget, as of August 2007" (GAO, 2008). GAO attributed this, *inter alia*, to the fact that recent refugee outflows and de-Baathification had reduced the number of skilled workers. As for the capital budget, only 17 percent was spent in 2006 but this improved to about 50 percent by the end of 2007 after budget execution was identified as a priority (SIGIR, 2009: 268).

The impact of the brain drain on the health sector was severe, as doctors and medical workers were specifically targeted. Unlike Saddam Hussein's era, when doctors left Iraq because they were individual victims of the regime, in the Iraq of post-2003, doctors as a group were targeted. They were kidnapped for ransom and were tortured and killed to disrupt the basics of civil society. Because they had to move around in public and in and out of clinics and hospitals, they became an easy target for their attackers. Nurses were also a target; between 2003 and the end of 2006, it was estimated that 160 nurses were murdered and more than 400 wounded (*IRIN*, 2006).

According to one estimate, 23 percent of all academics murdered in Iraq were doctors, 90 percent of whom were medical doctors, 6 percent veterinary surgeons, 2 percent dentists and 2 percent pharmacists. Almost 50 percent of those murdered were specialists; 14 percent were surgeons. The vast majority (98 percent) were Muslims (no identification of Sunni or Shi'a, but one could assume a high percentage of the former) from the Baghdad region (Jalili, 2006a).[10]

As mentioned before, there are no official or accurate statistics about the number of doctors who left the country. Whatever the exact number of those who left and those who are still working, there are two definite observations. First, Iraq lost thousands of its physicians and with them the country lost a wealth of experience. Second, Iraq's health system has crumbled, and the health conditions (physical and mental) of Iraqis have deteriorated dramatically in the six-year period following the invasion.

The implications of this brain drain for all patients in Iraq were severe. Two Iraqi doctors from Diwaniya and Kufa Colleges of Medicine wrote in the *British Medical Journal*: "Medical staff working in emergency departments admit that more than half of those killed could have been saved if trained and experienced staff were available. Our experience has taught us that poor emergency medicine services are more disastrous than the disaster itself" (al-Sheibani, Hadi and Hasoon, 2006: 847).

Iraq today has a ratio of 6 doctors per 10,000 compared to Egypt and Jordan who have 24 doctors per 10,000 respectively (Laub, 2008). A recent study published by the World Health Organization (WHO), based on a large survey it conducted in Iraq, indicated that 16.5 percent of those surveyed suffered from mental disorder, yet only 2 percent of those affected had received any medical treatment. The main reason is that following the exodus of the majority of medical staff, it is estimated that about 430 psychiatric and social workers were left to deal with the whole population (WHO, 2009: 21).[11] In addition, the Iraqi health system is no longer able to provide proper care for victims of violence, particularly those with severe burns or who are in need of prosthetics surgery, and many of them head to Jordan for treatment if they can afford it.

As for education, the quality of higher education and research has been steadily deteriorating since the late 1980s. The real drop was in the 1990s as a wave of brain drain took place. Concurrently the research community suffered total isolation from the international academic community due to the sanctions.

It is important to keep in mind that Iraq's higher education has been in steady decline since the early 1990s. In the immediate aftermath of the 2003 invasion, universities were among the first institutions to face looting. By summer 2003, almost none were spared: from the veterinary college in Abu Ghraib, which lost all its equipment, to the faculty of education in Waziriya, a suburb of Baghdad, which was raided daily for two weeks (Munthe, 2003). Two years after the end of Saddam Hussein's regime, a report by the United Nations University stated that 84 percent of Iraq's higher education institutions had been burned, looted or destroyed. According to the report, the infrastructure that survived mostly had unreliable water or electricity supplies, was badly equipped and lacked computer facilities. Overall, the teaching staff was under qualified: 33 percent held only bachelor's degrees, despite rules requiring a minimum of a masters degree; 30 percent held masters degrees; and only 28 percent of the teaching staff had PhDs (United Nations University, 2005). Students complained that Iraq's university system had significantly declined, dragged down by chronically canceled lectures and decrepit equipment (Cave, 2007). Thus, it is important to emphasize here that the issue is not the quantity but the quality. While statistics published in Iraq clearly indicate that the number of students is continuously increasing and new universities and educational institutes are opening their doors, the level of education is lagging behind due to the lack of qualified academics. There is no doubt that replenishing the lost human capital will take time.

At the same time, an atmosphere of terror and violence began to dominate the campuses and the day-to-day lives of all academics. Similar to the doctors, lecturers and university staff were being targeted. Scores of Iraq's best minds were exiting the country, running away not just from the violence but also from the creeping control of the religious parties, through their militias, over the lives of the universities. In Basra, the militias forced segregation between males and females in classes. As a result, many academics fled to northern Iraq, where Kurdistan is a haven. According to the Kurdish Regional Government's figures, about 1,900 university lecturers from outside Kurdistan have joined universities in the Kurdish area, and more than 3,700 students from Baghdad and Mosul study there (KRG, 2008).

Can Iraq's brain drain be reversed, and how does it compare with the experiences of other countries? What are the long-term implications for the country? The brain drain in Iraq, as mentioned earlier, is not a new phenomenon for the country, and it happens all over the world. In Iraq, this wave took place over a short period of time (2006–7), and unlike other countries, Iraq is not being compensated for the loss of its human capital by the exiles' remittances. This is a critical point when one looks, for example, at the brain drain in Lebanon, Egypt or India. Remittances are, in many countries, an important source of foreign exchange for the country and income to their families at home.[12] Very few Iraqis have found work abroad or are earning enough to remit back a portion of their income. On the contrary, there is reverse remittance whereby refugees are reliant on their own savings in Iraq or remittances from their families to support them given the lack of employment opportunities in the host countries.

With its loss of human capital, Iraq lost its middle class. Two economists who researched the middle class reached the conclusion that the middle class is the driver of democratization and has a crucial role in consolidating democracy (Acemoglu and Robinson, 2006: 38–43).[13] Following the invasion and subsequent violence, the weakness of Iraq's middle class meant that its private sector also faltered. Hampered by a decimated infrastructure, a lack of foreign investors and a flood of imports that undercut local businesses, the private sector failed to flourish. The US efforts to develop the sector did not materialize, and the Iraqi government "has been sustaining the economy by the way it always has: by putting citizens on its payroll" (Robertson, 2008). A positive element has been the relative increase of foreign investments (about $900 million in 2008) in Iraqi joint ventures that might spur the creation of small and medium-size enterprise (*The Economist*, 2009b). However, the private sector, which failed to take root after 2003 for the reasons mentioned above, will struggle to thrive unless security continues to improve.

The US, which invaded Iraq to create democracy, did not take enough steps to protect and expand the middle class, thus losing the major contributor to, and beneficiary of, having a democratic state. In fact, it is interesting to note that while the US media highlights the number of casualties among US troops, they rarely mention the number of Iraqis killed or maimed, except for occasional reports of death tolls as a result of large scale attacks: "Rarely, if ever, do they mention such disparate issues as the massive brain drain that has taken place in Iraq, the staggeringly high unemployment rates, or the growing destitution of Iraqi refugees in Syria" (Ferris, 2008).

One final aspect in considering the brain drain is the examination of the reactions of the Iraqi government to this crisis. A tragic but critical point from the end of the 2003 invasion is that Iraqi authorities are reluctant to recognize or admit that there is indeed a humanitarian crisis, and do so only under pressure from international organizations and media (Oxfam, 2007). Even in September 2007, the *Azzaman* newspaper accused the government of being "in total denial about the daily killings, the uprooting of millions of Iraqis ... and even the imminent imploding of a whole nation" (al-Shaboot, 2007). Partly due to international pressure, but more importantly because of the desperate need for some of the best minds to return home, the Iraqi government launched the first conference in Baghdad in December 2008 aimed at attracting Iraqi expatriate professionals back to Iraq. About 200 professionals participated in the conference, which was held under the banner "Capacities and Expertise." It is still too early to judge how many of the attendees will eventually return to Iraq. However, it is interesting to note that many of those who attended were not part of the brain drain post-2003 but Iraqis who left their country in the 1980s and 1990s (Jamal, 2009). Overall, the Iraqi government has failed to take political, economic and social factors into consideration and examine the country's capacity to absorb large number of returnees; "instead, it has made the return of displaced Iraqis a component, as opposed to a consequence, of its security strategy" (Refugees International, 2009).

If violence comes to a halt or ebbs, would these professionals return to their country? It is doubtful whether many of those who went to the West (top specialists and members of the different minorities) will return to Iraq. Research done worldwide indicates clearly that only a relatively small percentage of educated skilled professionals return to their home countries, assuming political and economic conditions ameliorate. Also, the longer these professionals stay abroad, the less likely they are to return to their home countries (Shinn, 2002). One could safely assume that most who found their way to Sweden and Europe will not return to Iraq in the near future, if ever. In the Arab countries, the case is somewhat different; most of the academics and doctors were unable to find suitable jobs in their host countries (a situation defined by economists as brain waste) (Özden and Schiff, 2006: 227–44), and this is particularly true in Syria and Jordan. As many of those professionals have not managed to get jobs that meet their qualifications, a large number feel frustrated with their professional life. But even for them, a number of basic conditions need to take place before large numbers head home.

Apart from a reduction or cessation of violence, ethnicity and sectarianism would need to diminish significantly from daily life. Those in exile will consider employment opportunities but need to be confident that jobs and opportunities would be given on merit rather than according to affiliation to the right party and clan. Academics have to feel free to write and express their opinion without being intimidated by religious groups. Other considerations would be access to essential services (water, electricity, etc.) and the quality of education for their children. The current situation of Iraqi women is not conducive for those living abroad to return home. (In March 2009, the Minister in charge of Women Affairs, Nawal al-Samarri, resigned due to the lack of progress with regard to issues relating to Iraqi women.) Last, but not least, is the critical factor of property rights and the ability to return home. As in the post-Balkan conflict, property disputes are a key issue and can be politically explosive. Property disputes could linger for many years and spark more violence. The current Iraqi government is not willing to deal with this problem in a serious way. Needless to say, all of this assumes that the refugees will return due to "pull" factors in Iraq rather than "push" factors in their refugee countries.

A critical "pull" factor is the economy. Today, the level of oil production in Iraq is unchanged or slightly up; revenues rose in 2007—five times the pre-war level—but that is due only to the dramatic increase in oil prices (from mid-2007 to summer 2008). The electricity supply is barely back to the pre-2003 levels, although it improved towards the end of 2007 after severe shortages in the period between 2004 and mid-2007. No major industries sprang up, and an analysis of Iraq's economy would indicate that the price of oil spiked, from $25 to $30 per barrel in 2003 to a peak of $147 per barrel in July 2008, masking the government's incompetent management and the corrosive corruption. One could argue that the country would have probably imploded if oil prices had not gone to $100 and above and had the US presence not supported the Iraqi government in spite of all its shortcomings. The rentierism nature of the economy has not changed in the last six years. Thus, Iraq continues to rely on oil for more than 95 percent of its revenues and no real development of new industries has taken place. The deterioration in the agricultural sector has continued, and farmers lack suitable irrigation, proper seeds and modern equipment; farm labour has shrunk because of immigration to cities, and high soil salinity has stifled productivity. If the government does not spend the resources to develop agriculture, industry and other sectors, it will not be able to stimulate employment. This will mean fewer "pull" factors to attract back the professional and skilled emigrants who have fled their country. This is even more true in early 2009, given that oil prices have plummeted to $40, and the Iraqi government will face tough times balancing its budget and creating employment opportunities.

Some economists argue that the power-sharing arrangement between different political groups in Iraq, whereby each party is interested in controlling as much as possible of the rich resources of the country in order to increase its power base, is leading to more emphasis on Iraq's oil resources: "The creation of a consociational democracy in Iraq in the post-invasion period has increased rent-seeking amongst the various ethnic and confessional groups" (Dibeh, 2008).

The emigration of the highly skilled is not always a brain drain for their home countries. In certain cases, countries benefit from more investment in education as a result of emigration; while in other circumstances, the remittances become an important factor in the home economy. In some cases, emigration is only temporary and the professionals return with new skills gained in jobs overseas. In Iraq's case, the exodus has been a brain drain and the emigration of the skilled professionals has irreparably harmed the basic needs of the country (Lucas, 2005: 103–44). It is remarkable that Jordan and Syria, the two main hosts of the refugees, are not taking advantage of the many skilled Iraqi professionals and trying to integrate them into their economies. This "brain waste" does not bode well for those countries and definitely not for the refugees themselves in the long term. Kurdistan is probably the only region that has benefited from and taken advantage of the exodus of skilled professionals from central and southern Iraq.

Long term, the brain drain issue must be addressed, since Iraq's oil wealth and the US's investments will not be able to compensate for the human capital loss. Apart from paying lip service, the government must launch the right projects to attract Iraqi talent back from abroad. At present, the systems are not in place to handle a large number of returnees, and the country's infrastructure is far from ready. Violence must diminish, and professionals living in exile must feel that they could return to work in a safe environment without undue pressure from militia groups and religious fanaticism. Property rights need to be resolved and infrastructure has to improve dramatically. Overseas governments and international organizations must be involved and can play an important role, as "Iraqis need training of civil servants, scholarships and agreements with foreign universities" (Malley, 2008).

Notes

1 For a detailed analysis of the refugees' situation after the 2003 invasion, see Sassoon, 2009.
2 For a detailed analysis of rentierism in Iraq, see various articles by Isam al-Khafaji. See, for example, his article "A Few Days After: State and Society in a Post-Saddam Iraq," in *Iraq at the Crossroads: State and Security in the Shadow of Regime Change*, edited by Toby Dodge and Steven Simon.
3 For a review of the impact of wars and sanctions, Alnasrawi, 2002b.
4 This issue has been widely discussed and analyzed by journalists and academics. For Bremer's point of view, see Bremer, 2006: 39–42 and 343–44; Phillips, 2005: 143–53. See also the shortcomings of the CPA discussed in the Report of the Special Inspector General for Iraq Reconstruction (SIGIR), 2005. October 30, 2005. Pages 77–78.
5 Erhard introduced the currency reform in Germany in 1948 that paved the way for its economic recovery, and became West Germany's Economics Minister.
6 See the Report of the International Advisory and Monitoring Board for the period May 22, 2003, to June 28, 2004. The report criticized the CPA for its weak controls over oil extraction, weakness in the administration of resources, and inadequate spending controls in Iraqi ministries (p. 8). See also O'Hanlon, 2006.

7 Back in October 2003, the National Security Adviser, Condoleezza Rice, took over responsibility for the CPA from Donald Rumsfeld (Bremer, 2006: 186–88).
8 See the history of the American-led reconstruction of Iraq in SIGIR, 2009.
9 Recently, when anti-corruption officials accompanied by Iraqi soldiers went to the Trade Ministry to arrest nine senior officials on charges of corruption, gunfight broke out and the minister and other officials fled the scene. See Dagher, 2009a.
10 See also Jalili, 2006b.
11 The WHO survey identified 136 psychiatrists, 224 psychiatric nurses, 29 psychologists, 46 social workers and 2 psychotherapists serving Kurdistan and the South/Central regions; see WHO, 2009.
12 In 2006, migrants from poor countries sent home $300 billion, about three times the world's foreign aid budgets combined. See Jason Deparle, 2007.
13 A poll conducted by *The Economist* showed that the middle class is more supportive of democracy than the poor (*The Economist*, 2009a).

References

Acemoglu, Daron and James A. Robinson (2006). *Economic Origins of Dictatorship and Democracy*. New York: Cambridge University Press.

al-Khafaji, Isam (2003). "A Few Days After: State and Society in a Post-Saddam Iraq," in *Iraq at the Crossroads: State and Security in the Shadow of Regime Change*, edited by Toby Dodge and Steven Simon. Pages 77–92. London: Adelphi Papers.

al-Khalidi, Ashraf, Sophia Hoffman and Victor Tanner (2007). "Iraqi Refugees in the Syrian Arab Republic: A Field-Based Snapshot." Washington, DC: The Brookings Institute-University of Bern Project on Internal Displacement. June.

Allawi, Ali (2007). *The Occupation of Iraq: Winning the War, Losing the Peace*. New Haven, CT: Yale University Press.

Alnasrawi, Abbas (2002a). *Iraq's Burdens: Oil, Sanctions and Underdevelopment*. Connecticut: Greenwood Press.

——— (2002b). "Long-term Consequences of Wars and Sanctions," in *Iraq's Economic Predicament*, edited by Kamil A. Mahdi. Pages 343–48. Reading, PA: Ithaca Press.

al-Shabibi, Sinan (2002). "An Economic Agenda for a Future Iraq," in *Studies on the Iraqi Economy*. Pages 24–25. London: Iraqi Economic Forum.

al-Shaboot, Mohammed (2007). "Maliki's Government Is in Denial." *Azzaman*. September 6.

al-Sheibani, Bassim Irheim Mohammed, Najah R. Hadi and Tariq Hasoon (2006). "Iraq Lacks Facilities and Expertise in Emergency Medicine," *British Medical Journal*. Vol. 333, October 21: 847.

Bremer, Paul (2006). *My Year in Iraq*. New York: Simon & Schuster.

The Brookings Institution (2009). "Iraq Index, Tracking Variables of Reconstruction & Security in Post-Saddam Iraq." February 26. Available at: http://www.brookings.edu/saban/iraq-index.aspx.

The Brussels Tribunal (2008). "List of Killed, Threatened or Kidnapped Iraqi Academics." Available at: http://www.BRusselstribunal.org/academicsList.htm.

Cave, Damien (2007). "Cheated of Future, Iraqi Graduates want to Flee." *The New York Times*. June 4.

Dagher, Sam (2009a). "Gunfight Breaks Out as Iraqi Soldiers Try to Arrest Trade Officials." *The New York Times*. May 2.

——— (2009b). "Iraqi Report on Corruption Cites Prosecutors' Barriers." *The New York Times*. May 6.

Deparle, Jason (2007). "Western Union as a Player in Immigration Debates." *International Herald Tribune*. November 22.

Diamond, Larry (2005). *Squandered Victory: The American Occupation and the Bungled Effort to Bring Democracy to Iraq*. New York: Owl Books.

Dibeh, Ghassan (2008). "Resources and the Political Economy of State Fragility in Conflict States: Iraq and Somalia." United Nations University, Research Paper no. 2008/35. April.

The Economist (2009a). "What Do You Think? A Special Poll on Middle-Class Attitudes." February 12. Available at: http://www.economist.com/specialreports/displaystory.cfm?story_id=13063322.

——— (2009b). "Searching for a Phoenix in Basra." April 30. Available at: http://www.economist.com/world/mideast-africa/displaystory.cfm?story_id=13579106.

Economist Intelligence Unit (2009). "Iraq Monthly Report." January.

Ferris, Elizabeth G. (2008). "The Looming Crisis: Displacement and Security in Iraq." Washington, DC: Brookings Institution, Policy Paper, IX. August.

Glanz, James and Riyadh Mohammed (2008). "Premier of Iraq Is Quietly Firing Fraud Monitors." *The New York Times*. November 18. Available at: http://www.nytimes.com/2008/11/18/world/middleeast/18maliki.html.

Herring, Eric and Glen Rangwala (2006). *Iraq in Fragments: The Occupation and Its Legacy*. London: Hurst & Company.

Integrated Regional Information Networks (IRIN) (2006). "Iraq: Neglected Nurses Fight Their Own War." November 19. Available at: http://www.irinnews.org/PrintReport.aspx?ReportID=61948.

——— (2007). "Iraq: Justice Delayed as Lawyers Live under Threat." April 30. Available at: http://www.irinnews.org/PrintReport.aspx?ReportID=71864.

——— (2009) "Iraq: Growing Unemployment Threatens Stability, UN Says." February 18. Available at: http://www.irinnews.org/Report.aspx?ReportId=82993.

Jalili, Ismail (2006a). "Plight of Iraqi Academics." Paper presented to the Madrid International Conference on the Assassinations of Iraqi Academics, April 23–24 (data was updated by Dr Jalili May 1, 2006). Available at: http://www.jalili.co.uk/Community?HR/IraqiAcademics_60501_PPT.ppt.

——— (2006b). "Iraqi Academics and Doctors: Innocent Victims of a Wider Geological Struggle." *TAARII Newsletter*. The American Academic Research Institute in Iraq, No.1–2, Fall.

Jamal, Randa (2009). "Iraqi Expatriate Professionals Back in Iraq for the First Conference on Iraq's Capacities and Expertise." *Relief Web.* January 5. Available at: http://www.relief.int/rw.

Kurdish Regional Government (KRG) (2008). November 20. Accessed February 19, 2009 at: http://www.krg.org/articles/details.asp?lngnr=12&smap=02010100&rnr=223&anr=26811.

Laub, Karin (2008). "Health Chiefs Battle to Bring Back Iraqi Doctors." *USA Today.* September 7.

Lucas, Robert E.B. (2005). *International Migration and Economic Development: Lessons from Low-Income Countries.* Cheltenham, UK: Edward Elgar.

Malley, Robert (2008). "Testimony to the Senate Armed Services Committee." Washington, DC: United States Senate, Committee on Armed Services. April 9. Available at: http://armed-services.senate.gov/statemnt/2008/April/Malley%2004-09-08.pdf.

Merza, Ali. (2007). "Iraq: Reconstruction under Uncertainty." *International Journal of Contemporary Iraqi Studies.* Vol. 1, No. 2: 173–212.

——— (2008). "Policies and Economic and Social Trends in Iraq: 2003–2007." Paper presented at the International Association of Contemporary Iraqi Studies, 3rd Annual Conference, SOAS, University of London. July 16–17.

Misconi, Humam (2008). "Iraq's Capital Budget and Regional Development Fund: Review and Comments on Execution Capacity and Implications." *International Journal of Contemporary Iraqi Studies.* Vol. 2, No. 2: 271–92.

Munthe, Turi (2003). "Will Harsh Weed-out Allow Iraqi Academia to Flower?" *The Times Higher Education Supplement.* July 25.

Office of the Special Inspector General for Iraq Reconstruction (SIGIR) (2005). "Report of the Special Inspector General for Iraq Reconstruction (SIGIR)." October 30.

——— (2008). "Anticorruption Efforts in Iraq: U.S. and Iraq Take Actions but Much Remains to Be Done." SIGIR Report 08-023, July 29.

——— (2009). *Hard Lessons: The Iraq Reconstruction Experience.* Washington, DC: United States Government Printing Office.

O'Hanlon, Michael (2006). "We Can't Stop Rebuilding Iraq." *Washington Post,* January 24.

Oxfam (2007). "Rising to the Humanitarian Challenge in Iraq." July 30. Available at: http://www.oxfam.org/sites/www.oxfam.org/files/Rising%20to%20the%20humanitarian%20challenge%20in%20Iraq.pdf.

Özden, Çağlar and Maurice Schiff (eds.) (2006). *International Migration, Remittances and the Brain Drain.* Washington, DC: World Bank and Palgrave Macmillan.

Packer, George (2005). *The Assassin's Gate.* New York: Farrar, Straus and Giroux.

Phillips, David L. (2005). *Losing Iraq, Inside the Postwar Reconstruction Fiasco.* Colorado: Westview.

Refugees International (2009). "Iraq: Preventing the Point of No Return." April 9. Available at: http://www.refugeesinternational.org/policy/field-report/iraq-preventing-point-no-return.

Reuters (2009). "Iraq Inflation Seen at 10 Percent End-2009." April 30.

Robertson, Campbell (2008). "Iraq Private Sector Falters; Rolls of Government Soar." *The New York Times*, August 11. Available at: http://www.nytimes.com/2008/08/11/world/middleeast/11baghdad.html?partner=rssnyt&emc=rss.

Sassoon, Joseph (2009). *The Iraqi Refugees: The New Crisis in the Middle East*. London: I.B. Tauris.

Schmidt, Eric and David E. Sanger (2003). "Reconstruction Policy: Looting Disrupts Detailed US Plan to Restore Iraq." *The New York Times*, May 19.

Shinn, David (2002). "Reversing the Brain Drain in Ethiopia." Paper delivered to the Ethiopian North American Health Professionals Association, November 23.

United Nations Development Programme (UNDP) and the Ministry of Planning and Development Cooperation (2005). "Iraq Living Conditions Survey 2004." Baghdad, Iraq: vol. II. Analytical Report.

United Nations Office for the Coordination of Humanitarian Affairs (OCHA) (2009). "Iraq Labour Force Analysis 2003–2008." Inter-Agency Information and Analysis Unit. January. Available at: http://www.iauiraq.org/reports/Iraq_Labour_Force_Analysis.pdf.

United Nations University (2005). "UNU calls for World Help to Repair System." April 27. Available at: http://update.unu.edu/archive/issue37_16.htm.

United States Department of Defense (2006). "Measuring Stability and Security in Iraq." Washington, DC: Report to Congress. February. Available at: http://www.defenselink.mil/home/features/Iraq_Reports/docs/2006-02-Report.pdf.

United States Government Accountability Office (GAO) (2008). "Iraq Reconstruction: Better Data Needed to Assess Iraq's Budget Execution." Washington, DC: Report to Congressional Committees, GAO-08-153. January. Available at: http://www.gao.gov/new.items/d08153.pdf.

United States House of Representatives (2007). *Resolution 734*. Washington, DC: Committee on Oversight and Government Reform, Testimony given by Stewart Bowen (SIGIR), 110th Congress, First Session. October 11. Available at: http://www.oversight.house.gov.

Women's International League for Peace and Freedom (2006). "Iraq: Unemployment Forces Female Professionals into Domestic Work." July 25. Available at: http://www.peacewomen.org/news/Iraq/July06/women_forced_to_domestic.html.

World Health Organization (WHO) (2009). "Iraq Mental Health Survey 2006/7." March 7. Available at: http://www.emro.who.int/iraq/pdf/imhs_report_en.pdf.

8
IRFFI
A Multi-Donor Initiative

Carla Angulo-Pasel

The International Reconstruction Fund Facility for Iraq (IRFFI) was launched at the request of donors seeking to fulfill their obligations under United Nations Security Council (UNSC) Resolution 1483. The May 2003 resolution sought assistance from donor states and international financial institutions (IFIs) toward post-conflict reconstruction and development efforts in Iraq. At an Iraq Donors Meeting held in New York on 24 June 2003, donors requested the development of a fund to facilitate the channeling and coordination of donor resources. Subsequently, the United Nations Development Group (UNDG) and the World Bank began developing the IRFFI to assist donor countries in the coordination of reconstruction and development projects.

The development of IRFFI is important for several reasons. First, it was recognized that there was a need for a multilateral effort to support the rebuilding and development of Iraq. Moreover, there was an understanding among several donors that there needed to be a mechanism to help pool resources and coordinate reconstruction activities. Western countries especially had a vested interest in promoting a successful reconstruction effort to ensure a degree of stability and security in the region. Most importantly, IRFFI has proven to be an effective mechanism to promote international cooperation. In 2003, when the idea of a Multi-Donor Trust Fund (MDTF) was first introduced, it was a precarious time, as many nations around the world opposed the United States' (US) occupation of Iraq. Consequently, most donor countries were hesitant to invest funds in reconstruction projects, believing that they would be dominated by the US. European countries such as France and Germany were especially concerned with the lack of United Nations (UN) presence in Iraq. The creation of the IRFFI helped address these concerns by assuring international donors that their funds would be managed by an international organization rather than by the US.

The aim of this chapter is to advance the understanding of IRFFI as a multilateral reconstruction mechanism. Following an initial section outlining the IRFFI's structure, this chapter will examine the challenges involved with the coordination of this multilateral exercise. A variety of actors are involved in reconstruction efforts in Iraq, including donor governments, international organizations and non-governmental organizations—all working with the Iraqi government toward national priorities. Moreover, there are significant bilateral reconstruction projects that frequently compete with multilateral efforts. Canada's involvement in Iraq's reconstruction will also be analyzed, because the Canadian International Development Agency (CIDA) is a major actor advocating membership in the IRFFI. As with any exercise, several lessons may be learned for future multilateral donor funds and Iraqi reconstruction. This chapter does not seek to evaluate the effectiveness or implementation of individual IRFFI reconstruction projects on the ground in Iraq, but rather it undertakes a macro-level assessment of the coordination and management of the Iraqi reconstruction process.

The IRFFI Structure

Formerly launched in 2004, the IRFFI's governance structures were designed in consultation with key donors and Iraqi authorities. In these consultations, the Iraq Core Group included representatives of Iraq's Governing Council, Iraqi Sector Ministries and the Coalition Provisional Authority (CPA) (UNDP and the World Bank, 2003a). In post-conflict situations, multi-donor trust funds function according to certain principles; the IRFFI is no different. For instance, to achieve funding approval each project needs to conform to the priorities of a needs assessment carried out in consultation with Iraqi authorities, donors and partners. Local capacity plays an important role in the execution of projects given that activities financed by the donor community have to be implemented, as much as possible, by Iraqis. This Iraqi participation is paramount. One of the principal aims of IRFFI is to provide sustained support to the Iraqi Government throughout the country's transition, fostering sustainable local capacity building, with the goal of full Iraqi administration of all development programs and donor coordination (UNDP and the World Bank, 2008). The other goals of this multi-donor initiative are to ensure transparency and accountability while avoiding gaps and funding overlaps.

The complex structure of IRFFI is clarified in the Terms of Reference (TOR), a document originally developed by the fund in 2003. In 2007, the TOR was revised at the request of the Government of Iraq to reflect a clearer Iraqi leadership role. The revised TOR was approved at the Sixth Donor Committee Meeting held in Bari, Italy. Both versions will be employed in this explanation. Because this fund was to be a coordinated effort with Iraqi input, it was important to first clarify which priorities should take precedence. To that end, a needs assessment was carried out in 2003 by the World Bank and the UNDG in consultation with the International Monetary Fund (IMF). The assessment helped define the short- and medium-term priorities for reconstruction projects. The findings and recommendations of the needs assessment were approved by the Iraqi Governing Council and the Iraqi Ministers of Planning and Finance. The revised TOR also stipulated IRFFI's alignment not only with the needs assessment but also with Iraq's National Development Strategy (NDS) and the International Compact with Iraq (ICI).

In total, IRFFI has five different components. There are two trust funds that donors may use to channel their aid: the World Bank Iraq Trust Fund (WB-ITF) and the United Nations Development Group Iraq Trust Fund (UNDG-ITF). As the administrators, each have their own procedures; they are responsible for maintaining appropriate records and accounts as well as disbursing the funds to specific projects. The WB-ITF operates on three specific areas, with only some nuanced differences between the 2003 TOR and the revised TOR from 2007. The first remains unchanged: the "capacity building of Iraqi counterparts in areas that will help facilitate sound implementation." The second area is more interesting, as the revised TOR includes "sectoral programmes that may include a menu of specific projects, which can be expanded." This has been altered from the original, less appealing, "which can be expanded opportunistically *as circumstances improve* [emphasis added]," likely referring to the security situation. The exclusion of the statement from the latter version could indicate a conscious effort to remove any reference to a dangerous post-conflict security situation. The last stipulated area is "projects and policies that aim to establish building blocks for sectoral and structural policy reforms and larger scale development" (UNDP and the World Bank, 2003a; 2007). Overall, the WB-ITF operates with these three elements in mind. Although it may operate in all priority sectors specified in the needs assessment, it pays particular attention to areas in which it has a comparative advantage, namely, investment and capital expenditures as well as technical assistance and training. As of 2009, donors have supplied a total of US$496 million to the WB-ITF projects, with minimum contributions set at US$1 million.

The second available avenue for donors is the United Nations Development Group Iraq Trust Fund (UNDG-ITF), which is administered by the United Nations Development Programme (UNDP). The role of UNDG-ITF stems from the UN mandate in Iraq, which comes from UNSC Resolutions 1483, 1511 and most recently 1770. Resolution 1770 continues to actively encourage IRFFI, noting that the Special Representative of the Secretary-General supports "active donor coordination of critical reconstruction and assistance programmes through the International Reconstruction Fund Facility for Iraq (IRFFI)" (UNSC, 2007). Unlike the World Bank, the UNDG focuses more on development projects. As per both the 2003 and revised 2007 TOR, these project areas include improving capacity for human development and social justice, delivery of social services, civil society empowerment, protection and reintegration of IDPs and refugees, water resources and food security, human rights and the rule of law, private sector development and employment generation (UNDP and the World Bank, 2003; 2007). Each individual donor contribution must amount to at least US$200,000. As of 2009, the UNDG-ITF has received approximately US$1.35 billion and has funded over 180 different projects.

The IRFFI also requires an effective governance structure to function properly. This governance structure, consisting of a Donor Committee, an Executive Committee and a Secretariat, was also changed to a certain extent to facilitate an increase in Iraqi leadership. These changes were stipulated clearly in the revised 2007 TOR. Although 25 donor countries have pledged funds to the IRFFI, only those whose contributions amount to at least US$10 million—to either or both funds—may be included in the Donor Committee (see Appendix 8.1 for full resource allocation of each member country). In addition, the Donor Committee has the discretionary ability to appoint two seats to countries that do not meet these criteria. The World Bank, UNDG, IMF and the Ministry of Planning and Development Cooperation (MoPDC) have observer status. Being a member of the Donor Committee is significant since it is expected to provide strategic guidance to the UNDG and the World Bank. While these international organizations manage the funds and implement the projects on the ground, the Donor Committee makes certain that the Government of Iraq's overall reconstruction priorities are met. Moreover, the Donor Committee must ensure coherence and collaboration between the Facility, NDS and ICI, review the progress of the Facility's operations and report this progress to all its donors, ensure that Facility can adapt to changes in priorities and work to attract new funding opportunities and new members (UNDP and the World Bank, 2007). Meetings of the Donor Committee are held on a semi-annual basis, though it may be decided that they occur more frequently.[1]

The Donor Committee Chair is appointed by the international donor members. The primary role of the chair is to act as a coordinator, introducing ideas and pursuing different initiatives with the two executing agencies and the major donors. When IRFFI was first established, the chair position lacked a formal mandate. Though considered to be a prestigious position, the IRFFI never devised a formal mandate for this role. The responsibilities were not articulated until the revised TOR. Annex C of the TOR outlines both the chair's responsibilities to the Donor Committee and the Executive Committee. Overall, the Chair's primary role is to act as the representative of the Donor Committee by ensuring all requests and concerns of the Donor Committee are expressed to the World Bank, the UNDG, the Executive Committee and the Government of Iraq.

Along with the Donor Committee, the Executive Committee also acts as a governance mechanism. When the IRFFI was first established, this body was called the Facility Coordination Committee (FCC) and consisted of representatives from the UNDG and the World Bank, with the IMF having observer status. This body was to ensure close coordination with Iraqi counterparts, but it did not include Iraqi representatives. As the Iraqi government became more autonomous and requested a more prominent role, the FCC was expanded and transformed into the Executive Committee. It is chaired by the Chairperson of the Iraqi Strategic Review Board (ISRB) and includes the Chair of the Donor Committee as well as UNDG and World Bank representatives. The ISRB not only chairs the Executive Committee but must approve each IRFFI project to avoid overlaps or gaps in activities. One of the most significant contributions made by the Executive Committee is to provide effective coordination. Thus, while the Donor Committee primarily addresses the concerns and objectives of donors, the Executive Committee ensures that the IRFFI programs are coordinated with programs funded from the national budget or bilateral donors while promoting the objectives of the NDS and ICI. In the same respect, the Executive Committee's close working relationship with the Iraqi government provides an understanding of national needs and priorities, allowing the executive to make recommendations to donors on appropriate resource allocation. Finally, the Executive Committee is expected to act as an oversight mechanism, making certain that monitoring and evaluation of all reconstruction activities is undertaken.

The Secretariat is the last component within this structure. It is staffed by representatives of the donors, the World Bank, the UNDG and the MoPDC, and reports directly to the Chairperson of the Executive Committee. The duties of the Secretariat are mainly logistical and administrative in nature; it assists in the coordination and public dissemination of information.

Challenges of Coordination

Being a multi-party trust fund, IRFFI has encountered many challenges with regard to donor governments, international organizations, bilateral projects, conflicting needs and priorities, and encouraging Iraqi leadership and capacity. The management of funds is administered by the UNDG and the World Bank, but difficult security circumstances have impeded the attainment of optimal levels of direct management. The UNDG and WB personnel, under normal circumstances, would have been more actively involved but are hampered by deteriorating security conditions in Iraq. The lack of presence on the ground is extremely challenging when trying to implement a system of reconstruction. Iraqis expect reconstruction personnel and the Chair of the Donor Committee to be more dynamically involved, frequently visiting Baghdad. However, maintaining a presence on the ground between 2005 and 2007 was difficult, and at the beginning of 2005, the World Bank did not have active personnel in Iraq (Bell, 2009).

There were instances in which the credibility of the IRFFI system was undermined. The example of the UN can be used to illustrate this point. As the coordinating mechanism for UN agencies, the IRFFI is responsible for soliciting funds and then determining which projects should be prioritized and implemented. Although this process was supposed to ensure organization among all reconstruction projects, it was circumvented by many UN organizations. UN agencies, like the World Health Organization (WHO), the United Nations Educational, Scientific and Cultural Organization (UNESCO) and the United Nations Children's Fund (UNICEF), solicited funds independently of IRFFI. Each drafts a project idea and speaks directly to Iraqi ministries. These agencies assert their autonomy as entities with their own authority that can operate independently of the IRFFI structure (Bell, 2009). This undercuts the purpose of the IRFFI system. If agencies of the UN are willing to work outside the scope of IRFFI, what prevents other international organizations or donor governments from doing the same?

Another major challenge for the IRFFI coordination concerns existing tension between international organizations like the UN or the World Bank and donor governments. For instance, at the beginning of the IRFFI exercise, there was a certain precipitancy from some donor countries. In particular, the British required that their funding be spent promptly. Britain was disappointed with the slow pace with which projects were implemented on the ground by the international organizations. The World Bank deliberately took a more cautious approach with the disbursement of funds, taking care to sufficiently prepare prior to the commencement of any project (Bell, 2009). Another primary reason for the delay of reconstruction efforts was the unstable security situation. As then-President of the World Bank James Wolfensohn told the BBC in 2004, "if you want [reconstruction] going full pace, that will only happen when you get some sense of security in the country" (Schifferes, 2004). He warned that the main problem was not one of resource restraint but one of physical safety, which prevented personnel deployment in Iraq.

Similarly, political aims exist that create tension among the donor governments. After the invasion, various conferences took place concerning post-conflict reconstruction in Iraq. For instance, the Iraq International Conference, held in Brussels on June 22, 2005, was organized by the European Union (EU), the United States and the Iraqi Government. More than 80 countries and organizations were in attendance, including the UN Secretary General, the Arab League, the Organization of Islamic conference, NATO, all UN Security Council members and the G8. The three main issues of discussion included the political support for the new Iraqi government, the new constitutional process taking place and encouraging international support for the democratic process in Iraq. Areas included the economy, reconstruction programs and donor countries' contributions, and the rule of law and consolidation of law and judiciary in Iraq. Iraqi Foreign Minister Hoshyar Zebari elucidated the point that, with Iraqi presence at the conference, the Iraqi government would be treated on equal footing with other parties and Iraqi priorities would have a prominent voice at the conference (BBC, 2005b).

According to the Conference Statement, this gathering was meant to renew the international partnership with Iraq. However, the US decision to invade Iraq was becoming increasingly unpopular with the international community, and the US encouraged this conference, hoping to achieve more support in Iraq. The earlier Madrid Conference of 2003, which served as a donor conference to raise funds for Iraq, yielded poor results (see the following chapter by Momani). At the Brussels meeting, this prompted Iraqi Finance Minister Ali Allawi to express disappointment that little of the financial assistance promised in Madrid had materialized, and Prime Minister Ibrahim al-Jaafari asked donors to fulfill the aid pledges they had already made (Weisman, 2005). A prominent example, disclosed at the Brussels conference, was that the US had only spent US$7 billion of the US$19 billion in economic aid that Congress appropriated two years prior. Similarly, only US$2 billion of aid from other countries had materialized out of the US$13 billion pledged in Madrid (Maddox, 2005).

Thus, this conference was an opportunity for many donor countries to express symbolic and rhetorical support rather than providing tangible assistance. Many countries made speeches outlining the urgent need to provide more aid to Iraqis and to help them rebuild their country. US Secretary of State Condoleeza Rice, among them, claimed that nations needed to stand with the "brave people of Iraq," improve security and liberalize the economy. But there were many dissenting voices at the conference who agreed that the meeting lacked significance; one British official stated that their intention was simply to orchestrate the expression of "warm feelings" (Maddox, 2005). Other countries underscored the important principle of multilateralism. Iranian Foreign Minister Kamal Kharrazi was quick to point out how the US now wanted the help of the international community in Iraq as it became clear that US unilateralism was failing (BBC, 2005b). The Irish government was also critical of the US leadership role in rebuilding Iraq, claiming that the US had alienated and isolated Iraqis and therefore should not have been in charge of any key areas (Walsh, 2005). In the end, the conference, although never intended specifically as a pledging conference, did not materialize substantial aid but relatively minor offers of help. EU High Representative Javier Solana was asked by the media about pledging money for Iraq to which he answered that the real pledging conference was to be held in a couple of months at the Dead Sea Donor Committee meeting. However, this future meeting was never intended to be a pledging conference but simply a donor meeting, especially since the

Donor Committee believed it would not acquire any new funding (Bell, 2009). The best outcome a pledging conference would have accomplished involved debt forgiveness. Most Gulf States—which hold a large amount of Iraq's debt—were unprepared to forgive this debt (see the following chapter).

Iraq's reconstruction efforts are often hampered by the strain caused between multilateral and bilateral project initiatives. As of 2009, the United States has pledged approximately US$48 billion in reconstruction aid for Iraq. The portion of this sum allotted to the IRFFI, however, is only US$10 million per year, the minimum contribution needed to achieve major stakeholder status on the IRFFI Donor Committee. Furthermore, it is clear that the US has exerted its power in Iraq and, given a choice between a bilateral or multilateral project, it will always choose the bilateral option. These bilateral arrangements allow the US more control in defining project priorities while permitting the US to award contracts to American companies. Yet despite having billions of dollars to control and dispense in Iraqi reconstruction, the US still desires to maintain a powerful stakeholder position in the IRFFI that would allow it to control the strategic direction of these projects as well. Another reason for this position may be due to the growing pressure within the US to promote at least a facade of multilateralism. The reversal in US position regarding the International Compact with Iraq—one of the major documents used to determine priorities for IRFFI—may be further evidence of this. At a meeting in Baghdad with the Europeans, US representatives were hesitant about the idea of a compact in which donors would undertake to accomplish certain initiatives in return for Iraqis to accomplish certain others. Three months after this meeting took place, the US changed its position and advocated for the ICI (Bell, 2009).

The IRFFI has been executing projects in Iraq for six years. Inevitably, there has been a certain amount of adaptability in the process, especially when a new and elected Iraqi government came to power in 2005. Not only did potential new priorities come to light, but there was also an increasing Iraqi presence and capacity in the decision-making process. The IRFFI established a number of priorities in a needs assessment performed in October 2003. There were several reasons for undertaking this needs assessment. For instance, since the 1980s, public infrastructure and investment had been neglected. The resulting deterioration was exacerbated by the conflict, which further damaged buildings, communication equipment and transportation links. Health and education in Iraq were once regarded as among the best in the Middle East, but have severely declined due to a lack of resources. Moreover, income per capita had risen to over US$3,600 in the early 1980s due to the increase in the price of oil; however, by 2001, it had fallen to the range of approximately US$770–1,020. The needs assessment was administered against this backdrop, and the report highlighted 14 key priority sectors for IRFFI projects to tackle.[2] The report also divided each priority sector into either an immediate or medium-term priority. It estimated that the total reconstruction costs for all priority sectors would be approximately US$36 billion, of which US$9 billion needed to be addressed in 2004 (UN and the World Bank, 2003b). To date, the IRFFI has received only US$1.85 billion in total funding.

Several of the identified priority sectors may be used to demonstrate some IRFFI obstacles. For instance, for health, education and employment creation the report stipulates restoring indicators to the levels obtained in the 1980s. In 1989, the education budget was approximately 6 percent of the GDP or US$2.5 billion. Similarly, the infant mortality rate in 1989 stood at 40 per 1000 births; this number more than doubled from 1990 to 1996. Since the 1990s, however, Iraq has experienced a substantial decline in professionals such as teachers, doctors and nurses. As Sassoon discusses in his chapter, the brain-drain phenomenon has crippled Iraq's middle class. Likewise, the development of vital infrastructure to provide basic services like water and sanitation has also been hampered because of the security situation in Iraq. Not only is the safety of personnel on the ground being threatened, but rebuilt infrastructure is often susceptible to militia attacks.

After the needs assessment was performed, additional documents began to influence IRFFI's reconstruction efforts. The National Development Strategy (NDS), for instance, was formulated as Iraqi leadership became more prominent. This document was prepared first through consultations that took place with the Iraqi Interim Government and continued with the Iraqi Transitional Government. It was submitted for comments to both the World Bank and the UNDG and was formally discussed at the IRFFI Donor Committee's Dead Sea Meeting in July 2005. Having a more prominent Iraqi presence was always a principal goal for IRFFI and the Donor Committee. However, there are also certain challenges to the overall coordination of IRFFI with another prominent player in the system. Specifically, when the NDS was formulated it called for "significant resource transfers" from development partners and advocated for a "larger more inclusive 'Consultative Group' type forum to supplement the more restrictive IRFFI Donor Coordination Meetings" (Republic of

Iraq, 2005: 40). Clearly, Iraqi ownership is prevalent throughout the document. Similarly, Iraqis were insistent on determining development priorities when they met periodically with the UNDG and the World Bank. Evidently, Iraqis wanted to be seen as determining strategic priorities; unfortunately, they lacked adequate capacity to execute these priorities. One reason may be that Iraq is still a developing country. Second, and more importantly, many qualified people were simply not available due to the decision made by Paul Bremer to dismantle the political infrastructure of the Baath Party (Bell, 2009).

This is not to say that donor governments should be given the opportunity to formulate their own priorities irrespective of the local government in power, however, the local government may not always have the ability and leadership capacity needed to determine strategic priorities. For example, in one instance the MoPDC had approximately 95 engineers readily available but they were not utilized due to the lack of coordination in projects (Bell, 2009). This scenario shows that although there may be a wish to be seen as achieving a leadership role, the reality demonstrates that this leadership role is often cosmetic and devoid of real substance due to capacity issues. Similarly, during a discussion concerning the Chair of the Donor Committee, the Iraqi Government wanted the appointed chair to be from the Government of Iraq—which suffered from a logical inconsistency since the chair position was intended to be filled by donors to enable them to better coordinate their strategies in order to hold the UN and World Bank accountable to the financiers (Bell, 2009). At the Istanbul Donor Committee meeting in 2007, a compromise was reached to have co-chairs—one from the Iraqi Government and one from Italy. Ambassador Gianludovico de Martino was selected for Italy. He was a former Ambassador to Iraq and the Coordinator of "Task Force Iraq" through the Ministry of Foreign Affairs. This co-chairmanship, however, was an interim arrangement for one year. It has since been replaced with its original composition—having the chair selected from the contributing donors. Ambassador de Martino remained in the chairmanship post until February 2009. Ambassador Mikael Winther from Denmark has since been appointed Chair of the Donor Committee.

Overall, IRFFI has adapted to a procedural change. The needs assessment was supplemented by both the NDS and the ICI. Although the identified needs have not necessarily changed, the prioritization seems to have shifted. There appears to be more emphasis placed on economic recovery and private sector development. In Iraq's NDS, the first four sections of the document focus on economic development and growth, fiscal frameworks, banking and finance, and privatization and restructuring of state-owned enterprises. The last two sections focus on improving the quality of life and strengthening good governance. Similarly, in the ICI the primary focus is to "build a framework for Iraq's economic transformation and integration into the regional and global economy" (Republic of Iraq, 2008). Both documents also highlight a greater emphasis on the Iraqi government being actively involved in the reconstruction process.

CIDA and IRRFI

The Canadian experience in IRRFI and Iraq has had mixed results. Prior to the 2003 US invasion, Canada was adamant about not participating in the military operation with the "Coalition of the Willing." Then-Foreign Affairs Minister Bill Graham stressed that "no country is going to commit their soldiers or their treasury or their taxpayers' money unless they believe they have some role in making a decision about how that money will be spent" (Koring, 2003). Once the reconstruction efforts began, however, there was a sense that Canada could and should contribute in Iraq. The Chrétien government was a strong supporter of a multilateral regime that involved the UN in reconstruction: "Canada is always behind any form of aid that will come through the multilateral way, not unilateral" (Thompson, 2003). There was a feeling that Canada had to contribute something to Iraq since it did not contribute troops. Therefore, when the opportunity to join IRFFI was presented, Canada was willing and able to provide assistance. Becoming active in IRFFI was seen as fulfilling a commitment to be helpful without deploying troops (Bell, 2009). In fact, Canada was one of the first countries to provide aid to Iraq in the sum of $300 million.

In the same respect, the Canadian International Development Agency (CIDA) was equally eager to demonstrate its willingness to the reconstruction effort. Moreover, not only was Canada prepared to contribute significant funds to IRFFI (approximately $100 million) to make it the fourth largest donor for IRFFI, but it went on to hold the position of Chair of the Donor Committee for two years (2005–2007). CIDA emphasized the importance of Iraq's reconstruction, focusing on multilateral institutions and acquiring support from the international community. At the same time, once on the ground, there was a certain amount of passiveness on behalf of the Canadian government. There was a feeling that Canada had done its part in Iraq by contributing to the IRFFI and attaining the Chairmanship of the Donor Committee, which provided a certain profile. Consequently, there seemed to be a lack of commitment to becoming more involved in the substance of the IRFFI exercise (Bell, 2009). Moreover, although CIDA claimed that it encouraged multilateral projects, $200 million of aid was disbursed through other avenues, including bilateral projects, in effect competing with IRFFI projects.

The lack of commitment was further hampered by the cautious approach taken toward any project or new idea as a result of the security situation. For example, Graham had stated that the opening of the Canadian Embassy in Iraq would send the message that "we're active in that region, we have responsibilities in that region, [and] we want to contribute to the better stability of that region" (Leblanc, 2003). Nonetheless, even though Canada had acquired the premises for the embassy, the security costs became prohibitive in terms of Ottawa's foreign policy priorities. The government decided to close the Baghdad Embassy, opting instead to represent Canadian interests in Iraq through the embassy in Amman, Jordan (Bell, 2009). Similarly, in the Martin government, there appeared to be a sense of fear about the escalating violence. It was suggested that Canada was "sitting on the sidelines" watching as Iraq descended into chaos; to this Martin responded that Canada was playing a significant role based on the resources it had to contribute (MacKinnon, 2004). It cannot be overlooked, however, that on the ground there was a growing anxiety about kidnappings and increased casualties. Canadian government policy meant that traveling to Iraq and especially working outside of the Green Zone was thus severely restricted for Canadians involved in reconstruction projects under the IRFFI or otherwise. Even Canadian companies, who were first banned by the US from bidding on lucrative Iraq reconstruction contracts, were not willing to risk the safety of their contractors, except in relatively secure Kurdistan (MacNamara, 2004). Once the Italian government, with Ambassador de Martino, was appointed as chair, there were fewer restrictions on travel into Iraq.

A final detriment to the Canadian participation in the IRFFI and Iraqi reconstruction came with the Harper government. When Stephen Harper was the Leader of the Opposition he supported the idea of joining the US in Iraq. However, once in power, the political decision not to join the coalition had been made and he focused his foreign policy efforts on Afghanistan. In fact, once prime minister, Harper stated that "the Iraq war destroyed at least temporarily, or disrupted, NATO's sense of commonality of purpose in Afghanistan" (Maniquet, 2009). While at the London G20 meeting in April 2009, he added that, "ultimately, whether it was right or wrong, the war in Iraq was a diversion from the central, the original mission to Afghanistan" (Blanchfield, 2009). Thus, Harper's failure to prioritize Iraq signifies that, in practice, there was still less support for an activist role for Canada as the Chair of the Donor Committee (Bell, 2009). Iraq is currently not a foreign policy priority for the Canadian government.

Lessons Learned

The primary lesson learned is that the Chair of the Donor Committee should have had a more active mandate and should have dealt with the macro issues of the IRFFI. There seems to be a general awareness of a "malaise" regarding the overall performance at the macro-level, but this obstacle never received due attention. There was only marginal effectiveness in organizing and attending meetings and following an agenda; these became ends rather than means, limiting the probability of positive tangible outcomes (Bell, 2009). Although the meetings went relatively smoothly and those involved felt like they had been heard, there were few deliverables. In essence what was needed was a more activist approach by the Chair of the Donor Committee, one in which the chair was more assertive, playing more of a leading role, respecting priority areas and working more dynamically with individual donors and international organizations to execute them.

In the latest Donor Committee Meeting, which took place in Naples, Italy in February 2009, a "Stocktaking Review" assessment was prepared and presented. This assessment supports several prominent observations. The primary observation concerns the delays and reduced scope of projects that have undermined outcomes. Not only was this a result of the field conditions like security but also deficiencies in planning, management and oversight. There was lack of coordination among all parties involved in the IRFFI, which made it difficult to develop synergies and use the fund to its full potential. In addition, the Government of Iraq was not able to exercise full ownership of the fund. The ISRB has remained weak and has experienced high staff turnover, which limits its capacity to fulfill its mandate of decision making on IRFFI projects. Unfortunately, the political process in Iraq is "immature," and there has not been a "unifying political consensus for reconstruction and development" (ScanTeam, 2009: 58). Likewise, the assessment also affirmed that the Donor Committee did not provide enough strategic guidance during the period of 2004 to 2007. In order to counter the lack of Iraqi ownership, stronger participation was needed. Unfortunately, meetings were too few and on an irregular basis; more importantly, guidance of IRFFI projects on a strategic level was insufficient.

There was often no oversight by the Donor Committee or its chair of project execution on the ground partly because there was simply no effective physical presence in Iraq. There was discussion among the donors about many IRFFI projects, but since the UNDG and World Bank were primarily employing locals to execute these projects, management was removed from implementation. Furthermore, the lack of efficient reporting structure did not provide an adequate situation analysis (ScanTeam, 2009). In this sense, the Chair of the Donor Committee could have been the best candidate to provide the "glue" between all parties involved.

Conclusion

The International Reconstruction Fund Facility for Iraq has made significant contributions in advancing the understanding of Multi-Donor Trust Funds (MDTFs). At a time of international political turbulence regarding the situation in Iraq, IRFFI offered a multilateral solution for reconstruction efforts. This mechanism allowed the international community to begin rebuilding Iraq in a constructive and productive manner. Nevertheless, IRFFI is a very complex structure with several prominent players, which can cause various challenges.

On the one hand, there are donor countries, some of which are primary stakeholders in the Donor Committee, that have certain preferences when determining reconstruction priorities. Often these preferences clash with the international organizations that are prominently involved in executing projects. Moreover, having an international organization involved, like the UN, creates other logistical hurdles, especially when other UN agencies seek independent funding and work directly with Iraqi authorities, undermining the coordinated approach. Similarly, countries also participate in bilateral reconstruction initiatives with Iraqi authorities, effectively competing with IRFFI as a multilateral mechanism.

On the other hand, the IRFFI process has had to adapt to changes from 2003 to the present. Initially a needs assessment was carried out by the UNDG and the World Bank, outlining the key priority sectors for immediate and medium-term timeframes. Ideally, this assessment was meant to solidify the most pressing needs of the Iraqi people and also set realistic budgetary allocations for each sector. In 2005, the National

Development Strategy of Iraq was prepared, clearly stating the need for more prominent Iraqi participation in the development agenda. The International Compact for Iraq also supported the notion of national ownership. Iraqi authorities, however, did not possess the capacity needed to take full ownership of the development strategy. The lack of capacity proved difficult for IRFFI when determining priorities and executing projects as it often faced delays in implementation.

Lastly, the role of Canada and CIDA in IRFFI achieved mixed results. Although Canada did not contribute troops to the US-led military operation, the Chrétien government supported a multilateral effort in Iraq under the sponsorship of the UN. When IRFFI was created, Canada offered substantial funding and a Canadian was appointed Chair of the Donor Committee. Unfortunately, as sectarian violence escalated, security became paramount and still more caution was exercised regarding new project ideas and maintaining a presence on the ground. Finally, with the Harper government, the foreign policy priority fully shifted away from Iraq to Afghanistan. The Canadian government felt that Iraq was simply a diversion from the main mission, which further hindered the opportunity for Canada to play a prominent role in the IRFFI. If the Chair of the Donor Committee had been given the opportunity to play a more dynamic role with a more robust mandate, perhaps more significant results could have been achieved in providing strategic guidance regarding project priorities and contributing management and oversight in their execution.

Appendix 8.1 International Reconstruction Fund Facility for Iraq Donor Commitments to the World Bank Iraq Trust Fund and United Nations Development Group Iraq Trust Fund as of June 30, 2009 (amount in millions)

Donor	Donor Currency	World Bank Donor Currency	World Bank USD	UNDG Donor Currency	UNDG USD	Facility (WB+UNDG) Donor Currency	Facility (WB+UNDG) USD
Australia	AUD	22.00	16.14	36.00	28.37	58.00	44.51
Australia (Dept. of Immigration)	AUD	—	—	4.82	3.29	4.82	3.29
Australia	Total	22.00	16.14	40.82	31.67	62.82	47.81
Belgium	EURO	-	-	1.00	1.32	1.00	1.32
Canada	CAD	35.00	26.67	80.00	63.79	115.00	90.45
Denmark	DKK	—	—	73.18	12.41	73.18	12.41
European Commission*	EURO	139.99	176.17	436.55	560.24	576.54	736.41
EC (Rapid Response Mechanism)	EURO	3.00	3.57	19.00	24.98	22.00	28.55
EC (Human Rights)	EURO	—	—	6.00	7.26	6.00	7.26
European Commission	EURO	142.99	179.74	461.55	592.48	604.54	772.22
Finland	EURO	2.00	2.58	6.00	7.70	8.00	10.28
Germany	USD	—	—	10.00	10.00	10.00	10.00
Greece	EURO	—	—	3.00	3.63	3.00	3.63
Iceland	USD	1.00	1.00	0.50	0.50	1.50	1.50
India	USD	5.00	5.00	5.00	5.00	10.00	10.00
Ireland	EURO	—	—	1.00	1.23	1.00	1.23
Italy	EURO	—	—	30.90	39.23	30.90	39.23
Japan	USD	130.63	130.63	360.95	360.95	491.58	491.58
Kuwait	USD	5.00	5.00	5.00	5.00	10.00	10.00
Luxembourg	USD	—	—	0.20	0.20	0.20	0.20
Luxembourg	EURO	—	—	1.70	2.12	1.70	2.12
Luxembourg	Total	—	—	1.90	2.32	1.90	2.32
The Netherlands	EURO	5.00	6.19	5.00	6.70	10.00	12.88
New Zealand	NZD	—	—	5.00	3.37	5.00	3.37
Norway	NOK	45.00	6.72	45.00	7.01	90.00	13.73
Qatar	USD	5.00	5.00	5.00	5.00	10.00	10.00
Republic of Korea	USD	9.00	9.00	21.00	21.00	30.00	30.00
Spain	USD	20.00	20.00	20.00	20.00	40.00	40.00
Spain	EURO	—	—	55.10	73.17	55.10	73.17
Spain	Total	20.00	20.00	75.10	93.17	95.10	113.17
Sweden	SEK	40.00	5.81	97.00	13.66	137.00	19.46
Turkey	USD	1.00	1.00	9.00	9.00	10.00	10.00
United Kingdom	POUNDS	40.00	71.38	30.00	55.54	70.00	126.93
United States	USD	5.00	5.00	5.00	5.00	10.00	10.00
TOTAL			496.87		1,356.66		1,853.53

Source: UNDP and World Bank (2009), New York. Available at https://www.irffi.org.
*USD equivalent of commitments not yet deposited are estimated at operational exchange rates and are for indicative purposes only.

Notes

1 The Committee holds two meetings a year. However, in 2004 three meetings were held: in Abu Dhabi, United Arab Emirates (February 28–29), Doha, Qatar (May 25–26) and Tokyo, Japan (October 13–14). The Fourth Committee Meeting was held at the Dead Sea, Jordan, July 18–19, 2005; the Fifth Committee Meeting was held in Istanbul, Turkey, March 19–20, 2007; the Sixth Committee Meeting was held in Bari, Italy, October 19–20, 2007; the Seventh Committee Meeting was held in Baghdad, Iraq, July 7, 2008; and the Eighth Committee Meeting was held in Naples, Italy, February 18, 2009.
2 The sectors include education, health, employment creation, water and sanitation, transport and telecommunications, electricity, housing and land management, urban management, agriculture, water resources and food security, finance and private sector development, state-owned enterprises, investment climate and trade, mine action, government institutions, rule of law, civil society and media.

Works Cited

BBC Monitoring Middle East—Political (2005a). "Iraqi, Italian FMs on Coalition Troops, Regional Issues, Brussels Conference." *Al-Sharqiyah—Arabic.* May 25.

——— (2005b). "Iran's Foreign Minister Says US Turns to Multilateralism to Save Face in Iraq." *IRNA, Tehran.* June 23.

Bell, Michael (2009). Interview by Carla Angulo-Pasel. Ottawa, Ontario, Canada, May 21.

Blanchfield, Mike (2009). "Iraq's War 'Diversion' from Afghanistan: Harper." *Canwest News Service.* April 1. Available at: http://www.canada.com/news/Iraq+diversion+from+Afghanistan+Harper/1452022/story.html.

Kessler, Glen (2005). "Major Forum Yields Minor Pledges of Iraq Aid." *The Washington Post.* June 23.

Koring, Paul (2003). "Iraq Situation Critical, Graham says; Canada Prepared to Aid Rebuilding but U.S. Must Work with UN, He Urges." *The Globe and Mail.* September 11.

Leblanc, Daniel (2003). "Canada Pledges More Money for Iraq." *The Globe and Mail.* May 15.

Maddox, Bronwen (2005). "'Show Us the Money' Still the Loudest Plea." *The Times (London).* June 23.

MacKinnon, Mark (2004). "Martin Cool to Renewed U.S. Request for Assistance: Canada Stretched too Thin to Contribute Troops to Iraq, PM Says in Paris." *The Globe and Mail.* October 15.

MacNamara, Kate (2004). "Canadians Absent from Iraq Bidding: Massive Security Risk Will Be an Impediment to Canadian Firms Participating in Prime Contracts: Those Involved Are Small." *National Post's Financial Post & FP Investing.* February 2.

Maniquet, Scott (2009). "Transcript: Sheldon Alberts Interviews Prime Minister Stephen Harper." *National Post.* March 29. Available at: http://network.nationalpost.com/np/blogs/posted/archive/2009/03/29/transcript-sheldon-alberts-interviews-prime-minister-stephen-harper.aspx.

Republic of Iraq (2005). *National Development Strategy 2005–2007.* Baghdad, Iraq.

——— (2008). *The International Compact with Iraq.* Available at: http://www.iraqcompact.org/en/default.asp.

ScanTeam (2009). "Stocktaking Review of the International Reconstruction Fund Facility for Iraq—Final Report." Oslo. Available at: http://siteresources.worldbank.org/IRFFI/Resources/IRFFIReviewVol1FinalReport.pdf.

Schifferes, Steve (2004). "World Bank Warns on Iraq Delays." *BBC News.* May 18.

Thompson, Allan (2003). "Ottawa Readies Aid Package for Iraq." *The Toronto Star.* March 26.

UNDP and the World Bank (2003a). *International Reconstruction Fund Facility for Iraq—Terms of Reference.* New York. Available at: http://www.irffi.org.

——— (2003b). *Joint Iraq Needs Assessment.* New York. Available at: http://www.irffi.org.

——— (2007). *International Reconstruction Fund Facility for Iraq—Revised Terms of Reference.* New York. Available at: http://www.irffi.org.

——— (2008). *UNDG ITF & World Bank ITF Concept Note: Timeline and Mechanisms for the Closure of the International Reconstruction Fund Facility for Iraq (IRFFI).* New York.

Walsh, Jimmy (2005). "US Too Aggressive in Iraq, Says Ormonde (FF)." *The Irish Times.* May 26.

Weisman, Steven R. (2005). "A Pledge to Speed Iraq Aid; Nations Tell Bagdad Its Plaints Are Heard." *The International Herald Tribune.* June 23.

9
Iraq's Tangled Web of Debt Restructuring

Bessma Momani and Aidan Garrib

Throughout the debt crisis of the 1980s and early 1990s, debtor states faced a concerted group of creditors seeking to reap the largest possible amount of repayment; this classical sovereign debt regime, for lack of a better phrase, involved the International Monetary Fund (IMF) at the core (Kahler, 1993: 363). Meanwhile, Paris Club creditors, today a conglomerate of 19 official or state creditors, surrendered much of its power and control to the IMF by tying its debt rescheduling to IMF programs. In particular, the Paris Club required that IMF programs be put in place with all of their debt restructuring agreements and thereby "shifted the centre of gravity" to the IMF (see Callaghy, 2004). Private creditors, often represented by the London Club, similarly had a lot of faith in IMF assessment of debtors' capacity to repay and often followed the Paris Club and IMF's lead on the terms of repayment. The IMF, known for its hardline analysis of debtors, was entrusted with the dual role as judge of a country's capacity for repayment and as monitor of debtor economic and fiscal policies (Lipson, 1985). For a time, the IMF "linked the entire nexus" of creditors because it had provided the largest source of funds to debtors and was entrusted with these roles by the international creditor community at large (Germain, 2002: 22). However, the political implications of Iraqi success in debt restructuring changed the way in which the international debt negotiations regime has typically been structured.

Under the Baathist regime, Iraq's economy was clearly statist and inward looking. With exception of oil, Iraq's economy was far removed from global trade. Plagued by crony capitalism and rentier state behaviour, the Iraqi state was fraught with economic inefficiencies (see Sanford, 2003). Its economic isolation was made worse throughout the 1990s by ten years of United Nations–led sanctions and international isolation of Iraq. In the meantime, Iraq had accumulated nearly $120 billion in public debt: $38.9 owed to industrialized states represented at the Paris Club (of which $4 billion was owed to the United States); $60–65 billion owed to 26 countries that were not Paris Club members, primarily and most notably in the neighbouring Persian Gulf states; and $15 billion to private commercial creditors (see Table 9.1). This debt represented more than 400 percent of Iraq's annual Gross Domestic Product (GDP) earnings—a crushing debt-to-earnings ratio. Even before the United States (US) invaded Iraq, American political leaders understood the importance of Iraqi debt relief as a prerequisite to American "success" in Iraq.

Initially, the United States attempted to coax other creditors to forgive Iraqi debt on moral grounds. When this was rebuked, the Americans turned to the Paris Club and the IMF. The other Paris Club creditors, specifically France, Germany and Russia, refused to go along with the American and IMF program until they received "undisclosed concessions" from the Bush administration. These are widely believed to have included opportunities to participate in the reconstruction of Iraq, which had been previously limited to countries that had, in the words of US officials, "put boots on the ground." Eventually, however, the United States was able to use the United Nations Security Council to limit Iraq's reparation payments to its creditors. Then the US also managed to have the Paris Club offer its most generous of terms to any middle-income country ever received: 80 percent debt write-off and generous repayment conditions. With pressure exerted on the IMF, the US also managed to have the IMF underestimate the Iraqi ability to repay their debt. Thus the stage was set for subsequent negotiations with Iraqi creditors.

Private creditors, both sovereign and commercial, were tied to the terms of the Paris Club agreement based on the club's "comparability of treatment" clause. After a number of years, private creditors settled their claims to Iraq's satisfaction. The remaining creditors, and by far the largest, were the Arab Gulf neighbours: principally Saudi Arabia, Kuwait, the United Arab Emirates (UAE) and Qatar. The political and historical animosity between Iraq and its Gulf neighbours had effectively put the brakes on Iraq's easy ride with its creditors. Therefore, despite US power

Table 9.1 Iraq: Estimated External Debt Stock, 2004–10 (in billions of US$ unless otherwise indicated)

	2004 before debt reduction[a]	2004 before debt reduction[b]	2005	2006	2007	2008	2009	2010
Without the second and third stage of debt reduction[c]								
Paris Club creditors	36.6	23.8	25.0	26.3	27.6	28.8	29.9	30.6
Non Paris club creditors	76.4	53.5	56.2	59.0	61.9	64.7	67.1	68.6
Of which: official creditors	61.4	43.0	45.1	47.4	49.8	52.0	53.9	55.2
Multilateral creditors[d]	0.6	0.9	0.9	1.0	1.3	1.7	2.4	3.4
Total debt	113.6	78.2	82.1	86.3	90.8	95.2	99.4	102.6
Total debt (in percent of GDP)	444.9	306.2	279.8	221.2	200.9	185.3	179.6	170.1
Total debt service[e]	...	0.0	0.0	0.0	0.0	0.7	1.6	2.7
With the second and third stage of debt reduction[f]								
Total debt	113.6	78.2	51.1	53.5	56.3	31.0	32.9	34.1
Total debt (in percent of GDP)	444.9	306.2	174.3	137.2	124.6	60.3	59.4	56.6
Total debt service[f]	...	0.0	0.0	0.0	0.0	0.6	0.8	1.1

Sources: The Paris Club and staff estimates; IMF Article IV agreement. http://www.imf.org/external/pubs/ft/scr/2005/cr05294.pdf.
[a] Some debt has been reconciled, and the amount of reconciled debt is less than the initial claim. As a result, the estimates of debt outstanding prior to debt reduction are lower than those in the 2004 EPCA staff report (IMF Country Report 04/325).
[b] Assumes comparable debt reduction to all external debt.
[c] The projection assumes the deferral of payments of principal and most interests until 2011.
[d] The project includes new debt. Iraq cleared its arrears to the Fund and the Bank in 2004.
[e] Debt service is actual amount paid (not accrued), excluding repayment of arrears.
[f] Assumes no additional debt other than a larger disbursement of Fund credit.

and influence in the international political and economic system, Iraqi debt restructuring would hit an impasse when the time came to negotiate with its neighbours.

Bargaining Iraqi Debt Relief: The Paris Club and the IMF

More than a month prior to the US invasion of Iraq, the US Congress discussed the need for economic reforms in Iraq. Congress urged President Bush "to organize debtor and donor conferences in order to restructure Iraq's debt and post–Persian Gulf War obligations and accumulate sufficient resources to fund the needs of an interim government during transition" (United States Congress, 2003a). The March 2003 US invasion of Iraq would end decades of Iraqi economic isolation and force Iraq to confront the forces of globalization; however, the question of what to do with the heavy burden of Iraqi debt, with its strain on the Iraqi interim government and its successor remained unanswered.

In the first month after the US invasion and of the occupation of Iraq, the US government sent initial signals regarding the future of Iraq's public debt. A number of senior Bush administration officials, such as Deputy Secretary of Defense Paul Wolfowitz and Treasury Secretary John Snow, called on official creditors to cancel Iraqi debt. Similarly, US Congress approved a number of bills that deemed Iraqi debt to be odious and called on creditors, including the IMF and World Bank, to cancel outstanding claims (United States Congress, 2003d). At the behest of Congress, Secretary Snow also instructed the IMF's US Executive Director to oppose any loans to Iraq unless "there are sufficient safeguards in place to prevent the loan proceeds from being used to reimburse the persons and governments holding the debt, as of such date of enactment, for any losses with respect to the debt" (United States Congress, 2003c).

Snow noted that he would take the issue of Iraqi debt relief to the G7 meeting of finance ministers held in April 2003. He stated: "Certainly the people of Iraq shouldn't be saddled with those debts incurred through the regime of the dictator who's now gone" (Beattie, 2003). In effect, the United States did not want the new Iraqi regime to pay the burden of Iraq's past debt; instead, the United States wanted official creditors to share the burden of what it started to characterize as "odious debt." The term "odious debt" has no international legal standing, but it has been used in the past to characterize debt incurred by oppressive governments that, in turn, burden their oppressed citizens. By April 2003, US Congress had agreed to a resolution that pointedly asked France, Germany and Russia to cancel Iraqi debt (United States Congress, 2003b). The United States was taking the position that the international community now needed to share the burden of reconstructing Iraq.

Consequently, the United States proceeded to call and organize a Paris Club meeting of Iraq's official creditors in May 2003.[1] The Paris Club, established in 1956, has been used by creditor states to organize common stances on rescheduling the debt of those debtor states in arrears. France, Germany and Russia were the largest official creditors in the 2003 meeting.[2] When the meeting commenced, the Bush administration, influenced by the US Christian right movement, framed Iraqi debt forgiveness in moral terms (see Helleiner and Cameron, 2006). The future of the Iraqi people, President Bush argued, should not be mortgaged to the enormous burden of debt incurred to enrich Saddam Hussein's corrupt and repressive regime (Bush, 2003). Similar appeals were made by the White House Press Secretary: "They [Iraqis] should not be burdened with a debt of a brutal regime that had little interest in helping the Iraqi people, but had a lot of interest in building palaces and building torture chambers and pursuing weapon programs" (McClellan, 2003). Carefully framing debt relief in a moral imperative was intended to garner support for debt relief from the international community, most of whom had vehemently opposed the war. As one US Congressmen noted, "I believe there is money that needs to be spent in Iraq but not only our money...We had a coalition of the willing. Now we need a coalition of the wallet. Let them step up to the plate to share the financial responsibility to create stability and a democracy in Iraq" (Mikulski, 2003). Fearing an upcoming US election, the Bush administration met congressional calls for sharing the burden of the Iraqi reconstruction. The United States thus bent to domestic pressure and convened an international donor conference to raise funds for Iraq.

The October 2003 meeting in Madrid included 73 countries and 20 international organizations and resulted in pledges of US$33 billion in grants and loans (see Table 9.2 for breakdown of donor pledges). The majority of the pledged funds were in the form of loans by international financial institutions (IFI), mainly the IMF and World Bank. To enable the release of these IFI loans, however, debt restructuring would be needed. To assist in the process, the Paris Club introduced the Evian debt relief terms—some of the most generous, and politically charged terms of debt relief to be introduced at the forum (see Weiss, 2009). Consequently, two months later, President Bush appointed James Baker, a respected former Chief of Staff and Secretary of Treasury under the Reagan administration, and a former Secretary of State under the Bush Sr. administration, as his special envoy on Iraqi debt relief.[3] The appointment of Baker signalled a new, multilateral phase after the invasion of Iraq; perhaps an implicit message that America was ready to bargain. Baker soon began a whistle stop tour of Russia, UK, France, Italy, Germany, Japan, South Korea, China, Saudi Arabia, Kuwait, Qatar and the United Arab Emirates to bolster support for debt cancellation. Baker quickly reached a consensus with Iraq's main European creditors under the terms of the Paris Club agreement. The US, France and Germany released a joint statement agreeing to a substantial reduction of Iraqi debt (White House Press Release, 2003). Iraq's major European creditors would cancel a significant portion of Iraq's outstanding debt, and others indicated willingness to work within the parameters of the Paris Club. Table 9.2 summarizes pledges made at the International Donor's Conference for Iraq in Madrid, Spain, on October 23–24, 2003.

Table 9.2 International Donor Pledges[a] for Iraq (in USD millions[b])

Donor	2005	2005–2007	Unpecified by Year[c]	Total[d]
Countries	569.59	758.62	25,118.50	26,446.71
Australia	45.59	0.00	0.00	45.59
Austria	1.94	3.53	0.00	5.48
Belgium	5.89	0.00	0.00	5.89
Bulgaria	0.64	0.00	0.00	0.64
Canada	0.00	0.00	187.47	187.47
China	0.00	0.00	25.00	25.00
Cyprus	0.00	0.00	0.12	0.12
Czech Republic	7.33	7.33	0.00	14.66
Denmark	26.95	0.00	0.00	26.95
Estonia	0.08	0.00	0.00	0.08
Finland	5.89	0.00	0.00	5.89
Greece	0.00	0.00	3.53	3.53
Hungary	1.24	0.00	0.00	1.24
India	10.00	0.00	0.00	10.00
Iran[e]	5.00	0.00	0.00	5.00
Ireland	3.53	0.00	0.00	3.53
Iceland	1.50	1.00	0.00	2.50
Italy[f]	0.00	0.00	235.62	235.62
Japan[g]	0.00	0.00	4,914.00	4,914.00
Korea	0.00	0.00	200.00	200.00
Kuwait	0.00	0.00	500.00	500.00
Luxembourg	1.18	1.18	0.00	2.36
Malta	0.00	0.00	0.27	0.27
Netherlands	9.42	0.00	0.00	9.42
New Zealand	3.35	0.00	0.00	3.35
Norway[h]	4.29	8.58	0.00	12.87
Oman	0.00	0.00	3.00	3.00
Pakistan	0.00	0.00	2.50	2.50
Qatar	0.00	0.00	100.00	100.00
Saudi Arabia	120.00	380.00	0.00	500.00
Slovenia	0.27	0.15	0.00	0.42
Spain	80.00	140.00	0.00	220.00
Sri Lanka	0.00	0.00	0.00	0.00
Sweden	0.00	0.00	33.00	33.00
Turkey	0.00	0.00	50.00	50.00
United Arab Emirates	0.00	0.00	215.00	215.00
United Kingdom	235.48	216.85	0.00	452.33
United States[i]	0.00	0.00	18,649.00	18,649.00
European Community	235.62	0.00	0.00	235.62
EC+EU Member States + Acceding Countries	614.83	369.04	272.54	1,256.41
International Financial Institutions	1,350.00	4,200.00–7,900.00	0.00	5,550.00–9,250.00
IMF[j]	858.00	1,700.00–3,400.00	0.00	2,550.00–4,250.00
World Bank	500.00	2,500.00–4,500.00	0.00	3,000.00–5,000.00
Total	2,155.21	4,958.62–8,658.62	25,118.50	33,232.33–35,932.33

Source: UNDP, http://iraq.undg.org/uploads/doc/summary%20tables.pdf.

Table 9.2 cont'd

a A pledge is an indication of intent to mobilize funds for which an appropriate sum of contribution is specified. Most donors were not able to specify the type of grant assistance at the time of the Donor's Conference. The following countries offered in-kind assistance: Bahrain, Chile, Egypt, Germany, Jordan, Latvia, Mexico, Poland, Portugal, Slovakia, Sri Lanka, Switzerland, Thailand, Tunisia, Vietnam.
b Source for all exchange rates: IMF exchange rates in SDR terms for October 24, 2003.
c Many donors were not able to provide a breakdown by year.
d Amounts do not include identified humanitarian assistance (total of 115.17 M USD). Amounts do not include exports credits and guarantees: Austria 11.78 M USD, Saudi Arabia 500 M USD, and Denmark 154.54 M USD.
e In addition to the amount in the table above, Iran pledged an economic package, with an estimated value of 1,495 M USD, which includes credit facilities, restoration of religious sites, tourism and pilgrimage, technical and advisory services, trade, investment, market access and humanitarian assistance.
f Amounts unspecified between grants and loans are: Italy (235.62 M USD) and Qatar (100 M USD).
g Japan's assistance of 4.914 M USD consists of (i) grant assistance of 1,414 M USD for the immediate reconstruction needs of Iraq within the Japan's commitment, chiefly corresponding to the reconstruction needs anticipated through 2004; and (ii) assistance of up to 3,500 M USD, basically utilizing concessional yen loans, chiefly corresponding to the medium-term reconstruction needs for a period extending approximately through the year 2007, taking into account the situation of Iraq including security and the advancement of political process, the progress of the reconstruction projects, developments toward the solution of debt issue, and discussion of the international community, etc.
h In addition to the amount in the table above, Norway pledged up to 30 M NOK from NORAD's global facilities for promoting private enterprises.
i The US pledged 20.3 B USD at the Donor's Conference, subject to Congressional approval. Subsequently, the US Congress approved 18.6 B USD in grants toward security and reconstruction needs.
j The World Bank and the IMF announced a range of assistance.

The Paris Club creditors, however, were not the majority of Iraq's creditors (see Figure 9.1). Both commercial creditors, many represented by the London Club, and non-Paris Club creditors—mainly Arab Gulf states—were reluctant to reschedule Iraqi debt. As noted in a variety of media sources, many creditors saw Iraq as an oil-rich country that held promising chances of debt repayment. Many of these creditors, moreover, were reluctant to make a hard commitment regarding the amount of debt they would forgive until Iraq was deemed to be a sovereign state (transfer of power occurred on June 28, 2004) and until the IMF released a study of how much debt Iraq could bear to repay, called a Debt Sustainability Analysis (DSA).

The IMF's DSA report was released to the Paris Club in June 2004 and found that 67 to 95 percent of Iraq's debt was unsustainable. The IMF, it should be noted, used a controversial assumption in its DSA report: the price of oil was assumed to be $26 a barrel, yet market prices at the time were closer to $60 a barrel (Chung, 2005). The IMF's DSA greatly underestimated Iraqi income potential and therefore overestimated the amount of unsustainable debt. In the meantime, however, the United States managed to get the United Nation Security Council to protect Iraq from its creditors by protecting Iraqi assets and income from debt collectors. But the Bush administration still had to work to reach a consensus with Iraq's creditors on the amount of debt they would

Figure 9.1 Iraq's External Public Debt, December 2005

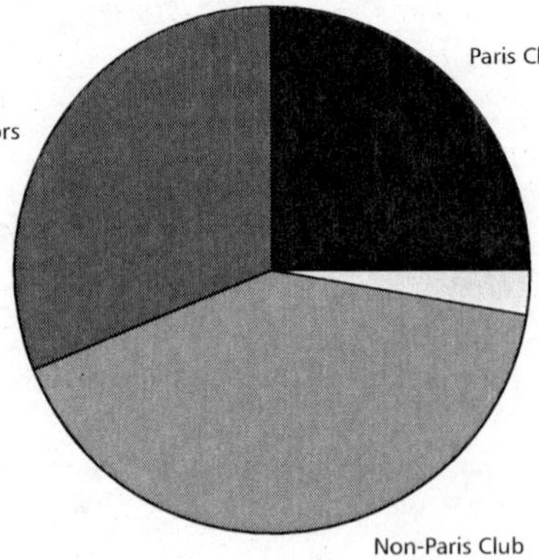

- Paris Club creditors 25%
- Multilateral creditors 3%
- Non-Paris Club official creditors 41%
- Commercial creditors 31%

Source: World Bank, Data Sheet for Iraq, 10 December 2006.

write off. As National Security Advisor, Condoleezza Rice declared to reporters soon after reading the IMF report, "We're going to work this now with people—again, people need to be clear that Iraq is not going to be capable of recovering if it has to pay a crushing debt burden. Eventually, this will go to the Paris Club, but we're still in discussion with members" (Rice, 2004). Paris Club members continued to debate in their capitals whether they would forgive 50 percent of Iraqi debt, a position favoured by Russia, France, and Germany, or 95 percent of Iraqi debt, favoured by the US and the United Kingdom (UK). In the meantime, Iraqi authorities entered into agreement with the IMF in September 2004.

The IMF's three-year Emergency Post-conflict Assessment (EPA) agreement with Iraq guaranteed $436 million loans to Iraq in exchange for conditions that outline the ways in which Iraq would liberalize its economy.[4] The Iraqi authorities did not intend to draw on the IMF loan; more importantly, the agreement would set targets and deadlines that would be used to gain the confidence of the Paris Club in Iraqi reform efforts. Specifically, under the EPA, Iraq was obliged to peg its Iraqi dinar to the US dollar and raise interest rates. Iraqi authorities were required to significantly curb spending on wages, pensions and other social programs. Structural adjustment, in the form of taking steps to privatize the country's financial sector and increasing private participation in the nation's oil industry, was also espoused. Price stability, which entailed increases in the price of gasoline, taxes on manufactured goods and cuts in consumer subsidies, was listed as an important facet of the IMF's conditions (see Looney, 2009).

Two months after the IMF approved the prerequisite program, the Paris Club agreed to cancel 80 percent of Iraq's debt. The US, Belgium, Canada, Italy and Japan were the first to react swiftly in the Paris Club. This would be one of the most generous debt write-offs for a middle-income country in Paris Club history; previously, former Yugoslavia had received 66 percent debt reduction after the overthrow of Milosevic. The US went further and announced it would also conditionally cancel 100 percent of its share of Iraq's debt (amounting to $4 billion). President Bush would later add that he hoped "more nations should do the same so that the Iraqi people are not held back by the crushing burden of debt accumulated by Saddam Hussein" (Lynch, 2006). The Paris Club Agreement would be implemented in three stages, and portions of Iraqi debt would be canceled upon successful completion of each stage. In phase one, 30 percent of debt owed to the Paris Club members would be canceled immediately. This amounted to a $11.6 billion write-off of the overall $38.9 billion owed to Paris Club members. In phase two, another 30 percent of Iraq's debt would be canceled when a new IMF standard program, called a Stand-by Agreement (SBA), was initiated (scheduled for end-2005). In the final phase, 20 percent of Iraq's debt to the Paris Club would be canceled upon meeting the terms of the new IMF SBA agreement (originally scheduled to end in September 2008, but achieved in December 2008 under a new IMF SBA signed in Dec 2007). As is customary practice, the IMF would be in charge of monitoring Iraqi progress on economic reforms and endorsing the completion of each phase. The IMF was now entrusted with the geopolitically important task of monitoring and assessing Iraqi progress on economic reforms.

With new Iraqi elections also slated to take place in December 2005, the IMF stepped up its press briefings about its objectives for the year, in the hopes that the incoming government would honour the commitments of the previous government and continue the progress of the program. In December 2005, the IMF Executive Board approved a 15-month Standby Arrangement of $475.4 million. Noting the difficulty of implementing the SBA, Deputy Managing Director and Acting Chair of the IMF's Executive Board Takatoshi Kato stated that: "The Iraqi authorities were successful in promoting macroeconomic stability in 2005, despite the extremely difficult security environment... [Inflationary] pressures moderated, although prices remained volatile. On the other hand, because of security concerns and capacity constraints, the implementation of structural benchmarks ... was slower than envisaged" (IMF, 2005b).

The 2005 SBA meant that the IMF recommended the implementation of phase two of the Paris Club arrangement. The fund, however, explicitly called for strengthened reforms on "controlling the wage and pensions bill, reducing subsidies on petroleum products and expanding the participation of the private sector in the domestic market for petroleum products" (IMF, 2005b). The IMF staff also stressed the enormous reconstruction needs and considerable risks facing the implementation of Iraq's IMF program, "including a continuing very dangerous security situation, political uncertainties associated with the implementation of the new constitution, a possible decline in export prices and a lower than projected expansion in oil production" (IMF, 2006a: 18). Iraq continued to struggle in meeting the IMF's economic reform targets that were required to initiate the final phase of Paris Club debt cancellation.

The fund agreed to a number of extensions to the SBA, as well as waivers on conditions not met, noting considerable deterioration and slippage in almost every category of reforms. Clearly, the deteriorating security situation continued to make it difficult for Iraqi authorities to implement reforms. Specifically, IMF staff reported that the security condition remained very difficult, economic growth continued to be below target, inflation had recently begun to accelerate, structural reform had been slowed by the delay in forming a government, the pensions bill required reform before going into effect, corruption was damaging the credibility of the government and the IMF program and private imports of gasoline had not yet been liberalized. In fact, only a few items in the report noted success in Iraqi targets: mainly stable exchange rates, fiscal surpluses and government commitment to reforms (IMF, 2006b: 3–7). Although the al-Maliki government had taken steps to bring the program back on track, the momentum of reforms slowed. Controlling inflation and institution building also stalled, while the negative effect of the IMF program on the poor increased (IMF, 2007). Nevertheless, the IMF has shown that it will continue to approve Iraqi reform measures in the interest of the greater good of assisting Iraq to meet its Paris Club terms of agreement and in helping its greatest economic and political benefactor: the United States. Finally, the IMF decided to terminate the 2005 SBA in December 2007 and signed a new two-year SBA to replace the old one. This effectively bought the Iraqis more time and allowed them to renegotiate the terms of their agreement with the fund.

Iraq's Private Creditors

Iraq's private debt amounts to claims by commercial interests of $20 billion. Most of these commercial claims were held by Western Europe and Asia (see Figure 9.2 for geographical distribution of claims). Meetings with Iraq's private creditors first took place in Dubai in May 2005 and were followed by a number of agreements and advancements in negotiations. Iraq tried to persuade its private creditors to accept the same 80 percent debt write-off agreed to at the Paris Club, vying to follow the principle of equal treatment of Iraqi creditors. With the assistance of Ernst and Young, the Iraq Debt Reconciliation Office (IDRO) was established to invite commercial creditors to submit their claims.[5] Iraqi private creditors were essentially divided into two groups: the majority were supplier credit issuers and the minority were foreign banks (see IMF, 2005a). The foreign banks formed their own coordinating body called the London Club Coordination Group (LCCG) in early 2005 and tried to invite the supplier credit issuers to join their group, so as to fully represent all of Iraq's private creditors (London Club Coordinating Group, 2005).

The LCCG of Iraq's bank creditors included Union de Banques Arabes et Franciases (UBAF) as chair, Arab International Bank (ALUBAF), British Arab Commercial Bank (BACB), Banca Nazionale del Lavoro (BNL), BNP Paribas, Gramercy Advisors and The Arab Investment Company. In June 2005, the LCCG stated their preferred outcomes:

1. A fair bilateral and transparent reconciliation exercise. We do not want validation of claims through a unilateral process (especially since missing files both on creditor and debtor side might jeopardize debt acknowledgement).
2. Recognition by the Iraqi Authorities of the LCCG as a representative creditors committee thus leading to good faith negotiations between both parties to achieve a successful private debt restructuring.
3. A realistic offer with new instruments, taking into account the comparability of treatment clause, which does NOT mean identical treatment, as comparable NPV [Net Present Value] can be reached with different financial terms treatment. (London Club Coordinating Group, 2005)

Overestimating their bargaining leverage, the LCCG initially resisted the Paris Club terms of an 80 percent write-off and opted to negotiate directly with Iraqi authorities. Already handicapped by a "2003 UN [United Nations] Resolution preventing creditors from resolving their

Figure 9.2 Geographical Distribution of Private Creditors, 2005

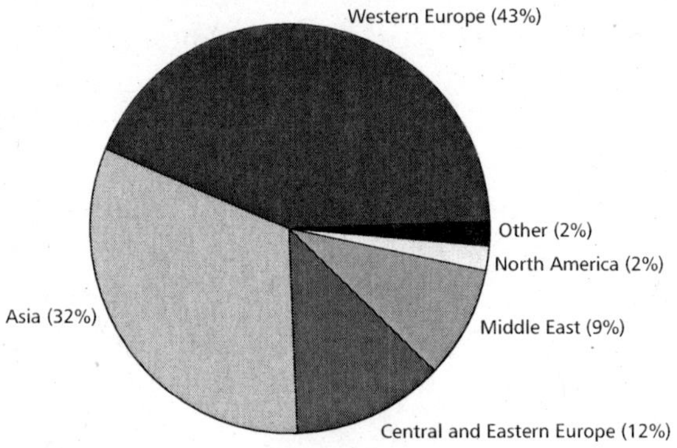

- Western Europe (43%)
- Other (2%)
- North America (2%)
- Middle East (9%)
- Central and Eastern Europe (12%)
- Asia (32%)

Source: Martin Weiss, "Iraq's Debt Relief" CRS Report for Congress, 2 October 2008, http://www.fas.org/sgp/crs/mideast/RL33376.pdf.

debt claims through litigation or attempting to attach liens on Iraqi energy resources until 2007" (Chung, 2005), the London Club was at the mercy of Iraqi authorities. Frustrated, complaining that Iraq "pursued a unilateral and coercive, take-it-or-leave-it approach" (Chung, 2005), the London Club was powerless and eventually succumbed to the Paris Club's rescheduling terms.

Responding to the London Club's presentation of its terms, the Iraq government offered many of its private creditors a cash buyback offer that amounted to 10.25 percent of the original loans for creditors with claims under $35million and a debt-for-debt exchange (issuing Iraqi government bonds) for creditors with larger amounts (Government of Iraq Debt Reconciliation Office, 2005). By mid-2006, 11,776 claims had been settled with 491 commercial creditors that amounted to $19.7 billion, or 96 percent of the value of Iraq's outstanding private credit (Government of Iraq Debt Reconciliation Office, 2006). The Iraqi government again offered the same settlement terms to the few remaining private creditors in early 2008 (closed in March 2008) and settled an additional $1.2billion in claims. The issue of Iraq's private creditors had been effectively settled.

Reasserting Power in the Gulf: Iraq's Remaining Creditors

Although much of the international community's focus concerning Iraq's debt restructuring centred on the Paris Club terms, it was non–Paris Club creditors, specifically the Persian Gulf states, that held the bulk of Iraq's outstanding debt. As such, the successful redevelopment of the Iraqi economy was heavily dependent upon securing debt relief from the Gulf States. Iraq's debt forgiveness reached a low point in December 2003, when Saudi Arabia, Kuwait, the UAE, and other Gulf nations refused US calls to forgive more than $40 billion in debt (*New York Times*, 2003). It was not surprising that the Gulf States were uncooperative; in part, this was because they had once been the target of Saddam Hussein's transgressions. These countries had also realized that their large creditor role gave them significant leverage in negotiating debt relief with the United States. Facing mounting domestic political pressure to end the war, it became clear to the Bush administration, that the only way to do so successfully, or while saving face at the very least, was to provide the conditions for the redevelopment of Iraq's economy, in the hopes that the possibility of a better future might quell the violence.

In May 2007, US Secretary of State Condoleezza Rice met with the Iraqi Prime Minister Nouri al-Maliki to discuss steps that the Iraqi leadership must take to secure debt relief from its Gulf neighbours. Among those commitments, Rice noted that Iraq must begin the process of national reconciliation, hold provincial elections and a constitutional review and dismantle militias (Kralev, 2007). This was echoed by America's Ambassador to the United Nations, who told the body, "Iraq's main creditors, including Saudi Arabia, will not write off billions of dollars in debt until they see progress on national reconciliation, economic reform and security" (Lederer, 2007b). At the same time, Vice President Cheney traveled to Egypt to urge nations in the region to cancel Iraq's debt (Xuequan, 2007).

Under the auspices of the United Nations and the World Bank, the US urged nations to join the International Compact for Iraqi debt forgiveness in a May 2007 meeting held in Sharm al-Sheikh, Egypt.[6] The meeting was attended by 60 nations, including many of Iraq's neighbours in the Gulf, and 12 regional and international organizations. Iraqi officials presented a five-year plan to implement democratic governance, economic reforms and commitment to work with the international political and economic community (Republic of Iraq, 2008). Specifically, the Iraqis signalled their intention to give Sunnis more political power by amending the constitution and allowing former Baathists to return to public life. The meeting produced commitments of $3 billon composed mainly of debt relief and bilateral agreements to apply Paris Club terms.[7] Moreover, a number of countries made new pledges of approximately $700 million in aid or grants. International support for the compact, however, was less than enthusiastic. Saudi Arabia, Kuwait, Russia, Qatar and the United Arab Emirates, holding a significant amount of Iraq's debt, refused to provide debt forgiveness or relief at the International Compact meeting.

By the second International Compact for Iraq meeting, hosted by Sweden in May 2008, Russia had announced that it would forgive part of Iraqi debt (60 percent of reduced debt stock of $4.5 billion). Similarly, China had stated in June 2007 in its official newspaper that it would also forgive Iraqi debt (reported by some to be worth $8.5 billion), but did not state how much would be forgiven and when. Chinese and Iraqi officials are said to have signed a memorandum of understanding, but little else has been disclosed, and this debt forgiveness, to date, has yet to be realized. Both the Russians and the Chinese wanted greater investment access to Iraq's oil industry. Moreover, both had lucrative oil investment contracts with the Saddam Hussein regime that were canceled by the transitional government. Revival or recognition of these contracts was a factor in both the Russian and Chinese bargaining over debt forgiveness and restructuring.

With little progress made in Stockholm, Rice went to Bahrain and Kuwait in April 2008 to join in meetings of Gulf leaders. Again, she urged them to provide Iraq debt relief and to open diplomatic missions in Baghdad. Subsequently, the United Arab Emirates announced 100 percent debt cancellation of $7billion owed in July 2008. This effectively left Iraqi debt owed to Saudi Arabia (estimated at $30 billion), Kuwait (estimated at $27 billion) and Qatar (estimated at $4 billion); the first two were effectively the largest overall creditors that were still uncommitted to debt forgiveness.[8] That said, prior to the 2007 International Compact meeting, Saudi Arabia's foreign minister had announced that the Kingdom would forgive Iraq of its debts along Paris Club terms, but made no public pledge during the meeting, dashing hopes of analysts and Iraqi officials. According to one UN official, part of the impasse had to do with disagreements between Saudi Arabia and Iraq on the total amount owed. Neither party kept written records of the transactions and no formal agreement had been kept (Lederer, 2007a). After the Stockholm meeting, the Saudis continued to hint that they would use the Paris Club terms to forgive Iraqi debt, but this failed to materialize again. To add insult to injury, both Saudi Arabia and Kuwait sent junior ministers to the Stockholm meeting, a move that has been interpreted as dismissive of the meeting.

Instead of reconstruction contracts or investment opportunities in Iraq, the remaining Gulf countries with debt owed to them demanded something more onerous: they demanded that national reconciliation become tied to the issue of debt relief. Fearing that civil strife in Iraq would cross into their respective territories, the Gulf States demanded Iraqi national reconciliation as their price for debt relief. Initially, this seemed to resonate well with the American political establishment, as both senior legislators and Bush administration officials had urged the Shi'a-led Iraqi government to start a process of national reconciliation in an attempt to pacify the violence ravaging the country and bring American troops home. The US obliged, and Condoleezza Rice urged Iraqi Prime Minister Nouri al-Maliki to meet these international demands and carry out its commitments to receive conditional international support in return. Besides paying lip service to the idea at the International Compact for Iraq meeting, the Iraqi regime was largely unresponsive. The political rift between Iraq and the US widened when al-Maliki publicly chastised President Bush, who was under significant pressure from US Senators who publicly demanded greater effort on national reconciliation (Karim, 2007).

The Gulf States were suspicious of the growing power wielded by Iran's influence over Shi'a leaders in Iraq, which also troubled Iraq's Sunni neighbours. Saudi Arabia continued to fear the influence Iraq's Shi'a would have on its own minority groups as well as the spill over of al-Qaeda-inspired militia into its territory (McMillan, 2006). Kuwait was also reluctant to forgive Saddam's debt, and understandably so, as much of it had been incurred through Saddam Hussein's attempts to annex the country. The Gulf States, many of which had felt the brunt of Saddam's aggression, were not about to give up Iraq's debt without gaining something in return. The Gulf States realized this position of strength early on, and refused to write off their share of Iraqi debt in line with the Paris Club conditions. In fact, calls for a write-off from the most senior US officials were, and perhaps will continue to be, politely ignored.

Conclusion

Clearly, the relationship between Iraq and its creditors can be characterized as a tangled web. For the greater part of the negotiations, the US and Iraq seemed to wield most of the leverage. The US negotiated with other Paris Club creditors to achieve lenient debt cancellation terms for Iraq. No doubt the US influence on the UN Security Council was instrumental in leading to the resolution that allowed Iraq to be shielded from its creditors early on in the debt restructuring process. This unprecedented move effectively gave Iraq an upper hand in subsequent negotiations and helped to rewrite the rules on how the international debt restructuring regime worked. The generous terms received at the Paris Club are attributable to the strong influence of the United States in the Club. Similarly, subsequent agreement of the IMF and continued waivers, extensions and, most importantly, a favourable debt sustainability assessment are all attributable to US pressure at the IMF, a familiar tactic for the United States in dealing with geostrategic countries in the Middle East (Momani, 2004). Iraq, an oil-rich nation with access to international liquidity that was abundant at the time, received generous Paris Club terms of repayment thanks to American intervention in the IMF staff's DSA analysis.

Iraq, for its part, took a strong hand with its private creditors, forcing them to accept unfavourable Paris Club conditions. Ultimately, all of Iraq's private creditors had settled with Iraq and on the terms that Iraq had dictated. Iraqi strength in its negotiations with the private creditors was attributable to the following factors. First, the geographical dispersion of the private creditors was wide, and the amount held per individual firm or commercial entity was relatively small. This allowed Iraq to effectively segment its private creditors to its satisfaction. In addition, the precedent set by the Paris Club to give such generous debt forgiveness had set the stage for Iraq to seek comparability of treatment among all its creditors. The private creditors were eventually forced to accept the generous Paris Club terms. Indeed, the Iraq case not only spurred legal debates over the role and use of odious debt, but the case would be remembered as a historically generous debt relief package (see Gulati and Skeel, 2007).

It was not until the Gulf States effectively ignored Paris Club terms, as well as US pressure, that the tables turned on Iraq. Both Saudi Arabia and Kuwait were effectively the largest creditors and have continued to politely ignore the conditions proposed by the Iraqis and the United States. After all, these two countries had little to gain in cross-border trade with Iraq and access to foreign investment contracts. For both of these Gulf states, the perception that Iran wields significant influence in Iraq's Shi'a led government and the belief that Iraq has yet to pay for its past aggressions were main factors in their dismissal of calls to forgive debt owed to them. Without political resolution of the issues raised by the Gulf States and a change in regional dynamics in the Gulf, the issue of Iraq's debt restructuring will remain unresolved. The case of Iraqi debt restructuring demonstrates that the reintegration of Iraq into the Gulf neighbourhood has yet to be realized.

Notes

1 At the same time, the US sponsored United Nations Security Council Resolution (UNSCR) 1483, which decreased Iraqi reparations to people and firms affected by Iraq's 1990–91 invasion of Kuwait. The new UN resolution required Iraq to place 5 percent, down from 25 percent, of its oil export earnings into a compensation fund. See http://www.foreignpolicy.org.tr/documents/210503.pdf.
2 Creditor states in attendance included: Australia, Austria, Belgium, Canada, Denmark, Finland, Germany, Italy, Japan, Republic of Korea, Netherlands, Russian Federation, Spain, Sweden, Switzerland, United Kingdom and United States of America.
3 The Baker appointment raised some controversy in early 2004 when it appeared that the Carlyle Group, a firm that Baker has vested financial and political interests in, was attempting to represent Kuwait in trying to retrieve all of its debt from Iraq. This conflict of interest was exposed by Naomi Klein (2004).
4 Soon after receiving the conditions of their debt relief, the Iraqi National Assembly declared that "[Iraq's] debts are odious and this is a new crime committed by the creditors who financed Saddam's oppression." See: al-Ali, 2004.
5 See *Government of Iraq Debt Reconciliation Office*, available from http://www.eyidro.com/.
6 A follow up meeting of the International Compact with Iraq (ICI) took place in Stockholm on May 29, 2008.
7 Egypt, Bulgaria, Poland, and Slovenia all agreed to debt forgiveness at the meeting.
8 Based on estimates by Jubilee Iraq, see: http://www.jubileeiraq.org.

Works Cited

al-Ali, Zaid (2004). "The IMF and the Future of Iraq." *Middle East Report Online*. December 7. Available at: http://merip.org/mero//mero120704.html.
Beattie, Alan (2003). "US in Push for Iraqi Debt Relief." *Financial Times Online*, In Depth: Iraq, April 11. Available at: http://search.ft.com/ftArticle?queryText=Alan+Beattie.+percentE2 percent80 percent9CUS+in+push+for+Iraqi+Debt+Relief percentE2 percent80 percent9D+Financial+Times&aje=true&id=030410008240&ct=0.

Bush, US President, George W. (2003). "President Bush Discusses the Economy at the Home Depot in Maryland." Maryland: Speech to the public. December 5.

Callaghy, Tom (2004). *Innovation in the Sovereign Debt Regime: From the Paris Club to Enhanced HIPC and Beyond.* Washington, DC: World Bank.

Chung, Joanna (2005). "Iraq's Debt Solution Ruffles Feathers." *Financial Times.* December 21. Available at: http://www.ft.com/cms/s/0/ba122474-71c5-11da-836e-0000779e2340.html.

Germain, Randall (2002). "Reforming the International Financial Architecture: The New Political Agenda" in *Global Governance: Critical Perspectives,* edited by Rorden Wilkinson and Steve Hughes. Pages 17–35. London: Routledge.

Government of Iraq Debt Reconciliation Office (2005). "Iraq Announces Terms of Commercial Debt Settlement Offer." Ernst & Young. July 26. Available at: http://www.eyidro.com/iraqterms.pdf.

——— (2006). "Iraq Announces Conclusion of Commercial Debt Settlement." Ernst & Young. July 18. Available at: http://www.eyidro.com/doc/Iraq_Annnounces_Conclusion_of_Commercial_Debt_Settlement.pdf.

Gulati, Mitu and David A. Skeel, Jr. (eds.) (2007). "Odious Debts and State Corruption." *Law and Contemporary Problems* (Special Edition). Vol. 70, No. 4 (Autumn).

Helleiner, Eric and Geoffrey Cameron (2006). "Another World Order? The Bush Administration and HIPC Debt Cancellation." *New Political Economy.* Vol. 11, No. 1 (March): 125–40.

International Monetary Fund (2005a). "Iraq: 2005 Article Consultation—Staff Report; Staff Supplement; Public Information Notice on the Executive Board Discussion; and Statement by the Executive Director for Iraq." International Monetary Fund, IMF Country Report No. 05/294. Page 13. Available at: http://www.imf.org/external/pubs/ft/scr/2005/cr05294.pdf.

——— (2005b). "IMF Executive Board Approves First Ever Stand-By Arrangement for Iraq." Washington, DC: International Monetary Fund, Press Release No. 05/307. December 23.

——— (2006a). "Iraq: Request for Stand-By Arrangement—Staff Report." Washington, DC: International Monetary Fund, IMF Country Report No. 06/15. January 13.

——— (2006b). "Iraq: First and Second Reviews under the Stand-By Arrangement." International Monetary Fund, IMF Country Report No. 06/301. August 3.

——— (2007). "Iraq: Third and Fourth Reviews under the Stand-By Arrangement." International Monetary Fund, IMF Country Report No. 07/115. March.

Kahler, Miles (1993). "Bargaining with the IMF: Two Level Strategies and Developing Countries" in *Double-Edged Diplomacy: International Bargaining and Domestic Politics,* edited by Peter Evans et al. Pages 363–92. Berkeley, CA: University of California Press.

Karim, Ammar (2007). "Iraqi Leaders Vow to Boost National Reconciliation." *Middle East Times*. August 27.

Klein, Naomi (2004). "James Baker's Double Life." *The Nation*. October 12. Available at: http://www.thenation.com/doc/20041101/klein.

Kralev, Nicholas (2007). "Conference on Iraq Lacks Relief for Debt." *Washington Times*. May 5.

Lederer, Edith M. (2007a). "No Immediate Debt Relief for Iraq." *Washington Post*. May 4. Available at: http://www.washingtonpost.com/wp-dyn/content/article/2007/05/03/AR2007050300991.html.

——— (2007b). "Iraq Debt Relief Depends on Progress." Associated Press. May 18.

Lipson, Charles (1985). *Standing Guard: Protecting Foreign Capital in the Nineteenth and Twentieth Centuries*. Berkeley, CA: University of California Press.

London Club Coordinating Group (2005). "Iraq: LCCG Presentation to Paris Club Creditors." Paris. June 15. Available at: http://www.clubdeparis.org/sections/communication/archives-2005/rencontre-du-club-de/downloadFile/attachment3_file/LCCGtoParisClubwebsitev2.pdf?nocache=1175506474.25.

Looney, Robert (2004). "The IMF's Return to Iraq." *Challenge*. Vol. 49, No. 3 (May/June): 68–82.

Lynch, David J. (2006). "Iraq Takes Another Step toward Conquering Debt." *USA Today*. January 18. Available at: http://www.usatoday.com/money/world/2006-01-18-iraq-usat_x.htm.

McClellan, Scott, White House Press Secretary (2003). "White House Press Briefing." Washington, DC: Speech to the White House Press Corps. December 12.

McMillan, Joseph (2006). "Saudi Arabia and Iraq. USIP Special Report." Washington, DC: United States Institute of Peace. January.

Mikulski, Barbara, US Senator (D-MD) (2003). "Iraq (Supplemental Appropriations on Iraq Debate)." Washington, DC: Debate at the United States Senate. October 15.

Momani, Bessma (2004). "American Politicization of the International Monetary Fund." *Review of International Political Economy*. Vol. 11, No. 5 (December): 880–904.

The New York Times (2003). "Easing Iraq's Debt Burdens." *New York Times Editorial*. December 21. Sec 4, Page 8 of the New York edition.

Republic of Iraq (2008). "The International Compact with Iraq." July 4. Available at: http://www.iraqcompact.org/en/default.asp.

Rice, Condoleezza, National Security Advisor (2004). "Press Briefing by National Security Advisor Dr. Condoleezza Rice on The President's Trip to Ireland and Turkey." Washington, DC: Speech to International Press. June 24. Available at: http://georgewbush-whitehouse.archives.gov/news/releases/2004/06/20040624-5.html.

Sanford, Jonathan E. (2003). *Iraq's Economy: Past, Present, Future.* Washington, DC: The Library of Congress, Report for Congress. June 3.

United States Congress (2003a). *S.J. Resolution 6 IS.* Washington, DC: 108th U.S. Congress. February 13.

—— (2003b). *House Resolution 198 IH.* Washington, DC: 108th U.S. Congress. April 11.

—— (2003c). *House Resolution 2080 IH.* Washington, DC: 108th U.S. Congress. May 13.

—— (2003d). *House Resolution 2482 IH.* Washington, DC: 108th US Congress. June 16.

Weiss, Martin (2009). *Iraq's Debt Relief.* Washington, DC: Congressional Research Service, US Congress. January 26. Available at: http://www.fas.org/sgp/crs/mideast/RL33376.pdf.

White House Press Release (2003). "Joint Statement Agreed to by President Bush, President Chirac, and Chancellor Schroeder." Washington, DC. December 16. Available at: http://www.america.gov/st/washfile-english/2003/December/20031216193206ssor0.5547907.html.

Xuequan, Mu (2007). "Mubarak, Cheney Talk over Regional Issues with Divergent Focuses." *Xinhua General News Service.* May 13.

10
The Iraq War and (Non)Democratization in the Arab World

Rex Brynen

When the United States (US) invaded Iraq in the spring of 2003, the Bush Administration justified its actions, in part, on the grounds that regime change in Baghdad would have a much broader transformative political effect on the Middle East. Outlining his "forward agenda of freedom" in November 2003, President Bush stated the policy, and the importance of Iraq, in the following stark terms (emphasis added):

> This is a massive and difficult undertaking—it is worth our effort, it is worth our sacrifice, because we know the stakes. The failure of Iraqi democracy would embolden terrorists around the world, increase dangers to the American people, and extinguish the hopes of millions in the region. Iraqi democracy will succeed—and that success will send forth the news, from Damascus to Teheran—that freedom can be the future of every nation. *The establishment of a free Iraq at the heart of the Middle East will be a watershed event in the global democratic revolution.* (Bush, 2003)

There has been much debate, of course, as to whether democratization was indeed a US war aim or, as Francis Fukuyama argues, an ex-post-facto justification for intervention that was motivated by a doctrine of pre-emption and other security concerns (Fukuyama, 2006). Nonetheless, some in the Bush Administration do appear to have believed that by toppling the Iraqi dictator, they might foster a series of broader regional political changes—changes that would reform authoritarian regimes in a way that served US interests. The notion of democratization as a way of advancing US foreign policy security and interests was, after all, a well-established component of neo-conservative thinking. It had been vindicated in neo-con circles by the critical role that regime transitions had played in the end of the Cold War, the collapse of the Warsaw Pact and the transformation of Eastern Europe. In the aftermath of 9/11 (September 11, 2001), this logic was applied to the Middle East too. Hostile authoritarian regimes, such as Iraq, Syria and Iran, supported terrorist groups and sought to acquire weapons of mass destruction. Even friendly dictatorships potentially threatened the US through the growing of radical, militant oppositions within their own societies.[1] This logic was not only a contributing factor to the decision to overthrow Saddam Hussein but was also expressed in a number of other ways in the years following 9/11. These included the launching of the Middle East Partnership Initiative (a series of US aid programs designed to "support the expansion of political opportunity throughout the Middle East") in 2002 (US Department of State, 2003) and the declaration of a common "Partnership for Progress and a Common Future with the Region of the Broader Middle East and North Africa" at the G8 summit in June 2004, together with its associated "Plan of Support for Reform" (G8, 2004a; G8, 2004b). In President Bush's words, "As long as freedom and democracy do not flourish in the Middle East, that region will remain stagnant, resentful and violent—and serve as an exporter of violence and terror to free nations" (White House, 2003).

The April 2003 toppling of Saddam's statue in Firdos Square did not, however, prove to be a democratizing domino that unleashed a chain reaction of political reform across the region. On the contrary, far from resulting in a wave of successful political openings, modest pressures for reform (most of which predate the 2003 invasion) have been offset by authoritarian rollbacks and regime consolidation. One commonly cited set of quantitative indicators by Freedom House suggests that civil liberties and political rights in the Middle East and North Africa showed only miniscule improvement between 2003 and 2006, and no significant shift (and even a slight retrenchment) since then (see Table 10.1). Moreover, political changes in just two countries—Iraq itself and the so-called 2005 "Cedar Revolution" in Lebanon that ended Syrian occupation—account for most of this small change. To this day, the Middle East and North Africa remain the most authoritarian regions in the world by a substantial margin (see Figure 10.1).

Although the absence of substantial political reform in the Middle East is evident, the precise relationship—if any—that might exist between

Table 10.1 Average Freedom House Scores of Political Rights and Civil Liberties for the Middle East and North Africa, 2003–2008

	2002	2003	2004	2005	2006	2007	2008
Political Rights	5.68	5.58	5.58	5.42	5.47	5.53	5.53
Civil Liberties	5.53	5.47	5.21	5.11	5.00	5.00	5.05

Rights are scored from 1 to 7, with 7 being the most restrictive.

Source: Calculated from Freedom House 2009, with the inclusion of data for the Palestinian territories.

the war in Iraq and authoritarian stagnation in the region is less clear. Did regime transition and the advent of electoral politics in Iraq have no impact on politics elsewhere? Or might this effect have been masked, overwhelmed or offset by other factors? Fully answering this question, of course, would require a sophisticated model of what accounts for authoritarian persistence in the Middle East—a puzzle over which there has been much academic debate since the early 1990s, and very little agreement. Consequently, I will set myself the rather more modest task of answering the following question: have the political changes in Iraq

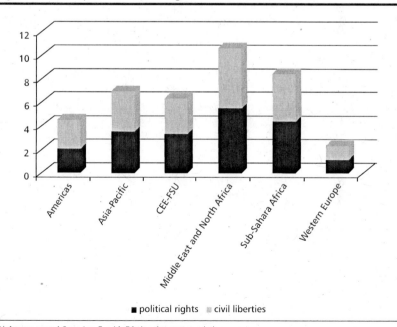

Figure 10.1 Comparative Political Rights and Civil Liberties, 2008

Rights are scored from 1 to 7, with 7 being the most restrictive.

Source: Calculated from Freedom House 2009.

had a positive effect on the prospects for political reform in the region, or have they been negligible or even negative?

Specifically, I will argue that the primary repercussions of the war on the prospects for regional reform have been threefold. First, while the overthrow of Saddam Hussein and the establishment of electoral politics in Iraq did have some minor demonstration effects, their impact on the region was severely constrained by the way in which political transition occurred, the violence that followed it and a general suspicion of US intentions. This both coloured and constrained Arab regional perceptions of Iraqi events, severely undercutting whatever positive effects they might have had. Second, the war in Iraq spurred recruitment by radical jihadist organizations, both inside and outside of the country. Not only were, and are, these movements anti-democratic in orientation, but they have also tended to provoke anti-democratic responses by the governments that they challenge. Third, the war also aggravated the rift between more moderate Islamist movements and the West, lessening the possibility that such movements would either play, or be allowed to play, a central role in regime democratization.

The focus of this chapter will be on post-2003 political changes in Iraq and their effects and not the earlier liberalization and partial democratization that took place in Iraqi Kurdistan following the 1990–91 Gulf War and the collapse of Baathist control in the north. While such changes were momentous—not least of all for Iraq's long-suffering Kurdish population—they had negligible effects on political views and discourse in the Arab Middle East. Instead, the establishment of Kurdish autonomy under the protection of the US "no fly" zone, when it was considered at all, was widely seen as an American plot to dismember Iraq (or the Arab nation more generally) rather than as a positive development worthy of emulation.

It should be noted that it is only a few years since the US invasion, and Iraq's precarious political system is still in a process of evolution. Consequently, by way of conclusion, this chapter examines several possible Iraqi futures and thereafter suggest what the implications each of these might have for political development in the broader Middle East.

Regime Transition in Iraq: The Limits of Demonstration Effects

In many parts of the world, regime transitions and democratic reforms have proven contagious, giving rise to the democratic "waves" that Samuel Huntington identified (Huntington, 2003; for empirical analysis of the geographic and temporal clustering of democratic change, see also O'Loughlin et al., 1998). This was certainly the case in Latin America in the 1970s and 1980s, and later and even more dramatically in Eastern Europe in the 1990s.

This contagion can be born of several factors. In the category of what can be termed immediate *demonstration effects*, regime transition or democratization in one country may encourage populations in neighbouring countries to believe that they too can bring about such changes. Given that the stability of authoritarian regimes is often dependent on the aura of invincibility, and a widespread passive acquiescence among the population rooted in a profound sense of political powerlessness, evidence that authoritarian leaders are something less than all-powerful can have substantial effect on the willingness of people to engage in pro-democracy activities. Populations and activists may also be exposed, by observing events in other countries, to new tools and techniques that they could use in their own struggles for political change in a kind of anti-authoritarian learning. The growth of new information and communication technologies—from satellite television to the internet to SMS texting—has the potential to "snowball" such developments, increasing both the rate and scope of their diffusion and thereby accelerating the momentum for political change.

Demonstration effects, in turn, may shift the political calculations of actors and groups that are essential to the maintenance of the old order. Regime allies may defect, or at the very least hedge their bets by fence-sitting. Within the regime leadership itself, the rapid growth of pressures for political change may exacerbate splits between hard- and soft-liners, leading some of the latter to urge regime opening rather than a more repressive response to protests.

Finally, in the somewhat longer term, demonstration effects are compounded and reinforced by what can be termed *neighbourhood effects*, as more and more democratic regimes are established. These newly established democratic regimes tend to favour democratic over authoritarian governance in nearby states, putting further pressures on neighbouring authoritarian governments. Another factor is the influence of democratic norms, which gradually become more widespread and established (Brinks and Coppedge, 2006). In Eastern Europe, for example, the European Union (and the prospects for EU membership) has played a powerful role in supporting post-communist democratic consolidation, both through example and through the material incentives that EU accession represents. This effect has even extended to the Middle East in the case of

Turkey, where the prospects for greater engagement with Europe and possible EU accession have certainly played a role in encouraging democratic transition and greater respect for human rights. While the role of the Organization of American States has been less profound, it has nonetheless also helped to strengthen a broader emerging norm of democracy in the Americas (Pevehouse, 2005).

In light of these contributing factors, it immediately becomes clear how and why demonstration effects from Iraq have had so little impact in spurring democratic changes elsewhere in the region despite widespread approval of democracy as a system of government among populations in the region (Tessler and Gao, 2005). First, the transition in Iraq was achieved by external (US) military force rather than indigenously by the Iraqi population. Consequently, Middle Eastern populations did not see events in Iraq as either pointing to the potential vulnerabilities of the authoritarian state, or suggesting any replicable way in which change might be advanced elsewhere. While Iraqi elections—together with the ubiquitous picture of a proud and smiling voter emerging from the polls with his or her thumb dyed with purple ink—were widely and generally positively covered in the Arab media in 2005, the bloody terrorism and political violence that engulfed Iraq after Saddam Hussein's overthrow diminished the appeal of developments there. Put simply, Iraq, with almost 100,000 civilians dead since 2003 (Iraq Body Count, 2009), and 2.3 million internally displaced and another two million or more refugees worldwide (UNHCR, 2007), did not appear to be a model that many Arabs wished to emulate. Indeed, Iraq may have reinforced views among Arab publics that, whatever complaints they might have against the authoritarian status quo, the stability that they provide is preferable to anarchy, violence and uncertainty. In this regard, it is perhaps noteworthy that popular support for democracy in the region is somewhat weaker in countries that experienced violent domestic conflicts in the past, such as Algeria (Tessler, 2004: 201).

Compounding these constraints on the potential demonstration effects of events in Iraq was the deep suspicion that most in the region harboured towards the Bush Administration and US policy. As a consequence, many Arab observers simply did not accept that elections in Iraq were genuine and meaningful. Instead, the Iraqi government was widely seen as a puppet installed under the oppressive force of an American occupation. According to a recent (2008) University of Maryland/Zogby survey of public opinion in five Arab countries, some 65% do not believe that democratization is a real American objective in the region.[2] The survey also found that, with specific regard to Iraq:

Only 6% of Arabs polled believe that the American surge has worked. A plurality (35%) does not believe reports that violence has in fact declined. Over 61% believe that if the US were to withdraw from Iraq, Iraqis will find a way to bridge their differences, and only 15% believe the civil war would expand. 81% of Arabs polled (outside Iraq) believe that the Iraqis are worse off than they were before the Iraq war. (Anwar Sadat Chair for Peace and Development and Zogby International, 2008)

At the level of regime elites, events in Iraq by themselves did little to foster reform, and arguably served to retard it. Regimes at odds with Washington, such as Syria and Iran, grew increasingly worried about a US agenda of regime change and showed increasing intolerance to their own domestic critics. Regimes friendly to Washington certainly felt some pressure to open up, although more as a consequence of the broader "freedom agenda" and the brief period of Western interest in political reform that followed it, than because of any particular effect of the invasion. On the contrary, the 2003 US invasion of Iraq—like the bloody civil war in Algeria a decade earlier—undoubtedly convinced many regime hard-liners and soft-liners alike of the dangers of radicalism, violence, ethnic and sectarian tension, and terrorism that might arise from loosening authoritarian controls. This perception would have been further amplified by the occasional spill over of Iraqi violence further afield, most notably in the November 2005 Amman bombings conducted by al-Qaida in Iraq (AQI).

In Latin America, in particular, most democratic openings were the subject of carefully constructed political pacts intended to assure that the initial transfer of political power (typically, to the centre or centre-right) took place in a way that assuaged many of the concerns of outgoing military juntas. In the Middle East, Iraq's transition sent a very different signal to those holding power. It was understood that reform would lead to chaos. The narrow survival strategies of authoritarian leaders, the difficulty and dangers of negotiating any exit, the Islamist challenge, and the relative security of the status quo all militated strongly against any sort of change. The weaknesses of civil society and the absence of substantial domestic pressure for change further reinforced these trends.

Finally, Iraq's transition took place in a regional environment that contained only some encouraging elements, but mainly discouraging ones. In the former category was the Arab media environment. Much of the Middle East shares both a common Arab language and a popular, largely independent direct broadcast satellite media (notably al-Jazeera and al-Arabiya, both of which covered Iraqi events in considerable detail).

This might have acted to amplify the positive demonstration effects of Iraq, and indeed the Arab news networks extensively and generally positively reported on Iraq's successful elections. However, they also extensively reported the violence and other negative aspects of US policy and the Iraqi experience, thereby contributing to a general popular sense that events in Iraq were hardly a replicable experiment.

This led to periodic accusations from US officials during the Bush Administration that coverage by al-Jazeera in particular was "vicious, inaccurate and inexcusable.... It's disgraceful what that station is doing" (then US Secretary of Defense Donald Rumsfeld, quoted in Scahill, 2005). Certainly, opinion surveys suggest that journalists tended to be more Arab nationalist, and even more cynical than the already cynical Arab public about American commitment to democratization. However, cynicism regarding political rhetoric is hardly an uncommon characteristic of professional journalists. Regarding Iraq in particular, the same opinion surveys show that the (negative) attitudes of journalists largely mirrored that of the general Arab population (Pintak, 2009: 199; for a broader discussion of the new Arab media and the Iraq wars, see Lynch, 2006).

In other respects, the regional environment was profoundly hostile to any reformist momentum generated by political developments in Iraq. Regional states were both suspicious of the changes in Iraq and threatened by, and hence hostile to, any agenda of democratic change. Of the immediate neighbours, Iran was perhaps the most open to Iraqi democracy, largely because the demographic weight of the Shi'a majority seemed likely to produce governments that were (at least) unthreatening and (at best) friendly to Tehran. Saudi Arabia, by contrast, has viewed the prospect of Iraqi democracy—especially a Shi'a majority Iraqi democracy—as threatening, for exactly the same reason. Jordan has also viewed Iraq as a source of security threat. For Syria, Iraq was a potential springboard to US designs against Damascus. Finally, increasingly democratic Turkey has viewed almost everything in Iraq through the parochial lens of its own Kurdish "problem."

Iraq and Radical Jihadist Movements

There can be little doubt that the US invasion of Iraq served to both spur and radicalize militant Islamist movements in the Middle East. As was evident in public statements, jihadist websites and elsewhere, radical organizations saw Washington's actions as proof of nefarious Western intent and capitalized on widespread opposition to US policy in the

Arab and Muslim world to recruit supporters. As the 2006 US National Intelligence Estimate on *Trends in Global Terrorism* concluded, "The Iraq conflict has become the 'cause célèbre' for jihadists, breeding a deep resentment of US involvement in the Muslim world and cultivating supporters for the global jihadist movement" (National Intelligence Council, 2006).

Moreover, not only did the war in Iraq increase radical Islamist recruitment, but it also created a flow of foreign (Sunni) radicals into Iraq, where they hoped to take part in the jihad against the American "Crusaders" and their "puppet" Iraqi government. The so-called "Sinjar records"—AQI personnel records for some 576 foreign fighters smuggled via Syria that were obtained by US forces in September 2007—shows that they originated in some 21 different countries, with Saudi Arabia (41%), Libya (19%), Syria (8%), Yemen (8%), Algeria (7%) and Morocco (6%) accounting for the largest shares (Felter and Fishman, 2008: 34).[3] Most recruitment took place through local jihadist networks (35%) or friends (29%) and family (7%) (Felter and Fishman, 2008: 45). Quite apart from the damage done by these foreign fighters to Iraq itself— where they made up only a small proportion of the combatants in the various Iraqi insurgencies against Coalition forces, but where they represented a disproportionate share of suicide bombers targeting Iraqi civilians—some left Iraq with newly acquired paramilitary skills that could be put to use in other places. Perhaps the most dramatic example of this was to be seen in the fighting in the Nahr al-Barid Palestinian refugee camp in Lebanon in 2007. There, militants of Fateh al-Islam fought the Lebanese Army for over three months. Some of these militants drew on their experience fighting in Iraq, and others had hoped to eventually join the jihad there; most were not from Lebanon at all. Over 400 people, most of them militants or soldiers, died in the fighting. The camp itself, once home to some 30,000 Palestinian refugees, was largely destroyed.

The growth of such movements has had several effects on the prospects for regional democratization. First, such movements are themselves largely anti-democratic and anti-pluralist in nature. Second, the growth of violent jihadist movements provides both a reason and a pretext for existing regimes to tighten their authoritarian controls. Finally, those same regimes have been able to use post-9/11 Western fear of radical jihadist movements as a way of deflecting external pressures for democratization.

Iraq and the Islamist Mainstream

Of course, relatively few Islamist movements in and outside of the Middle East are radical jihadist groups espousing violence, nor do such groups enjoy majority support within these countries. Instead, the groups that have tended to attract widespread public support are those such as the Muslim Brotherhood (Egypt), the Muslim Brotherhood/Islamic Action Front (Jordan) or the Justice and Development Party (Morocco). These movements have called for democratic reforms and peacefully participate in electoral politics. These movements have also been somewhat strengthened by the public backlash against American intervention in Iraq, although domestic political issues—notably public dissatisfaction with corruption and poor governance—have been far more significant in bolstering their local support.

Such groups have certainly been vociferous critics of American involvement in Iraq, in addition to taking up a range of other issues (most notably Palestine and US support for Israel, intervention in Afghanistan, Western support for authoritarian Arab regimes and International Monetary Fund-supported structural adjustment policies). Mainstream Islamist movements such as the Muslim Brotherhood have, on occasion, implicitly endorsed Iraqi Sunni insurgent movements by upholding the right of Iraqis to engage in resistance against a foreign "occupier." In doing so, they have shown little regard for the will of the (elected) Iraqi government—criticizing, for example, the new Status of Forces Agreement between Iraq and the US (Akef, 2008).

At the same time, however, mainstream Islamist movements have condemned both sectarian violence and the terrorism of AQI. Egyptian Muslim Brotherhood leader Mohammed Mahdi Akef, for example, has warned "Those raising the banner of jihad against the occupier did not provide our countries with anything other than bad things and division" (*International Herald Tribune*, 2006). With the decline of AQI, the "Anbar Awakening" in Iraq, the reduction of violence and the increasing involvement of Iraqi Sunnis in both the security forces (through the "Sons of Iraq") and politics, Iraq has become much less of an issue for mainstream Islamist movements than it was from 2003 to 2006.

What does all of this have to do with regional political reform? I would argue that it has had two effects. First, it highlighted an essential paradox of the Bush Administration's "forward agenda of freedom," namely that the likely beneficiaries of democratization in the region have been Islamist political parties that were strongly opposed to US foreign policy and much of the post 9/11 "global war on terror"—including US actions in Iraq. Second, authoritarian regimes in the Arab world were often able to use this first development to their advantage, capitalizing on the perceived dangers of moderate Islamist ascendance—much as they have done with the threat of radical jihadist groups—by using them to reduce or deflect external pressures for political reform.

The strong performance of Hizbullah in the 2005 Lebanese elections and the election of a Hamas government in the (US-supported) January 2006 Palestinian Legislative Council elections highlighted the first of these paradoxes. The Bush Administration pushed for an international boycott of the new Hamas-led government, and in so doing confirmed cynical Arab perceptions about the limits of Western support for democracy.

The second process was more than amply demonstrated in Egypt. There, Washington played an essential role in pressuring the Mubarak regime to agree to (semi)competitive presidential elections in September 2005. Later that year, however, Washington said little as the Egyptian government took a number of measures, through fraud and intimidation, to try to limit the Muslim Brotherhood's success in subsequent parliamentary elections. The party nonetheless won 88 seats, and would likely have won far more if it had been free to fairly contest all 454 seats in the People's Assembly. Since then, the Egyptian government has continued to harass the opposition by arresting its members and through other means.

Looking Back and Ahead

It is important to reiterate that the effects discussed above are far from the most important determinants of regional non-democratization in the Middle East in the post 9/11 period. Indeed, the failure of regime transition in Iraq to spur political reform elsewhere is more deeply rooted in the much-debated variables that have generally contributed to the persistence of authoritarianism in the Arab world for decades: rentier economies, weak civil societies, successful strategies of regime maintenance and cooption, regional militarization and perhaps some political-cultural factors too (for a discussion, see Brynen, Korany and Noble, 1995; Pripstein Posusney and Penner Angrist, 2005; and Carothers and Ottaway, 2005, among many others). Despite this inauspicious context, however, it is clear that—contrary to the declared ambitions of the Bush Administration—political change in Iraq has done little to hasten political reform further afield, and may even have served to retard it.

However, as Mao Tse Tung is said to have commented regarding the French Revolution, perhaps it is too early to tell. The unstable and uncertain political experiment that is Iraq is, after all, only six years old. Could it have more substantial effects on regional democratization in the future?

This, of course, depends on what the future holds for Iraq—a topic that itself could easily be the subject of several more papers. For the purposes of this analysis, however, it is possible to identify four possible broad scenarios over the next decade, each with significantly different potential regional ramifications.

The first of these—and the least likely of the four, in my view—would be the greater stabilization of Iraq, an end to endemic violence and the establishment of *democratic good governance*. A flourishing Iraqi political system would undoubtedly provide a positive model for populations and reformists elsewhere in the region. There is reason to doubt, however, whether the effects would be substantial. The Iraqi experiment would continue to be seen as born of original sin (US intervention) and intolerable chaos (violence, terrorism and sectarian strife). Continued close association of the Baghdad regime with Washington and/or Tehran would also tend to delegitimize it as a model, and Sunni regimes could also point to its perceived Shi'a majoritarianism as further evidence of its shortcomings. Indeed, were a successful Iraq to draw closer to Iran, some Arab governments (Saudi Arabia, Egypt and Jordan) might even encourage opposition Sunni groups as a way of offsetting perceived Iranian influence and undercutting the effectiveness of the central government.

The second possible outcome would be a *descent into violence*, potentially even greater than that of the 2003–6 period, and possibly involving a full-scale civil war with an ethno-sectarian core. Such a development would undoubtedly have a chilling effect on the prospects for political reform in the region. A bloodbath in a failed Iraqi democracy would further convince populations, key social groups and potential regime softliners of the dangers of opening up authoritarian regimes. It would also provide a further incentive for regimes to clamp down on their own domestic oppositions.

A third possible outcome is one of democratic reversal and *increasing authoritarianism* in Iraq, possibly as a reaction to growing violence and instability of the sort just mentioned. This might occur gradually, as ruling elites abuse their powers to weaken and intimidate their rivals, restrict civil society and skew the electoral system to suit their goals. Much less likely, it could also occur suddenly through a direct seizure of power. In both cases, the effect would also be to discredit Iraq as any sort of model for reform.

The fourth—and to my mind most likely—outcome of the next ten years is one of *muddling-through and more of the same*. Iraq would continue to enjoy competitive electoral politics, and while some political and civil rights might be compromised by periodic threats of violence or illiberal politics, elections would nonetheless continue to be both important in shaping public policy and generally reflective of the popular will. At the same time, Iraqi politics would also continue to be bedevilled by ethnic and sectarian tensions, corruption and poor governance. In such a case, the regional effects of the Iraqi experiment would continue to be much as they have been in recent years, neither having powerful demonstration effects for reform nor representing a democratic domino that would hasten a series of changes—Latin American or Eastern European style—in the rest of the region.

There are broader policy lessons in all of this, of course. Perhaps democracy can be brought in, or brought back, at the point of a gun through external intervention, as it was in Italy, Germany, Japan (post-1945), Grenada (1983) and Panama (1989), and even where the intervener has other, ulterior motives. Leaving aside both the ethics and efficacy of this approach, however, it is clear that such transitions have much more limited demonstration effects than the more usual transitions-from-within. The notion among some Bush Administration policy makers that Iraq was the first of a series of potential democratic dominos was therefore badly misplaced, both theoretically and in regional context. That Iraq has been a particularly problematic, bloody and uncertain transition has limited its reformist effects still more.

Ironically, despite President Bush's rhetoric about the importance of Iraq as a "watershed event in the global democratic revolution," the Bush Administration actually failed to act in the one case that might have proven to be a democratic domino of sorts: Egypt. Successful US pressure on Egypt to hold and abide by fully democratic parliamentary elections in 2005, despite the inevitable benefit of such elections to the Muslim Brotherhood, would have been seen in the region as a marked departure from past Western policy. It might have had important implications for the participation of other Islamist movements in the political process. It might also have had implications for the direction of a post-Husni Mubarak Egypt.

In Egypt, however, the more traditional security concerns won out—the value of Egypt as a reliable regional ally, and the cooperation of the

Mubarak regime in the "Global War on Terror" (GWOT). Although the Obama Administration has dispensed with the rhetoric of the "GWOT," there is little evidence that it will substantially revise either its diplomatic positions or aid strategies with regard to democratization.

Notes

1. This is not to argue that neoconservatives provided the only ideological foundation for this policy. Many liberals were also attracted to the idea of a campaign for Middle East democracy. Conversely, realist conservatives saw the export of American democracy as a diversion from necessary power politics.
2. The poll surveyed opinion in Egypt, Jordan, Lebanon, Morocco, Saudi Arabia and United Arab Emirates. Many of these views are not, it must be said, strikingly dissimilar from those of Iraqis themselves. Another 2008 survey showed Iraqis evenly split on whether the 2003 invasion was "right" (49%) or "wrong" (51%). Some 72% opposed the presence of coalition forces, 61% felt that US forces made the security situation worse, and 42% supported attacks against Coalition forces. Less than half had any confidence in the national government (ABC News et al., 2008).
3. The distribution of data for third country nationals actually held by US forces painted a slightly different picture, with the largest shares originating from Syria (19%), Egypt (19%) and Saudi Arabia (17%).

Works Cited

ABC News, BBC, ARD and NHK (2008). Survey undertaken by D3 Systems and KA Research. Conducted February 2008 and released March 2008. Available at: http://news.bbc.co.uk/2/shared/bsp/hi/pdfs/14_03_08iraqpoll march2008.pdf.

Akef, Mahdy (2008). "Interview with Muslim Brotherhood Chairman Mohamed Mahdy Akef." *Ikhanweb*. November 27. Available at: http://ikhwanweb.com/Article.asp?ID=18778&LevelID=1&SectionID=87.

Anwar Sadat Chair for Peace and Development and Zogby International (2008). "2008 Annual Arab Public Opinion Poll." University of Maryland, PowerPoint summary. March. Available at: http://sadat.umd.edu/surveys/index.htm.

Brinks, Daniel and Michael Coppedge (2006). "Diffusion Is No Illusion: Neighbor Emulation in the Third Wave of Democratization." *Comparative Political Studies*. Vol. 39, No. 4: 463–89.

Brynen, Rex, Bahgat Korany and Paul Noble (eds.) (1995). *Political Liberalization and Democratization in the Arab World: Volume 1, Theoretical Perspectives*. Boulder, CO: Lynne Rienner.

Bush, George W. (2003). "Remarks by the President at the 20th Anniversary of the National Endowment for Democracy." Washington. November 7. Available at: http://www.ned.org/events/anniversary/20thAniv-Bush.html.

Carothers, Thomas and Marina Ottaway (eds.) (2005). *Uncharted Journey: Promoting Democracy in the Middle East.* Washington, DC: Carnegie Endowment for International Peace.

Felter, Joseph and Brian Fishman (2008). "Becoming a Foreign Fighter: A Second Look at the Sinjar Records" in *Bombers, Bank Accounts, and Bleedout: Al-Qaida's Road In and Out of Iraq,* edited by Brian Fishman et al. West Point, NY: Combating Terrorism Center at West Point. Available at: http://www.ctc.usma.edu/harmony/pdf/Sinjar_2_July_23.pdf.

Freedom House (2009). Freedom in the World Comparative and Historical Data. Available at: http://www.freedomhouse.org/template.cfm?page=439. (last accessed May 7, 2009).

Fukuyama, Francis (2006). *After the Neocons: America at the Crossroads.* London, UK: Profile Books.

G8 (2004a). *Partnership for Progress and a Common Future with the Region of the Broader Middle East and North Africa.* June 9.

——— (2004b). *Plan of Support for Reform.* June 9.

Huntington, Samuel (2003). *The Third Wave: Democratization in the Late Twentieth Century.* Norman, OK: University of Oklahoma Press.

International Herald Tribune (2006). "Leader of Egypt's Muslim Brotherhood Urges All Iraqis, Sunni and Shiite to Stop Fighting." November 30.

Iraq Body Count (2009). Iraq Body Count. Available at http://www.iraqbodycount.org. (last accessed March 25, 2009).

Lynch, Marc (2006). *Voices of the New Arab Public: Iraq, al-Jazeera, and Middle East Politics Today.* New York, NY: Columbia University Press.

National Intelligence Council (2006). *Trends in Global Terrorism: Implications for the United States.* NIE 2006–02D. Washington, DC, Declassified summary. April. Available at: http://www.dni.gov/press_releases/Declassified_NIE_Key_Judgments.pdf.

O'Loughlin, John, Michael D. Ward, Corey L. Lofdahl, Jordin S. Cohen, David S. Brown, David Reilly, Kristian S. Gleditsch and Michael Shin (1998). "The Diffusion of Democracy, 1946–1994." *Annals of the Association of American Geographers.* Vol. 88, No. 4: 545–74.

Pevehouse, Jon (2005). *Democracy from Above: Regional Organizations and Democratization.* Cambridge, UK: Cambridge University Press.

Pintak, Lawrence (2009). "Border Guards of the 'Imagined' Watan: Arab Journalists and the New Arab Consciousness." *Middle East Journal.* Vol. 63, No. 2: 191–212.

Pripstein Posusney, Marsha and Michele Penner Angrist (eds.) (2005). *Authoritarianism in the Middle East: Regimes and Resistance.* Boulder, CO: Lynne Rienner.

Scahill, Jeremy (2005). "Did Bush Really Want to Bomb Al Jazeera?" *The Nation.* December 12. Available at: http://www.thenation.com/doc/20051212/scahill.

Tessler, Mark (2004). "The View from the Street: The Attitudes and Values of Ordinary Algerians." *Journal of North Africa Studies.* Vol. 9, No. 2: 184–201.

——— and Eleanor Gao (2005). "Gauging Arab Support for Democracy." *Journal of Democracy.* Vol. 16, No. 3: 83–97.

United Nations High Commissioner for Refugees (UNHCR) (2007). Statistics on Displaced Iraqis around the World. Geneva. September. Available at: http://www.unhcr.org/cgi-bin/texis/vtx/iraq?page=home.

United States Department of State (2003). *Fact Sheet, US–Middle East Partnership Initiative.* Washington. June 18.

White House (2003). *Fact Sheet: President Bush Calls for a "Forward Strategy of Freedom" to Promote Democracy in the Middle East.* Washington: Office of the Press Secretary. November.

11
Debating the Issues
A Roundtable Report

Carla Angulo-Pasel

Introduction

Iraq has endured decades of conflict, which has decimated infrastructure and spurred high levels of sectarian violence. Taking into account Iraq's complicated history, this chapter focuses on post-2003 Iraq, current problems that Iraqis are facing and the direction the international community should follow to build a sustainable state. This roundtable report, based on discussions that took place at The Centre for International Governance Innovation (CIGI), in Waterloo, Canada, on April 16–17, 2009, gathers the participants' views and reflections on issues of concern. The first section summarizes the dialogue on Internally Displaced Persons (IDPs) and refugees. Entitlements to basic services, rights of return and repatriation and property rights are relevant issues for millions of Iraqis. The second section recaps discussions of citizenship in Iraq and the feasibility of federalism given the state's ethnic heterogeneity and associated competing interests. The third section outlines the discourse regarding lessons from comparable cases and the potential they may have held for the development of the 2005 Iraqi Constitution. The fourth section sums up the exchange of ideas concerning the role for middle powers—such as Canada—in Iraq.

Internally Displaced Persons and Property Rights

The IDP problem and refugee crisis are pressing issues in Iraq, but they are in no way new. Twelve years of sanctions by the United Nations (UN) have led to a catastrophic humanitarian crisis. Since the United States-led invasion of 2003, however, conditions have worsened. Civilian displacement can be divided into three phases. Prior to 2003, Saddam Hussein's government forcibly displaced Kurdish communities in Northern Iraq and Shi'a communities in the southern provinces. The goal of this displacement was to alter the ethnic organization of these regions and neutralize Kurdish independence aspirations (IDMC, 2008: 6). Between 2003 and 2006, most of the displacement was caused by coalition military operations, generally in western, predominantly Sunni, areas. For instance, in the first months after the invasion began, "thousands of people were displaced by air strikes and urban warfare in Anbar, Thi'Qar, Basra and Baghdad" (IDMC, 2008: 7). In 2004, the fighting intensified in the cities of Fallujah, and in November of that year, nearly the whole population of Fallujah (approximately 200,000) fled the violence (UNAMI, 2004). Such military operations resulted in restrictions on freedom of movement, lack of access to humanitarian aid, disproportionate use of force and the destruction of property. The latest phase of forced displacement has taken place since 2006. Sectarian violence is the major cause of this displacement, and it is widely reported to have commenced after the explosion of the al-Askari Shi'a shrine in Samara in February 2006. The populations at risk have been Sunni and Shi'a, as well as families in Sunni/Shi'a mixed marriages (Human Rights Watch, 2006). This sectarian violence marked a shift in the conflict, indicating that various Iraqi groups are now competing for political and economic power.

The UN High Commission for Refugees (UNHCR) estimates Iraqi IDPs at approximately 2.8 million people. This is in addition to approximately 3 million externally displaced persons, or refugees (UNHCR, 2009). The main difference between IDPs and refugees is that refugees have crossed an international border. Both groups share the same plight, but IDPs legally remain under the protection of their own government. Including minorities, there are approximately 15 categories of people forced to leave their homes from several areas within Iraq.[1] While some were given shelter in the homes of others, many found themselves in provisional camps or informal settlements. Without even basic infrastructure, such settlements are characterized by makeshift buildings and lack access to water, sewage systems and electricity. According to one displaced Iraqi who lives in an abandoned building in Bagdad, "it is living in misery… The government gives us 50 litres of heating and cooking oil each month, but we run out of it very soon, and then we have to try to find money to buy more so we can cook and try to stay warm" (Jamail,

2009). Ideally, IDPs and refugees could return to their homes, however, of the homes that have not been destroyed, many have been confiscated, transferred to party members or sold and then re-sold again. Consequently, there is a title crisis in Iraq.

Many of the issues raised at the roundtable had a complex, normative debate underlying them. Do IDPs have the right of return to their original homes? What if the right of return conflicts with the right to peace and security? It was noted that, until now, these decisions have been made mainly by the US army and they have, in essence, facilitated the ethnic reorganization of Iraq. Indeed, no longer are there mixed communities but rather a patchwork of segregated sectarian enclaves separated by concrete walls. This, as noted by one participant, amplifies existing ethnic cleavages and undermines Iraq's tradition as a diverse mosaic (see Lamani in this volume). This normative debate also has legal dimensions, like those surrounding property rights and legal entitlement. The right of return is not an absolute law—it must be balanced with property entitlements but avoid conflict where differences are irreconcilable.

The right of return and property rights are complex and sensitive topics. A major point of debate at the roundtable contemplated which actors would make such decisions and what political incentives and limitations they might face. The Iraqi government would like to remediate the displacement problem post haste, thus there is political pressure for the displaced to return to their homes. To promote a facade of progress, the government is underreporting the amount of IDPs and refugees. IDPs are no longer being registered by the government, and government refugee estimates total no more than 400,000 refugees in Syria and Jordan (Refugees International, 2009: 2). There exists a clear discrepancy between Iraqi numbers and UN estimates of 500,000 refugees in Jordan and 1.5 million refugees in Syria, respectively (UNHCR, 2009). The Iraqi government provides returnees with assistance of about US$800 per family, which is insufficient and unevenly distributed (Refugees International, 2009: 2). In January 2009, the government undertook to evict squatters from government property, giving occupants 60 days to vacate while promising financial assistance to find alternate living arrangements (Jamail, 2009). Among the displaced, there is also a disproportionate number of Iraqi minorities. The division of power between Shi'a, Kurd and Sunni created a real problem of insecurity and displacement for other minorities, as examined in Mokhtar Lamani's chapter in this volume. Lacking any force to protect their communities, smaller minorities face additional impediments to resettlement.

The Government of Iraq, moreover, does not possess the capacity, or the will, to provide basic services and property restitution to IDPs and returning refugees because corruption is rampant and because it is not a government priority. Furthermore, it lacks the cohesion to develop a coherent strategy to address this problem. Political factions within the Iraqi government make it extremely difficult to reach a consensus. With a Shi'a majority government and a Ministry of Displacement and Migration controlled by Shi'a and Kurds, there is little opportunity or incentive to include Sunnis in the dialogue. As a result, Sunnis feel disenfranchised and under-represented. As noted at the roundtable discussion, recent government policy entitles certain IDPs to assistance upon return to their original homes on the condition that they were displaced between January 2006 and December 2007. This period coincides with the surge in Shi'a displacement following the Samarra bombings in 2006, and therefore primarily benefits displaced Shi'a. This has the effect of excluding many other Iraqis, mainly Sunnis, who were displaced between 2004 and 2005 (Refugees International Field Report, 2009: 2). This biased policy, coupled with general insecurity, creates a political vacuum that provides justification for the existence of sectarian non-state actors such as warlords and militias. Furthermore, there is no judicial entity mandated to deal with post-2003 property disputes. The Iraq Commission for Resolution of Real Property Disputes (CRRPD) does exist, but its mandate is limited to pre-2003 claims, limiting its usefulness in the current crisis. In Iraq, a variety of actors and groups with overlapping jurisdictions are handling such disputes. These groups consist of the Iraqi army, the Iraqi National Police and the local militia groups—all believed to contain sectarian inclinations. For comparison, the Dayton Accords in the Balkans—which facilitated the recovery of property titles and housing swaps—were effective because the North Atlantic Treaty Organization (NATO) provided implementation as an impartial international mediator, free of encumbering local political pressures.

The Government of Iraq has taken steps to stop mass exodus from the state. In 2007, for example, the regime asked Syria to close its borders to stem the outflow of Iraqi refugees. Likewise, the Iraqi regime has offered incentives to coax Iraqis home, providing buses and planes for transportation, and supplying small sums of money upon return (Refugees International, 2009). The policy of enticing refugees back to Iraq, despite the insufficient capacity to manage the existing internal displacement crisis, appears to be politically motivated. Both the Iraqi government and the US can use returning refugee statistics as evidence of increasing stability within the state and, by extension, as an indicator of a successful security strategy. However, the real indicator should be the safety of the people who choose to come home. In reality, few people return, because they do not feel safe, and those that do return despite widespread insecurity, return because of the adversity of refugee life in neighbouring states. A 2008 report from Refugees International highlights other pull factors. For example, some refugees and IDPs are returning partly because of ceasefires enacted by Sunni and Shi'a militias and for the security such groups provide. Many militias have established fiefdoms for their associated sect, providing not only security but also food and non-foodstuffs (Refugees International, 2008: 12). In many cases it is these phenomena rather than the success of state security strategies and resettlement policies that are bringing Iraqis home.

Citizenship and Federalism

The second topic examined during the roundtable discussion centred on the idea of citizenship in Iraq. The Iraqi constitution established in 2005 represents progress toward political reconstruction, but this constitution needs further clarification and amendments. The issue of "Iraqi identity" and the future of Iraq's federal state are among the most complicated matters. Is there an agreement on the terms of citizenship? What is ethnic federalism? There was no consensus on how best to answer these questions. One participant put forward that in international law, there is no pre-standing and objective definition of "citizenship"; the definition varied by each academic discipline. What does exist as a framework, however, is the relationship between the citizens and the state. Another participant stated that "citizenship" as a term can be dependent upon how it is defined within one's sect. This sect-centric view, however, is difficult to accept given the various other affiliations— ideological, tribal, professional, demographic and rural–urban—that shape identities and attitudes toward citizenship (Cameron, 2007).

In terms of the political system, proponents of decentralization would like to see Iraq's federal state consist of Shi'a, Sunni and Kurd, but even within each of these main political factions, there are divergent views on such policies. A "corporate consociational" arrangement, as noted by McGarry and O'Leary, is not only unstable but unfair, since "they privilege certain ascriptive identities and exclude those who hold other group identities or no group identities" (2007: 691). Corporate consociation is encouraged by accommodationist democratic states, which favour multiple public identities within one federal state and therefore promote federal institutions that share power proportionately among predetermined communities. Consociation accommodates groups

(a) by involving all sizeable communities in executive institutions provided they wish to participate;
(b) by promoting proportionality throughout the public sector, not just in the executive and legislature but also in the bureaucracy, including the army and police;
(c) through autonomy of either the territorial or nonterritorial variety; and
(d) through minority vetoes, at least in those domains the minority communities consider important. (McGarry and O'Leary, 2007: 671)

This concept differs from integrationist states, which seek to construct a single overarching federal identity, one that is impartial and centralized with no power sharing.

In Iraq, divergent views on political organization constitute an additional stumbling block to progress. The Kurdish Alliance, for example, emphasizes Kurdish identity and advocates a degree of secularism. Within the United Iraqi Alliance, the Sadrists exhibit the strongest support for a unified state, but some Shi'a leaders would like to avoid a return to a strong central government; politically, there is little agreement. Lastly, the Arab Sunni Leadership, especially the Tawafuq and Hiwar parties, oppose the current degree of decentralization and may find it difficult to accommodate Kurdish separatism (Marr, 2007). These few examples indicate the divergence in policy preferences within Iraq and underscore the absurdity of treating the main political factions as three distinct and cohesive groups, each with uniform preferences. Further complicating the dynamic situation is the nature of regional boundaries, which will inevitably pit a much smaller Kurdistan against the rest of Iraq. This highlights the necessity to strengthen the rule of law and human rights in all districts of the country.

One consensus reached at the roundtable was the need for clearer implementation of political reconciliation conditions. This was hampered, as one participant pointed out, by Nouri al-Maliki, whose advisors are all from his own party. This has alienated other groups. In truth, the 2005 Constitution and therefore the current definition of "federalism" were only fully endorsed by two groups: Shi'a and Kurds. During the 2005 elections, there was a 59 percent voter turnout; however, the Sunni population was apathetic and turned out in low numbers at the polls (see Table 11.1). As a result, the new constitution, as Marr similarly notes, ensures a high degree of decentralization. Subsequently, there has been a shift from a relatively unified country with nationalist orientations to a political dynamic based on ethnic and sectarian identity (2007: 42). This of course is problematic coupled with low Sunni representation in the creation of the federal state, which has further embroiled and solidified the Sunni resistance movement.

According to Cameron (2007), there are three possible scenarios for the future of federalism in Iraq. One focuses on the concept of "partial federalism," which in his view represents the current reality. Though Baghdad continues to be the political focal point, it is weak, and the Kurdish region is experiencing a high degree of autonomy. The most dangerous scenario involves a radically decentralized federation. This type of federation would not only have a very limited list of executive powers, it would also create a weak revenue-raising capacity, encourage exclusive identities and thus generate a real risk of fragmentation. Given the current situation in Iraq, the last option of balanced federation is also unlikely to occur: this option involves a strong central authority that would assert and retain control as well as act as a counterbalance to regional aspirations (Cameron, 2007: 163). But whether related to the first, second or third option, the key element considered was the likelihood of power-sharing. As one roundtable participant noted, once the Shi'a came into power they argued, "it's our time to run the country."

Lessons could be learned from power-sharing in Bosnia-Herzegovina. In effect, the Bosnia-Herzegovina government is presided over by a rotating presidency composed of one Bosniak and one Croat from the Federation of Bosnia-Herzegovina and one Serb from Republika Srpska. This is similar to the provisions of Iraq's Constitution (Article 138), which contains a three-person Presidential Council, with a president and two vice-presidents. The main difference between the Iraqi and the Bosnia-Herzegovina cases is that Iraqi leaders are elected by a two-thirds majority in the Council of Representatives, and there is no requirement stipulating that they come from a particular ethnic or religious group (McGarry and O'Leary, 2007: 670). It could be argued, however, that since the majority of the Iraqi government is from one group, there is an ethnic component at play. Moreover, there is a sense of symbolic power-sharing between the Shi'a, Kurds and Sunni. All groups maintain that the government is political and not sectarian; in reality, however, there is an atmosphere of "complete mistrust and near-absolute absence of serious dialogue between the different actors" (Lamani, 2009). Even within each of these groups, there is an "unprecedented fragmentation," which

Table 11.1 Iraqi Voter Turnout for January 30, 2005 Elections

Province	% Voter Turnout
Baghdad	48
Ninawa	17
Dehuk	89
Sulaymaniya	80
Arbil	—
Tamin	—
Salah ad Din	29
Diala	34
Anbar	2
Babil	71
Karbala	73
Najaf	73
Wasit	66
Qadisiyah	69
Dhi Qar	67
Muthanna	61
Basrah	—
Missan	59

Source: Based on information obtained from the Independent Electoral Commission of Iraq.

produces substantial disagreements not only about sharing but about what to share. There is a complete lack of will toward establishing terms for sharing administrative power. Political reconciliation and Iraqi reconstruction efforts will fail if the system is based on ethnic or religious exclusion; what is needed is a form of democratization that promotes a "respect for pluralism and difference" (Lamani, 2009).

Lessons from Comparative Cases

Seeking comparative cases, participants highlighted Bosnia and Herzegovina. In the 1990s, a violent conflict erupted between Serb, Croatian and Bosnian armed forces and militias after the collapse of the Socialist Federal Republic of Yugoslavia. The causes of this conflict are complex and beyond the scope of this chapter; however, genocide, war crimes and ethnic cleansing contributed to approximately 2.2 million IDPs and external refugees (UNHCR, 2007). In an aim to maintain ethnic and territorial continuity between Serb-majority areas of Bosnia and Herzegovina and neighbouring Serbia, paramilitary and militias supported by the Serb Army began expelling Bosnian Muslims (Bosniaks), Croats and other minorities. This caused large-scaled forced displacement (IDMC,

2008a). Perhaps the most prominent example of the conflict was the Srebrenica massacre in 1995. UN safe havens had been created for Bosnian Muslims seeking refuge, but Srebrenica was overrun by Bosnian Serb forces and thousands of men were executed despite the UN presence. This prompted an intensive two-week NATO air campaign against Bosnian Serb targets.

The Dayton Peace Agreement (DPA) was signed in 1995. It effectively maintained a ceasefire and created two political entities: the Federation of Bosnia-Herzegovina and Republika Srpska. The Federation of Bosnia-Herzegovina consists of Bosniak and Croat ethnic groups, while Republika Srpska consists of the Bosnian Serb ethnic group. The DPA also outlined that there be a strong NATO-led military force, and Annex VII of the agreement focused on the right to return for IDPs and refugees. Further, it designated UNHCR as the lead implementing agency for property rights issues. Although a significant amount of returns occurred shortly after the signing of the agreement, these returns have decreased substantially since 2003—primarily due to the lack of economic opportunity for returnees (UNHCR, 2007). The situation in Bosnia is often advanced as an example to be used in the reconstruction of Iraq. The roundtable also discussed the extent to which outside influences and systemic issues have impacted the 2005 Iraq Constitution. Clearly, ideas from Bosnia were emulated; however, there were lessons that were not absorbed into the formulation of the Iraqi Constitution. Specifically, the Iraq Constitution cannot actually be considered a peace agreement like the Dayton Peace Accords, because some groups (namely, the Sunnis) were excluded from the negotiation process.

Given the context of the Balkans, it is difficult to draw straight comparisons, but roundtable participants explored similarities and differences. Two inferences were noted from the Bosnia experience: one relates to IDPs and property rights and the other to creating a nation state. The Dayton Agreement forcibly displaced hundreds of thousands of people into areas where they constituted the majority, thereby allowing the violence to subside and state building to begin. Learning from this Bosnian experience, many scholars have advocated the concept of "soft-partitioning" in Iraq. However, there is substantial debate on its implementation. For example, Micheal O'Hanlon and Edward Joseph advocate for a complete ethnic separation of Iraqis and the establishment of a property swap program—the ultimate goal being to create militarily defensible sub-regions (2007). This type of policy would require substantial oversight to implement. Lessons from Bosnia, moreover, suggest that many of the forcibly displaced were actually temporary evacuations. In Bosnia, there was a mechanism set up for property restitution and a system in which all the forcibly displaced had the right to return and reclaim their former homes and properties regardless of the local sectarian group (Williams, 2008). Although this arrangement had unintended consequences—for example, many sold their original homes instead of returning—at least a formal mechanism existed that allowed them to do so. Property restitution not only restored a degree of economic autonomy in Bosnia, but it also absorbed a significant amount of grievances resulting from the war (Williams, 2008). According to the roundtable participants, the Bosnian case could have helped Iraqi policy makers. Iraqis have not taken it into account, and, again, there is no agreement on how to establish a system and process that guarantees Iraqis the right to reclaim their property.

Another unintended consequence, stemming from an oversight in the formulation of the 2005 Constitution, relates to the creation of an Iraqi state. Under the Dayton Accords, Bosnia and Herzegovina became a federal republic made up of two parts: Republika Srpska and the Federation of Bosnia and Herzegovina—each having their own government, president, parliament and police. The Iraq Constitution, however, is not clear in defining the powers of the central government. Advocates of "soft-partitioning" believe the greatest chance for a stable Iraq lies in further decentralization, increased regional autonomy and mutually accepted limits on power (Evland, 2009). This approach unfortunately marginalizes groups outside the main factions. Shi'a, Sunni and Kurds are not the only groups at the table. As Mokhtar Lamani describes in his chapter, there are many minorities groups involved in Iraq. Furthermore, no agreement has been reached in the constitution with regard to the sharing of oil revenues. Meanwhile Kurds, Turkmen and Arabs all covet the disputed oil-rich city of Kirkuk. Thus, while the Bosnian case clearly has heuristic value, empirical differences must be taken into account to avoid, as one discussant put it, "decontextualized learning."

Participants at the roundtable felt that similar contextual ignorance evident in the US reconstruction strategy led to what one contributor termed "blind driving." This describes the manner by which the US would push toward certain objectives despite clear evidence of failure. For instance, a *New York Times* article describes how the Special Inspector General for Iraq Reconstruction concluded that US$8.8 billion had been provided to Iraqi ministries that claimed pay for thousands of "ghost employees" (Eckholm, 2005). In defence of this, Paul Bremer argued that, in the post-invasion period, it was imperative to rebuild ministries and restore Iraqi salaries (Eckholm, 2005). Ostensibly, the goal was to immediately establish these ministries, regardless of proper institutional architecture or oversight mechanisms, in order to expedite the disbursement of reconstruction funds; allegations of fraud and malfeasance are therefore unsurprising.

Equally important at the roundtable were views on both the lack of civil planning and the mismanagement of the economy. The lack of civil planning created a "reconstruction gap." Projects to rebuild water, electricity, health and oil infrastructure to pre-war levels, had to be scaled back, chiefly due to security concerns. In 2005, State Department Inspector General Howard J. Krongard stated that in extreme cases, 80 percent of project costs were spent on security (Witte, 2005). Similarly, the economy was mismanaged to the point where billions of dollars are unaccounted for. Henry A. Waxman's 2005 congressional report, "Rebuilding Iraq: US Mismanagement of Iraqi Funds," outlines some staggering revelations pertaining to a total absence of oversight of reconstruction funds. The report covers the period from the US invasion (March 2003) to June 2004, when the US-run Coalition Provisional Authority (CPA) transferred power to the interim Iraqi government. The three principle findings presented include approximately $12 billion withdrawn from the Federal Reserve Bank and physically shipped to US officials at the CPA in Iraq. There were virtually no financial controls to account for this money, and no certified accounting firm was hired to audit disbursements. Moreover, key to the vault holding, these funds "[were] kept in an unsecured backpack." Lastly, with no proper financial control, evidence exists indicating that the disbursement of funds was characterized by waste and fraud. In one instance, $7 million in cash simply went "missing." In total, the CPA controlled $23.3 billion in Iraqi funds and spent or disbursed $19.6 billion (see Table 11.2) (US House of Representatives, 2005).

This section of the roundtable ended with a discussion of US withdrawal from Iraq. On the one hand, many believe that the decision to leave Iraq has already been made, especially considering the monthly direct and indirect costs of US$12 billion and US$3 billion, respectively. Deficit reduction is clearly a priority for President Barack Obama; however, it remains unclear *how* exactly US forces will carry out the drawdown. Originally, Obama had advocated for a speedier withdrawal, but the timeline will now be longer, without major reductions until the 2010 elections. Current troops stand at approximately 142,000 and it is expected that

Table 11.2 Iraqi Funds under Coalition Provisional Authority Control (rounded to thousands)

Deposits		
	Development Fund for Iraq (DF)	$20,706,395,000
	Treasury Special Purpose Account (TSPA)	$1,916,496,000
	Seized Iraqi Cash	$926,700,000
	(Transfer from TSPA to DFI)	($208,564,000)
	Total Iraq Deposits under US Control	$23,341,027,000
Withdrawals		
	Disbursements from DFI	$14,059,659,000
	Cash Shipped to Iraq from TSPA	$1,707,931,000
	Seized Cash Disbursed or Obligated	$774,400,000
	Commitments from DFI	$3,104,909,000
	Total Amount Disbursed or Obligated by US	$19,645,899,000
Balance		
	Transferred from CPA to Interim Iraqi Government	$3,695,128,000

Source: United States House of Representatives: Committee on Government Reform, 2005.

they will be reduced to approximately 35,000 to 50,000 by August 2010. (DeYoung, 2009). On the other hand, others note the hard political reality of persistent American interests in Iraq, and therefore doubt the probability of a total US withdrawal. The public face of the operation may leave, but the covert operations will likely remain. Further complicating matters is evidence from a recent US Government Accountability Office (GAO) report. Counterintuitively, withdrawals from previous conflicts have resulted in cost increases rather than reductions in the near term, especially when it comes to closing facilities and turning over military installations (GAO, 2009).

The Role for Middle Powers

Analyses on Iraq often focus on what major powers like the US and the United Kingdom (UK) are accomplishing in Iraq. The achievements or roles of middle powers, however, should also be acknowledged. The concluding discussion at the roundtable focused on this theme.

Although Canada was a focal point of the discussion, its relative lack of involvement was highlighted and compared with states like Norway and Sweden—potential models for future contribution. A general consensus formed among the participants that middle powers could fulfill important roles in Iraq so long as they possessed a certain level of determination. It was agreed around the table that determination and resources are what the Canadian government lacks, especially given its current interest and involvement in Afghanistan.

Billions of dollars are being spent on the Afghanistan mission, and recently Prime Minister Harper stated that, "the war in Iraq was a diversion from the central, the original mission to Afghanistan" (*Embassy Magazine*, 2009). This contradicts his earlier stance as leader of the official opposition, when he openly supported the US-led invasion. In 2003, Harper even advocated joining the US-led "Coalition of the Willing." Some participants speculated that the wrapping up of many Canadian peacekeeping operations had made Canada *persona non grata* in international circles. One participant noted how the concept of "human security" has faded from the lexicon at the Department of Foreign Affairs and International Trade (DFAIT). Human security was originally a concept and agenda advocated by Lloyd Axworthy under Chrétien's Liberal government. Today, however, the Human Security Program at DFAIT has been renamed the Glyn Berry Program for Peace and Security, in honour of the first Canadian diplomat killed in Afghanistan. Moreover, there is a new focus on "Democracy Support and Development." Some argued that such a policy shift is detrimental to Canada's diplomatic standing and may weaken Canada's chances of acquiring one of the two UN Security Council (UNSC) seats that become available in 2010. Furthermore, due to the Harper government's increased support for Israel at the UN, the 56-country Organization of the Islamic Conference will probably vote in a united front against Canada (Edwards, 2009).

Both Norway and Sweden were mentioned by the participants as models for middle-power involvement. The Norwegian government has been very helpful in the efforts to re-build Iraq, both from a military and humanitarian standpoint. Despite abstaining from the 2003 invasion—primarily because there was no UNSC resolution to mandate the war—Norway did allocate US$55 million for humanitarian aid that year to Iraq. In March 2003, Prime Minister Kjell Magne Bondevik delivered a speech pledging Norway's assistance toward restructuring post-conflict Iraq. Furthermore, he stressed his support for peace and stability in the Middle East, including negotiations between Israelis and Palestinians (Government of Norway, 2003). Channelled mainly through the UN, the Red Cross and Norwegian non-governmental organizations (NGOs), Norway's humanitarian aid contributions have provided health care, clean drinking water and the rehabilitation of water treatment plants. In 2004, Norway also funded a United Nations Development Programme

(UNDP) project, Iraq Living Conditions Survey (ILCS), that sought to collect statistical information about living conditions in Iraq. Furthermore, at the request of the UN, the Norwegian government extended its contribution of personnel to help train Iraqi defence forces. Such Norwegian contributions and participation are in response to UNSC Resolutions 1483 and 1511. As Minister of Defence Kristin Krohn Devold put it, "Norway has consistently followed the line taken by the UN, and when the UN asks the world community to support the reconstruction and stabilization of Iraq, we in Norway will wish to respond to that request" (Government of Norway, 2006).

Roundtable participants indicated that Canada seems incapable of doing what the Norwegians have done. Although the experience with Quebec separatism may be relevant in Iraq, Canada's current unwillingness to commit time, talent and resources over the long term squanders an opportunity for a crucial contribution to Iraqi reconstruction. Some discussants remained optimistic, arguing that despite the current Canadian government, Canada could still offer valuable experience given its credibility and knowledge of diversity and federalism. Participants also noted what Canada and other middle powers can do in terms of refugees and IDPs. On the one hand, it was highlighted that Canada needed to put pressure on Prime Minister Nouri al-Maliki not to pass the responsibility onto Syria and Jordan. It was argued that the IDP and refugee situation is primarily Iraq's problem and so the prime minister must find a resolution. On the other hand, an opposing view took issue with Canada pressuring al-Maliki, especially given Canada's current lack of interest in the Iraq situation. Canada could easily play a role in Iraq similar to the Norwegian model, however this was never a priority for the Canadian government during the Bush era, and there is little indication that this will change with the Obama administration.

Another theme concerned the responsibilities of middle powers with regard to refugees, IDPs and assisting asylum-seekers for humanitarian reasons. Here, Sweden was raised as an example of a middle power that has eased the burden of over 2.8 million IDPs in Iraq. Similar to Norway, Sweden provided Iraq with significant humanitarian assistance. According to the Government of Sweden, between 2004 and 2007, it contributed more than US$66 million to Iraq and cancelled approximately US$190 million of Iraqi debt. For instance, the Swedish International Development Cooperation Agency (SIDA) has been working with Iraq's Ministry of Electricity to support long-term capacity building. SIDA has also been involved with United Nations Development Fund for Women

Figure 11.1 Top Five Destination Countries of Iraqi Asylum-Seekers (2008)

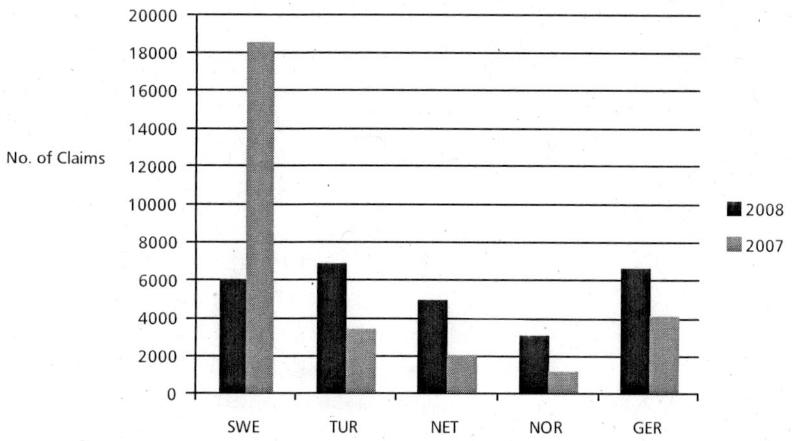

No. of Claims

■ 2008
▨ 2007

SWE   TUR   NET   NOR   GER

Source: UNHCR 2009.

(UNIFEM) to improve gender equality. Furthermore, as a leading donor to the UN personnel protection force, the Government of Sweden has strengthened UN activities in Iraq (Government Offices of Sweden, 2008). Given the considerable number of Iraqis currently living in Sweden this foreign aid is unsurprising.

In a 2007 interview, Tobias Billström, Sweden's Minister of Migration and Asylum Policy, indicated that a central reason for the high number of Iraqi refugees to Sweden relates to the mainly Kurdish Iraqi diaspora. Many Iraqi Kurds moved to Sweden during the 1970s and 1980s to escape the Saddam Hussein regime (Tabeling, 2007). As of 2008, Sweden had accepted more than 80,000 Iraqi refugees or over 50 percent of all the Iraqis who fled to Europe since the 2003 US-led invasion (Clark, 2008). Despite a population of over 30 times that of Sweden, the US accepted only 687 Iraq refugees between April 2003 and March 2007 (Congressional Research Service, 2007). Sweden, however, did state that the majority of Iraqis will have to return to Iraq when security and safety improve. In 2007, a decision was rendered by the Swedish Migration Court that changed asylum claims, noting that the situation in Iraq was no longer one of "armed conflict." Accordingly, when the figures of Iraqi asylum seekers declined by 33 percent between 2007 and 2008 in Sweden, they more than doubled in Norway, up 121% during the same period (UNHCR, 2009).

These types of "safe and voluntary" return policies place returning refugees and displaced persons at risk. Participants noted that the West should accommodate more Iraqi refugees for humanitarian and educational reasons. Canada rates poorly in terms of Iraqi refugee assistance. For instance, approximately 900 Iraqis were resettled in Canada in 2007, and the Canadian government committed to resettling up to 2,000 in 2008. Canada has only recently made a commitment to double the number of privately sponsored Iraqi refugees. This increase consists of an additional 1,300 people per year for the next three years for Iraqis living in Damascus and an additional 230 people for government-assisted refugee claims. The total resettlement figures amount to approximately 2,500 Iraqis per year for its private sponsorship program and 1,400 Iraqis for government-assisted refugees. All the refugees are from Damascus, as this is the area where most claims originate (Citizenship and Immigration Canada, 2009).

Although it was highlighted that refugee assistance is needed, participants were concerned that this continuous migration to the West would create an increasingly homogenous Iraq and would deplete its cultural mosaic. For instance, the Vatican is concerned because Iraq has lost more than half its Christian population. The last official Iraqi census in 1987 found that approximately 1.4 million Christians lived in the country. Subsequently, as of 2008, according to the US State Department, this number has dropped to between 500,000 and 800,000 Christians (Schemm, 2009). The Vatican would like to maintain a Christian presence in the Middle East and is urging the international community to ensure the protection and survival of the Christian population.

Conclusion

The reconciliation and reconstruction initiatives in Iraq are facing several struggles with respect to sectarianism, fragmentation and human rights. The roundtable sought to discuss the issues of concern in Iraq. The problem of IDPs and returning refugees permeated the discussion. It was a principal theme in this chapter and was also highlighted in the context of middle powers. The property rights of IDPs and returning refugees constitute a problematic issue; the Iraqi government will have to alleviate the strain on local capacity and provide hundreds of thousands people with sustainable housing solutions. Chief among the displaced persons are the minority groups who have also been forced out of their homes and suffer from extreme insecurity. Middle power countries like

Sweden and Norway provide support to ease the burden on Iraq, Syria and Jordan, but this assistance is temporary and policies have already been implemented to ensure that Iraqis return to Iraq.

The section on citizenship and federalism found divergent views on how to create a democratic Iraqi state based on citizenship and pluralism. There were several options proposed, and most involved substantial amendments to the current Iraqi Constitution. However, consensus was not reached on which option would be the most beneficial for Iraq. Whether centralized or extremely decentralized, the major issue is that political compromise among the key political factions is unlikely. The Constitution contains several outstanding issues that are yet to be resolved and needs clarification on other issues. Until the major actors decide what they would like Iraq to become, and exactly what they are willing to share in terms of power, Iraq will remain fragmented.

The lessons from the comparative cases section evaluated the case of Bosnia, which is often cited as an example for Iraqi reconstruction. The discussion pointed to the various similarities and differences in both countries. Different perspectives were found when discussing the Dayton Accords and their applicability to the Iraqi Constitution. There were proponents who advocated for a three-party approach for Iraq federalism, while others cautioned against this approach due to the major divisions that exist within the main political parties in Iraq. In many cases of foreign intervention, proper assessments and evaluations of the country are not performed, which often leads to mistakes on the ground. The case of Iraq is no different, as there were both errors in civil planning and the mismanagement of reconstruction funds.

Finally, the roundtable discussed the role of middle powers. Canada possesses extensive knowledge regarding federalism and separatist issues due to the experience with Quebec nationalism. Canada's reluctance to become involved in Iraq—essentially due to the political decision made in 2003 not to enter Iraq without a UN resolution and, in turn, taking part in the Afghanistan mission—prevents this potentially valuable knowledge from being applied in the Iraqi context. Sweden and Norway have been able to provide humanitarian, refugee and reconstruction assistance despite, or perhaps owing to, both states maintaining a neutral stance on the 2003 invasion and neither state endorsing the war. Conversely, Canada's situation diverges from that of Sweden and Norway in that, although it did not join the US-led invasion, current Prime Minister Stephen Harper advocated joining the war as leader of the opposition. This was negatively perceived among the Arab states and continues to affect Canadian foreign policy in the Middle East; consequently, Canadian neutrality has been compromised.

Note

1 Aside from Sunni, Shi'a and Kurds, Palestinians have also been displaced along with members of the following minority groups: Christian, Chaldean and Assyrian sects, Yazidis, Shabak, Turkmen, Sa-bean-Mandean, Bahai, Jews, Faili Kurds and Roma communities.

Works Cited

Cameron, David (2007). "Making Federalism Work" in *Iraq: Preventing a New Generation of Conflict*, edited by Markus E. Bouillon, David M. Malone and Ben Rowswell. Pages 153–68. Boulder, CO: Lynne Rienner.

Citizenship and Immigration Canada (2009). "News Release: Canada to Double Number of Iraqi Refugees." Ottawa, Canada. February 11. Available at: http://www.cic.gc.ca/english/department/media/releases/2009/2009-02-11.asp.

Clark, Mandy (2008). "Sweden Home to More Iraqi Refugees Than Other European Countries." *Voice of America*. February 20. Available at: http://www.voanews.com/english/archive/2008-02/2008-02-20-voa21.cfm?CFID=266340508&CFTOKEN=83724621&jsessionid=00305e8795f9a498baa31c58146d65474a22.

Congressional Research Service (2007). *Iraqi Refugees and Internally Displaced Persons: A Deepening Humanitarian Crisis?* Washington, DC: CRS Report for Congress. March 23. Available at: http://fpc.state.gov/documents/organization/82978.pdf.

DeYoung, Karen (2009a). "Obama Sets Timetable for Iraq." *The Washington Post*, February 28. Page A01.

——— (2009b). "GAO Calls Iraq Pullout a 'Massive,' Costly Effort." *The Washington Post*. March 25. Page A07.

Eckholm, Erik (2005). "The Struggle for Iraq: Capitol Hill; Lawmakers, Including Republicans, Criticize Pentagon on Disputed Billing by Halliburton." *The New York Times*. June 22.

Edwards, Steven (2009). "Support Grows for Canada's Spot on the UN Council." *National Post*. May 23.

Embassy Magazine (2009). "Iraq Was Distraction: Harper." April 8.

Evland, Ivan (2009). "Warning from Bosnia for Iraq." *The Independent Institute*. March 23. Available at: http://www.independent.org/newsroom/article.asp?id=2463.

Government Offices of Sweden (2008). "Iraq." Stockholm, Sweden. May 9. Available at: http://www.sweden.gov.se/sb/d/8899.

Government of Norway (2003). "Ready to Help Rebuild Iraq." *News of Norway*. March 24. Available at: http://www.norway.org/News/archive/2003/200301 iraq.htm.

——— (2006). "Norway Remains in Iraq." *News of Norway*. March 27. Available at: http://www.norway.org/News/archive/2004/200402iraq.htm.

Human Rights Watch (2006). "The Silent Treatment." November 27. Available at: http://www.hrw.org/en/reports/2006/11/27/silent-treatment.

International Displacement Monitoring Centre (IDMC) (2008a). "Bosnia and Herzegovina: Broader and Improved Support for Durable Solutions Required." Geneva, Switzerland: Norwegian Refugee Council. August 28. Available at: http://www.internal-displacement.org/8025708F004BE3B1/ (httpInfoFiles)/CE1A75CBBAA2EC23C12574B300362341/$file/Bosnia_ Overview_Aug08.pdf.

——— (2008b). "Challenges of Forced Displacement within Iraq." Geneva, Switzerland: Norwegian Refugee Council. December 29. Available at: http://www.internal-displacement.org/8025708F004BE3B1/(httpInfoFiles)/ 07A9E0C588CD5FECC12575240047DB82/$file/Iraq_Overview_Dec08.pdf.

Jamail, Dahr (2009). "Iraq: Still Homeless in Bagdad." *IPS* February 19. Available at: http://www.ipsnews.net/news.asp?idnews=45812.

Lamani, Mokhtar (2009). "Reconciliation in Iraq: Singular or Plural." *Turkish Weekly*. May 30.

Marr, Phebe (2007). "Iraq's Identity Crisis," in *Iraq: Preventing a New Generation of Conflict*, edited by Markus E. Bouillon, David M. Malone and Ben Rowswell. Pages 41–54. Boulder, CO: Lynne Rienner.

McGarry, John and Brendan O'Leary (2007). "Iraq's Constitution of 2005: Liberal Consociation as Political Prescription." *International Journal of Constitutional Law*. Vol. 5, No. 4: 670–98.

O'Hanlon, Michael E. and Edward P. Joseph (2007). "A Bosnia Option for Iraq." *The American Interest*. January–February. Available at: http://www.the -american-interest.com/article.cfm?piece=229.

Refugees International (2008). "Uprooted and Unstable: Meeting Urgent Humanitarian Needs in Iraq." Washington, DC. April 15. Available at: http://www.refugeesinternational.org/policy/in-depth-report/uprooted -and-unstable-meeting-urgent-humanitarian-needs-iraq.

——— (2009). "Iraq: Preventing the Point of No Return." Washington, DC. April 9. Available at: http://www.refugeesinternational.org/policy/field -report/iraq-preventing-point-no-return.

Schemm, Paul (2009). "In Iraq, an Exodus of Christians." *The Connecticut Post*, May 14.

Tabeling, Petra (2007). "Billström Interviewed on Iraq Refugees in Sweden." *Middle East Online*. September 26. Available at: http://www.middle-east-online .com/english/?id=22365=22365&format=0.

United Nations Assistance Mission for Iraq (UNAMI) (2004). "Emergency Working Group-Falluja Crisis: Update Note." November 13. Available at: http://www.uniraq.org/documents/Humanitarian%20Update%20on%20 Falluja%20-%2013%20Nov.pdf.

United Nations High Commissioner for Refugees (UNHCR) (2009). "Asylum Levels and Trends in Industrialized Countries; 2008: Statistical Overview of Asylum Applications Lodged in Europe and Selected Non-European Countries." Geneva: The UN Refugee Agency, March 24. Available at: http://www.unhcr.org/statistics/STATISTICS/49c796572.pdf.

——— (2007). *UNHCR Statistical Yearbook 2007*. Geneva: The UN Refugee Agency.

United States Government Accountability Office (GAO) (2009). "Iraq: Key Issues for Congressional Oversight." Washington, DC. March 24. Available at: http://www.gao.gov/new.items/d09294sp.pdf.

United States House of Representatives—Committee on Government Reform (2005). "Rebuilding Iraq: U.S. Mismanagement of Iraqi Funds." Washington, DC: Minority Staff, Special Investigations Division. June. Available at: http://oversight.house.gov/documents/20050621114229-22109.pdf .

Williams, Rhodri C. (2008). "Applying the Lessons of Bosnia in Iraq: Whatever the Solution, Property Rights Should Be Secured." Washington, DC: The Brookings Institution. January 8. Available at: http://www.brookings.edu/papers/2008/0108_iraq_williams.aspx.

Witte, Griff (2005). "U.S. Faces Iraq 'Reconstruction Gap.'" *The Washington Post*. October 19.

12

Reinventing Iraq
Binding the Wounds, Reconstructing a Nation

Nathan C. Funk

Whither Iraq? For three decades, Iraqis have experienced trauma on an epic scale, culminating in a tragic and relentless demolition of hope amid years of civil strife and occupation. Clearly, the Iraq that once was can offer only limited guidance for the future, because the past cannot be restored and reinstated. Too many lives have been lost, and too many shared dreams have been shattered. And yet possibilities remain. Even after years of internecine conflict and generations of tension between Sunni and Shi'a, Arab and Kurd, the *idea* of Iraq retains surprising vitality. Even in the wake of repeated political disasters, the endurance of a resourceful, capable and remarkably diverse people persists.

Despite the desperation and disarray of recent years, hasty conclusions about a nation's demise are unwarranted. Indeed, attentiveness to the *longue durée* of history suggests that it would be unwise to underestimate the resilience of a people who inhabit the heartland of numerous empires and whose ancestors' contributions to civilization include writing and the wheel. Neither desolation nor reconstruction is new to the Iraqi experience, and a land that only recently boasted one of the Middle East's most well-educated and professional workforces seems likely to rise again.

In the near term, of course, Iraq's challenges are formidable and its needs manifold. The American campaign to remake Iraq from the inside out provides a sobering, cautionary tale for those who would presume to change the course of another society by force of arms. Although the present shift in American priorities from occupation toward military withdrawal represents a welcome development, it would be naive to presuppose that the course of events in Iraq will now run smoothly. Iraq will need diverse forms of external engagement and support; in the absence of such support and engagement, the probabilities of relapse increase relative to the possibility of remission. Rudimentary international morality and enlightened self-interest appear united in calling for goodwill efforts to support the Iraqi people as they grapple with problems to which outsiders have undeniably contributed.

The analyses provided in this volume testify not only to great human suffering but also to the existence of a number of distinct challenges that are potentially responsive to new policy initiatives, by Iraqis as well as by members of the international community. There are many areas in which North Americans, Middle Easterners and peoples of other regions can offer partnership and assistance as Iraqis seek not only to advance the cause of reconstruction but also to reinvent and renew their society.

Desolation and Beyond

As Mokhtar Lamani and Bessma Momani note in the introduction, Iraq has never been a monolithic entity. The country's pluralism remains a deeply rooted reality, and its governance problems are longstanding. Despite tremendous progress in the domains of infrastructure and modernization, Philip Ireland's assessment in 1937 remained valid for decades:

> Within the country still lie the problems of the creation of a social class of citizens, now beginning to appear, capable and willing to assume political duties from a sense of public duty and not of personal aggrandizement, the evolution of a free Press motivated by public spirit rather than by individual or party grievances, the assurance of free elections, and the elimination of sectarian and sectional animosities which will eradicate the antipathies between tribesmen and townsmen, will bring the Shi'a into the body politic, will create a real bond between Kurds and Arabs, and provide adequate protection to all minorities within the State. (Ireland, 1937: 452–53)

Persistent and often heavy-handed state efforts to instil an authoritative Iraqi and Arab nationalism failed to correct and indeed often reinforced the underlying patterns of social, political and economic exclusion to which Ireland alluded. As a consequence, the Iraqi state failed to achieve political stability and social peace, and instead perpetuated conditions that were highly consistent with Edward Azar's theory of protracted social conflict. As Azar noted in numerous publications, most of the world's armed conflicts since World War II have transpired in developing nations plagued by deep social cleavages and by persistent governance problems linked to competition among communal groups for control of the state and privileged access to resources. The resultant patterns of discrimination, exclusion and government corruption serve to entrench rivalry between ethnic and cultural groups, and generate grievances linked to denial of basic human needs for identity, security, participation and development. Societies afflicted by these conditions, Azar proposed, are highly vulnerable to further destabilization caused by external pressures and international interventions (1990; see also Fisher, 1997: 77–97).

As a Lebanese-American political scientist, Azar's inquiry into the causes and dynamics of protracted social conflict was motivated in no small part by the painful events of Lebanon's civil war (1975–90), yet his formulations apply with equal force to an Iraq divided between Sunni Arabs and Shi'a Arabs as well as Arabs and Kurds, and within which diverse additional ethnic and religious groups also aspired toward identity, dignity and security. Although ideological conformity and profession of allegiance to Arab nationalism provided a route of upward mobility and allowed for the emergence of a well-educated, professional middle class within which intermarriage was not uncommon, underlying tensions and contradictions were never resolved.

Peter Sluglett's review of tragic developments in recent Iraqi history reveals how fragile these gains proved to be. By the 1990s, combined pressures and traumatic losses associated with war, stringent international sanctions and oppressive misrule had caused a widespread retreat from the state throughout Iraqi society, together with a concomitant reinvestment of loyalty in the primordial institutions of family, tribe, kin network and sect. With the US invasion of 2003, the collapse of shared national visions and the resurgence of sub-state loyalties accelerated dramatically. In the absence of a cohesive and truly national Iraqi opposition, only Shi'a and Kurdish parties were able to demonstrate coherence and viability on the country's chaotic and contested political stage. Sadly, liberation from the brutality of Saddam Hussein's rule inaugurated an even more harrowing period of transition during which the facade of peaceful coexistence among Iraq's many communities was torn away.

Nonetheless, despite manifold lesions and fractures in the Iraqi body politic, David Cameron rightly observes that the prospect of an Iraqi partition or dismemberment appears remote, with greater potential threats to territorial integrity arising from the regional environment than from within the boundaries of the fractious state. Bitter inter-communal politics and militia-based violence notwithstanding, commitment to the idea of Iraq remains widespread. Although such a heartfelt commitment is understandably absent in Kurdistan, the Kurdish leadership has nonetheless made a strategic choice to operate within a federalized Iraqi national framework, despite negative historical experiences. As Maria Fantappié emphasizes, the Kurdish Regional Government has adopted a strategy of maximizing autonomy while remaining loosely within the overall framework of the Iraqi state and attempting to influence policy in the nation's political centre.

The current reality of Iraq, then, is one of asymmetrical federalism, with the Kurdish region embracing the federal principle far more readily than the rest of the country, and with the current Shi'a leadership promoting a centralized political vision in which the Sunni community is reduced to minority status and some Kurdish gains reversed. As a result of the open-ended nature of the 2005 Iraqi Constitution, basic issues of internal political structure remain unresolved, as does the standoff between Kurdistan and the central government over the oil-rich region of Kirkuk. To date, the al-Maliki government has demonstrated little interest in either reconciliation or power sharing with other groups. Recognizing dangerous potential for renewed hostilities, David Romano wisely argues for concerted efforts to bridge the deep divide between Iraqi Kurds and Arabs, ideally in pursuit of a "grand bargain."

To this call for renewed efforts at political reconciliation, Mokhtar Lamani adds an additional plea for the construction of a common Iraqi identity predicated on equal citizenship and respect for human rights. The need for such a layer of shared identity as well as for affirmation of equal humanity and citizenship can be seen not only in the grave toll of civil war on the general Iraqi populace, but also in the disproportionate impact of violence and dispossession on Iraq's religious and cultural minorities. Heightened intolerance and war-induced dispersion pose a threat to the very survival of Iraq's smallest minority groups, many of which had subsisted in the land for millennia. The condition of these groups is yet another consequence of an Iraqi political culture in which distrust among political and religious groups has reached alarming heights. Lamani notes that, without the restoration of a shared vision and a measure of trust, diverse contenders for power will continue to react to one another and assert unreasonable demands rather than engage in more constructive forms of political advocacy and negotiation. Leaders who are willing to pursue a genuinely inclusive process of political reconciliation rather than seek to consolidate power bases are sorely needed.

Such a process of political and indeed social reconciliation is vitally needed if there is to be a sustainable economic recovery—a development that, Joseph Sassoon reminds us, will depend in no small part on a restoration of human security and a reversal of the Iraqi brain drain. After 2003, Iraq's already grave loss of human capital accelerated dramatically, causing the country to lose much of its former professional middle class. Consequences for health, management, higher education and politics have been profound; creating conditions for the return of exiled Iraqi talent is therefore one of the most important priorities for—and instruments of—national reconstruction.

Additional keys to an Iraqi recovery include international humanitarian assistance and further restructuring of the Iraqi national debt. Carla Angulo-Pasel documents notable international efforts to coordinate aid for post-war Iraq, as well as failures of political leadership and multilateral coordination. As Bessma Momani observes, international debt renegotiations have had similarly mixed results. The United States used substantial leverage to settle many outstanding Iraqi debts on favourable terms but failed to persuade Iraq's immediate neighbours in the Gulf region, particularly Saudi Arabia and Kuwait, to embrace debt forgiveness. This reluctance on the part of Iraq's neighbours is attributable in large part to lingering residues of past international confrontations, as well as to concerns about rising Shi'a power and growing Iranian influence. The al-Maliki government's resistance to integrating the Sunni community in the political process has become a significant source of tension with Iraq's Sunni-majority Arab neighbours.

Although the new Iraqi government has made progress in the direction of diplomatic acceptance within the Middle East, significant stumbling blocks remain. The country's new government still bears the stigma of having been created after the US invasion, and the turbulence surrounding its birth has reinforced regional ambivalence. As Rex Brynen argues, the overall demonstration effect of the US-led Iraq invasion has been minimal for most regional publics and regimes, and has thus far contributed little to the advancement of popular sovereignty and democratic rule in the region. The invasion has, however, contributed to recruitment into radical networks and deepened distrust of US intentions, even as the spectre of anarchy in Iraq has diminished public enthusiasm for potentially destabilizing political mobilizations and reinforced claims of the national security state vis-à-vis domestic and international critics. A renewal of democratic vigour and of conciliatory gestures in Iraq's experiment with competitive politics might not fully correct for these developments but (in combination with a lower American profile) would likely reduce regional ambivalence about cooperating with the new Iraq to enhance mutual security and develop a strategy for resolving the status of Iraq's three million refugees.

The uncertain future of Iraq's 2.8 million Internally Displaced Persons (IDPs) is another vital issue for Iraq's new government to confront. In her summary of insights from a roundtable discussion among contributors, Angulo-Pasel provides a compelling depiction of a society that has become more deeply factionalized than ever, with Baghdad's urban landscape transformed into a patchwork of "ethnically cleansed" sectarian neighbourhoods. The current Iraqi government lacks a coherent and impartial approach to problems of internal displacement and the associated title crisis, further adding to the grievances of the country's Sunni population while also contributing to the misery of other minority groups. Even if dealing with the IDP problem were a genuine priority, however, there are questions about the government's actual capacity to perform. No mechanism for property restitution or guaranteeing the right of return has been devised, nor has support for housing solutions been forthcoming.

The problem of IDPs underscores the vital importance of genuine political commitment to national reconciliation and to forging a sense of national citizenship capable of embracing Iraq's many competing communal identities. The persistence of political violence highlights the crucial question of how to bring the Sunni community back into the political process in a way that might correct its marginalization during the drafting of the 2005 Constitution and the elections that followed. Power sharing among Iraq's communities has become imperative, yet the current leaders of a once-oppressed Iraqi Shi'a constituency are not yet in a conciliatory mood and the level of US commitment to helping bridge the Sunni–Shi'a divide remains uncertain.

Seeking a Way Forward: Priorities for International Engagement

Iraq has made progress in recent years, yet the overall political situation in the country remains fragile, with many fundamentally important issues unresolved. In the absence of significant progress toward social as well as political reconciliation, apparent gains in the security sector and in state capacity are tentative and reversible.

At the present juncture, there is a need for the US to become more proactive in supporting national reconciliation measures as the Obama administration proceeds with a withdrawal strategy. Although military withdrawal should indeed proceed, US policy makers should be encouraged to resist the temptation to entrust stability and peace to Iraqi leaders who appear convinced that greater national unity can be achieved by centralizing authority and maximizing their own control of state power. For anyone with a memory of twentieth-century Iraq, this is a familiar strategy and yet one that has not demonstrably succeeded. Given continued signs of insurgency and the ongoing political marginalization of Iraq's Sunni community, the US exit strategy may fail unless Iraqi leaders can be persuaded to engage in serious negotiations on formulas for political coexistence, including power sharing as well as enhanced regionalism, institutional reform and broad-based economic empowerment measures.

Although only Iraqis can temper communal identity politics through adherence to rule of law, a wide range of potential interlocutors can encourage Iraq's leaders to draw upon traditional precedents and resources when making the argument for rule-bound coexistence as opposed to the rule of force. These precedents and resources include tribal law (*'urf*), historical Islamic practices associated with the accommodation of cultural diversity (Said and Sharify-Funk, 2003), and national pride in the law codes of the ancient Sumerians as was in the subsequent code of Hammurabi. Furthermore, Iraq's role as the cradle of civilization can be invoked to support an inclusive ethos of Iraqi citizenship as well as the rule of law, for both traditional Mesopotamia and the modern Iraqi state have always been multicultural (O'Leary, 2009).

Middle powers, such as Canada, can play a role in encouraging regional states to work constructively with the Iraqi national government, and to not play a spoiler role in the ongoing political transition. While advocacy of national reconciliation should be welcome, Iraq's fragile communal politics can easily be aggravated by Saudi partisanship on behalf of Sunnis, Iranian encouragement of Shi'a majoritarianism, Turkish intervention in Iraqi Kurdistan, and so forth. A theme that bears repeating is that a successful political transition in Iraq will bring benefits to all of Iraq's neighbours, including the prospect of refugee resettlement. Given its obvious interest in preserving present international borders and its growing role in regional conflict resolution efforts, Turkey might be encouraged to use its Sunni identity as a bridge for engaging the Arab world on matters pertaining to the future of Iraq (O'Leary, 2009).

In the long term, the ultimate success of these and other measures will depend on the extent of a deeper process of reconciliation within Iraqi society. This process cannot be imposed, but it can be supported and facilitated. Much thought should therefore be devoted to the content of new educational curricula emphasizing the many voices of Iraqis, as well as to the creation of spaces and forums in Iraqi society (including libraries and museums as well as community centres, parks and theatres) within which reconciliation might be discussed, meetings held, diverse heritages shared and new cultural symbols discovered (Said, 2004: 3–8; see also Said, 2009). In addition to encouraging the formation of a uniquely Iraqi truth and reconciliation commission modelled on values inherent in the Arab-Islamic tradition of *musalaha* (reconciliation) (Funk and Said, 2009) and supporting localized reconciliation processes, Iraqi leaders and their international partners can provide funds for exploring post-trauma healing and visions of a new Iraq through the arts (Said, 2004: 4–6).[1] Special efforts should also be devoted to enabling research on past modes of coexistence and to preserving Iraq's rich cultural and religious heritage sites as means of affirming the continuities of history and embracing the country's diverse contributions to civilization. Eventually, historical preservation efforts—alongside ecological restoration, as in the case of the southern marshes and the Marsh Arabs, and urban renewal—might pay dividends in the form of tourism and enhanced economic vitality (Said, 2004: 8–9).

A Role for Canada

In the years since the US invasion, Canada has not been a major player in Iraq. Although there are some who would argue that Canada's choice to abstain from involvement in the US-led war minimizes the country's potential contributions to Iraq-related diplomacy and reconstruction efforts, a case can also be made that the position taken in 2003 enhances possibilities for Canadian involvement in peacemaking should Canadian leaders seek to play a role.

In her chapter on the International Reconstruction Fund Facility for Iraq (IRFFI), Angulo-Pasel points out that Canada was among the first countries to engage with the IRFFI and offer aid to Iraq immediately after the end of hostilities in 2003. Canadian leaders were initially open to playing a significant role in multilateral as well as bilateral efforts to support Iraqi society. Soon, however, concerns about an increasingly volatile security situation added to an already deep discomfort with the war, curtailing serious Canadian involvement in reconstruction and humanitarian assistance activities. Under the Harper government, the shift away from involvement with Iraqi and other Middle Eastern issues continued, even as greater emphasis was placed on devoting Canadian resources and efforts to Afghanistan. Canada is now significantly less engaged with Iraq than other middle powers such as Norway and Sweden.

The rationale for Canadian–Iraqi engagement is strong. The direct and immediate stakes for Canada are modest, yet the opportunities to make a positive and noteworthy contribution are substantial. Indeed, the specificities of the Canadian historical experience and tradition of Middle East diplomacy provide diplomats with significant assets. These assets include rich experience with federalism, firsthand knowledge of challenges inherent in managing a multi-national state with a democratic separatist movement, a past commitment to Middle East refugee issues, historical activism as a middle power and substantial expertise on matters of human security (Heinbecker and Momani, 2007). At a time when the US is actively seeking to withdraw military forces from Iraq, there are fewer reasons not to engage. Through active efforts to forge linkages between governmental and civil society organizations, Canadians can support Iraqi efforts to develop institutions appropriate to their distinctive values, culture, and needs. Such engagement can include efforts to bolster "soft" capacity building and training by providing consultations and funds (O'Leary, 2009). Given major losses of capacity and expertise in Iraqi government institutions, such assistance is genuinely needed. By forging new relations and resonating with the contemporary Iraqi experience, Canadians may well find that there is much they have to offer, to share, and to learn.

Note

1 Said recommends that, "just as pictures and statues of Saddam used to stand at every corner, so too should Iraqi authorities with the financial assistance of the international community seek to create a new renaissance whereby images of ALL Iraqi faces adorn the society" (2004: 6).

Works Cited

Azar, Edward. (1990). *The Management of Protracted Social Conflict*. Hampshire, UK: Dartmouth Publishing.

Fisher, Ronald J. (1997). *Interactive Conflict Resolution*. Syracuse, NY: Syracuse University Press.

Funk, Nathan C. and Abdul Aziz Said (2009). *Islam and Peacemaking in the Middle East*. Boulder, CO: Lynne Rienner.

Heinbecker, Paul and Bessma Momani (eds.) (2007). *Canada and the Middle East: In Theory and Practice*. Waterloo, ON: Wilfrid Laurier University Press.

Ireland, Philip Willard (1937). *Iraq: A Study in Political Development*. New York: Russell & Russell.

O'Leary, Carole A. (2009). Personal communication/conversation with Nathan Funk. School of International Service, American University. September 23.

Said, Abdul Aziz (2004). "Unity in Diversity: The Cultural Mosaic of Iraq." Unpublished paper presented to the "First Cultural Forum on Iraq." UNESCO Headquarters, Paris. May 26–27.

——— (2009). "Educating for Global Citizenship: Perspectives from the Abrahamic Traditions," in *The Meeting of Civilizations: Muslim, Christian, and Jewish*, edited by Moshe Ma'oz. Pages 177–86. Brighton, UK: Sussex Academic Press.

——— and Meena Sharify-Funk (2003). *Cultural Diversity and Islam*. Lanham, MD: University Press of America.

Contributors

Carla Angulo-Pasel
Carla Angulo-Pasel is a Research Officer at The Centre for International Governance Innovation (CIGI), where she coordinates global and human security projects and oversees North American governance projects. She holds a Master of Arts degree in political science, specializing in international relations, from Wilfrid Laurier University. Her research interests focus on the implications of intra-state conflict on internally displaced persons (IDPs) and refugees.

Rex Brynen
Rex Brynen is Professor of Political Science at McGill University. He has authored, edited, or co-edited eight books on Middle East politics, including, *Persistent Permeability? Regionalism, Localism, and Globalization in the Middle East* (Ashgate, 2004) and *Political Liberalization and Democratization in the Arab World* (Lynne Rienner, 1995 and 1998).

David Cameron
David Cameron, FRSC, is Chair and Professor of Political Science at the University of Toronto. His professional career has been divided between public service—in Ottawa and at Queen's Park, Ontario—and academic life. A long-time student of Canadian federalism and Quebec nationalism, in the last decade he has turned his attention to ethno-cultural relations and constitution making in emerging or potential federal countries, such as Iraq and Sri Lanka.

Maria Fantappié
Maria Luisa Fantappié graduated from the department of Middle Eastern studies at Sciences po Paris with an MPhil dissertation about the role of irregular armed forces for state rebuilding in post-Saddam Iraq (2009). She is currently a PhD candidate at Sciences Po Paris and continuing her research about state rebuilding and the army establishment in contemporary Iraq.

Nathan C. Funk
Nathan C. Funk, Ph.D., is Assistant Professor of Peace and Conflict Studies at the University of Waterloo's Conrad Grebel University College, with previous appointments at American University and George Washington University. His writings on international affairs, the Middle East, and peace building include *Peace and Conflict Resolution in Islam* (University Press of America, 2001), *Ameen Rihani: Bridging East and West* (University Press of America, 2004), and *Islam and Peacemaking in the Middle East* (Lynne Rienner, 2009).

Aidan Garrib
Aidan Garrib is a Senior Risk Analyst with an investment firm in Toronto. He completed his MA in International Political Economy with a dissertation examining the reorientation of Canadian economic interests from protectionism to free trade. In addition to his MA, Aidan Garrib holds degrees in economics and political science, during which he analyzed competition in energy markets and the politics of international trade.

Mokhtar Lamani
Mokhtar Lamani is a Senior Visiting Fellow at The Centre for International Governance Innovation (CIGI), specializing in international affairs and conflict resolution. He is the former Special Representative of the Arab League in Iraq and Ambassador of the Organization of the Islamic Conference to the UN. His most recent publications include the *CIGI Special Report: Minorities in Iraq: The Other Victims* (2009).

Bessma Momani
Bessma Momani is Associate Professor at the University of Waterloo and Senior Fellow at The Centre for International Governance Innovation (CIGI), specializing on the Middle East and IMF. She is the author of *Twentieth Century World History* (Nelson Education, 2007), *IMF-Egyptian Negotiations* (American University in Cairo Press, 2005), the *CIGI-CIC Special Report: The Future of International Monetary Fund: A Canadian Perspective* (2009) and is the co-editor of *Canada and the Middle East* (WLUP, 2007). Dr. Momani has also published a dozen scholarly articles in numerous political and economic academic journals.

David Romano
David Romano is Assistant Professor of International Studies at Rhodes College and a Senior Research Fellow at the Inter-University Consortium for Arab and Middle East Studies. In addition to numerous articles on Middle East politics, the Kurdish issue, forced migration, political

violence, and globalization, he is the author of *The Kurdish Nationalist Movement* (Cambridge University Press, 2006). He has spent several years studying and conducting field research in Turkey, Iraq and Israel/Palestine, in addition to briefer research trips to other parts of the Middle East.

Joseph Sassoon
Joseph Sassoon, a Senior Associate Member at St. Antony's College Oxford, is currently a Visiting Scholar at Georgetown University. His recent book, *The Iraqi Refugees: The New Crisis in the Middle East* (Palgrave Macmillan, 2009) deals with Iraqi refugees after the 2003 invasion. Other publications under his name include *Economic Policy in Iraq, 1932–1950* (Frank Cass, 1987), and he has also written articles on Iraq and other Middle Eastern economies.

Peter Sluglett
Peter Sluglett is Professor of Middle Eastern History at the University of Utah, Salt Lake City. In addition to over 80 articles on Iraq, he is the author of *Britain in Iraq: Contriving King and Country* (I.B. Tauris, 2007) and co-author of *Iraq Since 1958: From Revolution to Dictatorship* (I.B. Tauris, 2001).

Index

A

Ahmad, Ibrahim, 22
Ahmad Chalabi, 14–15
al-Duri, Izzat Ibrahim, 28
Algiers Accord, 79
al-Hasan, Abd, 27
al-Karim, Abd, 53, 56
Allawi, Ali, 15
Allawi, Ayad, 15
al-Majid, Ali Hasan ("Chemical Ali"), 27
al-Maliki, Prime Minister Nuri, 25, 58–59, 63–65, 83, 88
al-Qaeda and 9/11, 37
al-Qaeda in Iraq (AQI), 29, 35, 43, 45, 92n18, 101, 108, 169
al-Sadr, Muhammad Baqir, 25
al-Sadr, Muhammad Sadiq, 15
al-Sadr, Muqtada, 24
ALUBAF. *See* Arab International Bank (ALUBAF)
Ansar al-Islam, 81, 92n18
AQI. *See* al-Qaeda in Iraq (AQI)
Arab International Bank (ALUBAF), 165
Arab–Israeli peace process, 26
Arab League, 68, 95, 141
Arab news networks reports, 182
Arab regional perceptions of Iraqi events, 178
Armenians, 105
Assyrian American National Federation, 106
Assyrian National Council of Illinois, 106
Assyrians, 40, 68, 98–99, 105
Axworthy, Lloyd, 203

B

Baathification of the Iraqi army, 76. *See also* de-Baathification
BACB. *See* British Arab Commercial Bank (BACB)
Banca Nazionale del Lavoro (BNL), 165
Barzani, Mas'ud, 22–23
Barzani, Mullah Mustafa, 53, 56, 60–61
Bazaaz Declaration 1966, 53, 56
BBC. *See* British Broadcasting Corporation (BBC)
bin Laden, Osama, 35
BNL. *See* Banca Nazionale del Lavoro (BNL)
Bosnia and Herzegovina, 198–99
Bosnia-Herzegovina government, 197
Bremer, Ambassador Paul: Baath Party, dismantle political infrastructure of, 145; as civilian administrator of CPA, 118; de-Baathification policy, 4, 42, 119, 121, 124; Iraqi army disbanded, 81, 92n19, 121; "vibrant private sector" objective, 119, 127
British Arab Commercial Bank (BACB), 165
British Broadcasting Corporation (BBC), 99, 141–42
Bush, President George H.W., 18, 20
Bush Administration, 2, 180, 185
Buzan, Barry, 5

C

Canada, 8, 136, 146–48, 150–51, 218–19

Canadian International Development Agency (CIDA), 51n11, 136, 146–48, 150
Central Intelligence Agency (CIA), 23, 113
Chalabi, Ahmad, 14
Chaldean American Chamber of Commerce, 106
Chaldean Federation of America, 106
Chaldeans, 68, 105
Chaldo Assyrians, 40
Chrétien government, 146, 150, 203
Christians, 8, 98–99, 101–2, 105–6, 108–9, 111
CIA. *See* Central Intelligence Agency (CIA)
CIDA. *See* Canadian International Development Agency (CIDA)
citizenship, 9, 68, 96, 100, 104, 108–9, 111
Coalition Provisional Authority (CPA): Congress approved $18.4 billion for Iraq's reconstruction, 119; crisis mode, nonstop, 119; Federal Reserve Bank, no financial controls to account for $12 billion from, 201; Iraq Core Group and IRFFI's governance structures, 136; Iraqi army disbanded by Paul Bremer, 81, 92n19; Iraqi funds controlled ($23.3 billion) and spent or disbursed ($19.6 billion), 201–2; Iraqi government, sovereignty transferred back to, 120; IRFFI's governance structures, 136; managers, shortage of competent, 119; money spent on small, vital projects, 119; Oil-for-Food Program, 14, 99, 119; Paul Bremer as civilian administrator of, 118; "Rebuilding Iraq: US Mismanagement of Iraqi Funds" report, 130n6, 201
Commission on Public Integrity, 123
Constitutional Review Committee, 38–39, 49
"Copenhagen School" of security studies, 5–6
corruption, 23, 69–70, 120–23, 129, 164, 184, 187
CPA. *See* Coalition Provisional Authority (CPA)
creditors: Iraq's remaining, 167–69; London Club, 9, 155, 165–66; non–Paris Club, 161–62, 167; Paris Club, 8–9, 155–59, 161–70; Paris Club meeting, 158; private, 9, 155–56, 165–66, 170; private commercial, 156–57; repayment, sought largest possible amount of, 155; UNSC Resolution prevented creditors from resolving their debt claims by litigation or attempting to attach liens on Iraqi energy resources, 156, 166, 170; US coaxed creditors to forgive Iraqi debt on moral grounds, 156
CRRPD. *See* Iraq Commission for Resolution of Real Property Disputes (CRRPD)

D

Dayton Peace Agreement (DPA), 199
Dead Sea Donor Committee meeting, 142, 144
de-Baathification policy, 4, 42, 119, 121, 124
debt restructuring, 155–57; conclusion, 170–71; creditors, Iraq's remaining, 167–69; debt stock (2004–10), estimated external, 157; Debt Sustainability Analysis (DSA), 161; donor pledges, international, 160–61; Emergency Post-conflict Assessment (EPA), 162; International Compact for Iraqi debt forgiveness, 167–68; International Monetary Fund (IMF), 155–65, 170; Iran's influence over Shi'a leaders in Iraq, 169, 171, 215, 217; Iraq Debt Reconciliation Office, 166; Iraqi

INDEX   227

debt relief as prerequisite to American "success" in Iraq, 156; Iraq's GDP, 156; Iraq's public debt, 156; Iraq's reparation payments and UN Security Council, 156; Kuwait, 156, 159–60, 167–79; London Club, 155, 165–66; London Club Coordination Group (LCCG), 165; non–Paris Club creditors, 161–62, 167; Paris Club, 8–9, 155–59, 161–70; Paris Club and the IMF, bargaining Iraqi debt relief, 157–64; Persian Gulf states, 156, 167; private commercial creditors, 156–57; private creditors, 155–56, 165–66, 170; public debt, external, 162; Qatar, 151, 156, 159–61, 168; sanctions, United Nations–led, 156; Saudi Arabia, 156, 159–60–161, 167–70; Stand-by Agreement (SBA), 163–64; United Arab Emirates (UAE), 156, 159–60, 167–68, 188n2; US and need to share burden of reconstruction, 158–59; US Congress organized debtor and donor conference, 157; US influence on the UN Security Council for debt relief, 170; US intervention in the IMF staff's DSA analysis, 170; US-sponsored UN Security Council Resolution 1483 to decrease Iraqi reparations, 165–66, 171n1

Debt Sustainability Analysis (DSA), 161–62

Debt Sustainability Assessment (DSA), 8, 170

Department of Foreign Affairs and International Trade, Canada (DFAIT), 203

DFAIT. *See* Department of Foreign Affairs and International Trade, Canada (DFAIT)

Diamond, Larry, 29–30

Donor Committee: Chair of the, 139–40, 145–46, 148–50; IMF as observer status on, 138; IRFFI, 8, 136–39, 142–45, 148–50; World Bank Iraq Trust Fund and UN Development Group Iraq Trust Fund, 151

donor pledges, international, 160–61

DPA. *See* Dayton Peace Agreement (DPA)

DSA. *See* Debt Sustainability Analysis (DSA); Debt Sustainability Assessment (DSA)

E

Eastern Europe: changes in late 1980s, 16; Communist Party in, 28; creditors, private, 166; democratic change, 179, 187; democratic consolidation, EU support of post-communist, 179; regimes in, collapse of, 17; state enterprises, party members and officials formed backbone of, 28; Warsaw Pact collapse and transformation of, 176

Edward Azar's theory of protracted social conflict, 212–13

elections: in 1992, free, 56; in 2010, 43–44; both national and provincial, 39, 43, 48; democratic, 36; of January 2005, 37; of January 2009, provincial, 44, 48; law crisis pushed minorities out of political process, 111

Emergency Post-conflict Assessment (EPA), 162–63

EPA. *See* Emergency Post-conflict Assessment (EPA)

ethnic cleansing, 2, 54, 56–57, 99–100, 120, 198

ethnic identity, 2, 68, 99

European Community, 160

European Union (EU), 141–42, 179–80

F

Facility Coordination Committee (FCC), 139
Faili Kurds, 108
FCC. *See* Facility Coordination Committee (FCC)
federal: arrangements, asymmetry in Iraq's, 48; consciousness, growth in, 45–47; developments, post-constitutional, 41; system, future evolution of new, 47–49
federalism, 7, 9, 36, 40–48, 54, 59, 68
Freedom House, 176–77
Fukuyama, Francis, 175

G

G7. *See* Group of 7 (G7)
G8. *See* Group of 8 (G8)
G20. *See* Group of 20 (G20)
GAO. *See* Government Accountability Office (GAO) [US]
GDP. *See* gross domestic product (GDP)
genocide, 24, 198
Glaspie, Ambassador April, 18
Global War on Terror (GWOT), 185, 188
Government Accountability Office (GAO) [US], 124, 202
Government of Iraq, 13–14, 54–55, 137, 139, 145, 148, 194
Graham, Minister Bill, 146
Graham-Brown, Sarah, 20, 22
"Green Line," 60
gross domestic product (GDP), 144, 156–57
Group of 7 (G7), 158
Group of 8 (G8), 141, 176
Group of 20 (G20), 147
Gulf War (1990–91), 41, 54, 56, 107, 117, 157, 178
GWOT. *See* Global War on Terror (GWOT)

H

Harling, Peter, 20
Harper, Stephen, 147–48, 150
Hashemite Monarchy, 75
Hizb al-Da'wa (Islamic movement), 24–25
HRW. *See* Human Rights Watch (HRW)
human cost of conflict, 44
humanitarian aid, 53, 192, 203
human rights: abuses against Iraqi Kurdistan, 54; protection mandated by UN conventions, 110; respect for, 36, 40, 68–70
Human Rights Watch (HRW), 192
Huntington, Samuel, 179–80
Hussein, Kamil, 27
Hussein, Saddam, 16, 21, 26–27, 29, 60, 64, 75, 77
Hussein, Saddam Kamil, 27
Hussein, Udayy, 27, 29

I

ICDC. *See* Iraqi Civil Defense Corps (ICDC)
ICG. *See* International Crisis Group (ICG)
ICI. *See* International Compact with Iraq (ICI)
IDMC. *See* International Displacement Monitoring Centre (IDMC)
IDPs. *See* internally displaced persons (IDPs)
IDRO. *See* Iraq Debt Reconciliation Office (IDRO)
IFI. *See* international financial institutions (IFI)
ILCS. *See* Iraq Living Conditions Survey (ILCS)
IMF. *See* International Monetary Fund (IMF)
infant mortality rate, 144
Integrated Regional Information Networks (IRIN), 121, 123–24
internally displaced persons (IDPs): assistance on return to homes, 194; Canada and refugees, 204; ceasefires enacted by Sunni and Shi'a militias, 195; Centre for International Governance Innova-

tion (CIGI), 191; Dayton Peace Agreement (DPA), 199; genocide, war crimes and ethnic cleansing contributed to, 198; Government of Iraq lacks capacity or will to proved basic services to, 194; government underreports numbers of, 193; IRFFI and, 138; land title crisis in Iraq, 193; middle powers responsibilities for, 204; number in Iraq, 192–93, 198, 204, 216; political commitment to national reconciliation, 216; property rights and, 191–95, 199, 206; roundtable report, 9, 198–99, 204, 206; UN High Commission for Refugees (UNHCR), 192
international aid agencies, 22
International Compact with Iraq (ICI), 137, 143, 167–68, 171n6
International Crisis Group (ICG), 65, 81
International Displacement Monitoring Centre (IDMC), 192, 198
international financial institutions (IFI), 135, 159–60
International Monetary Fund (IMF): assessment of debtors' capacity to repay, 155; creditors sought largest possible amount of repayment, 155; debt regime, classical sovereign, 155; debt restructuring agreements, 155; debt stock, Iraq's estimated external, 157; Debt Sustainability Assessment, US pressure to give favourable, 8, 161–62, 170; Donor Committee, observer status on, 138; donor pledges for Iraq, international, 160; in dual role as judge of country's capacity for repayment and monitor of debtor economic and fiscal policies, 155; Emergency Post-conflict Assessment (EPA), 162–63; needs assessment, 137; Paris Club, debt rescheduling plan for, 155; Paris Club used IMF formula for Iraq's debt forgiveness, 8; pledged funds in form of loans, 159; Stand-by Agreement (SBA), 163–64, 170; structural adjustment policies, supported, 184; US Congress pressured IMF to cancel outstanding claims, 158; US pressured IMF to underestimate Iraq's ability to repay debt, 156, 170; US urged creditors to forgive Iraqi debt on moral grounds, 156
International Reconstruction Fund Facility for Iraq (IRFFI), 135–36; Bremer dismantled infrastructure of Baath Party, 145; Canada and, 8, 136, 146–48, 150–51, 218–19; Canadian International Development Agency (CIDA), 51n11, 136, 146–48, 150; Chair of the Donor Committee, 139–40, 145–46, 148–50; Chair of the Executive Committee, 140; Chair of the Iraqi Strategic Review Board (ISRB), 139, 148; conclusion, 149–50; coordination challenges, 140–46, 148; Dead Sea Donor Committee meeting, 142, 144; deficiencies in planning, management and oversight, 148; donor commitments to World Bank Iraq Trust Fund and United Nations Development Group Iraq Trust Fund, 151; Donor Committee, 8, 137–50; Donor Committee meeting, Istanbul, 145; donor coordination of reconstruction and assistance programs, 138; donor funds managed by international organization vs. US, 136; Executive Committee, 138–40; Facility Coordination Committee (FCC), 139; governance structures, 136; Group Iraq Trust Fund (UNDG-ITF), 137–38;

230   INDEX

infant mortality rate, 144; internally displaced persons (IDPs), 138; International Compact with Iraq, 143, 150; international cooperation, as mechanism to promote, 135; International Monetary Fund (IMF), 137–39; Iraq International Conference, 141; Iraqi Transitional Government, 144, 168; Iraq's National Development Strategy (NDS), 137, 139–40, 144–45; kidnappings and increased casualties, 147; lessons learned, 148–49; Ministry of Planning and Development Cooperation (MoPDC), 121, 138, 140, 145; as multi-donor approach to Iraq reconstruction effort, 8; Multi-Donor Trust Funds (MDTFs), 135–36, 149; a multilateral reconstruction mechanism, 136; oversight lacking, no physical presence in Iraq, 149; rebuilt infrastructure susceptible to militia attacks, 144; reconstruction aid for Iraq, US$48 billion in, 143; reconstruction efforts, multilateral solution for, 149; safety of personnel on ground being threatened, 144; sectarian violence escalated, 150; structure of, 136–40; Terms of Reference (TOR), 134, 137–39; United Nations Development Group (UNDG), 135, 137–40, 144–45, 149, 151; UNSC Resolution 1483, 135, 138, 171n1, 204; UNSC Resolution 1483 and donors, 135; UNSC Resolution 1511, 138, 204; UNSC Resolution 1770, 138; US unilateralism, 142; World Bank, 135–41, 144–45, 149, 151; World Bank Iraq Trust Fund (WB-ITF), 137–38, 151

Iran: Ansar al-Islam, US army to destroy, 81; Ansar al-Islam and al-Qaeda guerrilla fighters on Iraq–Iran border, 92n18; Ba'th's stance against, 17; displaced persons returning from, 100; donor pledge to Iraq, 160–61; Faili Kurds, 108; Iranian Revolution in 1979, 25–26; Iranian troops entered area controlled by PUK, 23; Iran–Iraq War (1980–88), 6, 16–18, 25, 28, 79, 91n14, 98, 117; Iraqi democracy with Shi'a majority, supported, 182; Iraqis fled to, 21; Iraqi Shi'is in exile in Iran, umbrella organization of, 25; Iraq's politics, Iranian influence on, 9; Kurdish autonomous region, boundaries of, 56; "Kurdish autonomy" provoked, 23; Kurdish identity and, 22; Kurd population in, 31n15, 67–68, 70; Mandaeans in Southern, 103; "Oil for Soil" report, 65; Shi'a leaders in Iraq, Iranian influence over, 169, 171, 186, 215, 217; Shi'a power, Iranian influence over, 215, 217; Shi'is objective to create Islamic state in Iraq, 24; terrorist groups and weapons of mass destruction, support for, 176; US agenda of regime change in Iraq, 181

Iranian Kurdish Democratic Party (KDPI), 91n14

Iranian Revolution of 1979, 25–26

Iran–Iraq War (1980–88), 6, 16–18, 25, 28, 79, 91n14, 98, 117

Iraq: Baghdad's walled city, 2; brain drain of professional class, post-invasion policies caused, 8; British and Arab nationalists tried to craft an Iraqi state identity, 1; Bush Administration's rush to impose democracy, 2; centrist social order, violence for those that challenged, 6; citizenship, 9, 68, 96, 100, 104, 108–9, 111; civil peace, US-led coalition unable to keep, 4; "Copenhagen School" of security studies, 5–6; counter-insurgency operations, 5; de-Baathification policy, 4, 42, 119, 121, 124; democracy with Shi'a majority, 182; democratic process, lack of elite consensus for, 5; ethnic and sectarian politics, decentralized state marred by, 2; ethnic cleansing reflects radicalization of ethnic identity, 2; ethnic consideration in all aspects of governance, education policies to tax policies, 2; ethnic political parties and radicalization of interests, 2; ethno-political dynamics of Iraq's new institutions, 2; ethno-sectarian groups and future federalism, 7; ethno-sectarian lines organized along, 1; federalism, 9; funds and spent or disbursed by CPA, 201–2; GDP, 156; Green zone, 4; Gulf neighbours' reluctance to forgive Iraqi debt, 9; humanitarian law and Iraqi insurgency, 5; human toll of war on ordinary citizens, 4; IDPs and refugees, repatriation and property rights for, 9; Iraqi state as an Arab nation, myth of, 1; Iraqi state as decentralized and fragmented society, 5; Kirkuk and Ninawa province, status of, 2; Kurdistan and new oil law, 2; Kurds pursuit of decentralized Iraq, 7; Kuwait invasion in 1990, 7, 13–18, 26, 28, 56, 121; new Iraqi army, 8; oil revenues, state's distribution of political spoils from, 6; politics dominated by Iranian influence, 9; public debt, 156; public debt, external, 162; reconstruction can't be achieved without sustainable security, 2; Saddam Hussein, authoritarian rule of, 1; sanctions, twelve years of, economic, 6; security examined in literature, 3–6; Shi'a uprising in Iraq's south and in Kurdistan, 7; social order and Iraq's manufactured state identity, 1; Talabani, Jalal, 22–23, 31n14; US influence after US military withdrawal, 4; US invasion and mainstream Islamist movements, 9; US invasion and occupation in 2003, 1; US military worked to implement regime change, 4; US occupation, follies and challenges of administering, 4; US plans for Iraqi state-building exacerbate internal Iraqi divisions, 5

Iraq, reinventing, 211–12; Canada, role for, 218–19; communal identity politics, 217; desolation and beyond, 212–16; Edward Azar's theory of protracted social conflict, 212–13; inter-communal politics and militia-based violence, 214; Internally Displaced Persons (IDPs), numbers of, 216; internecine conflict of Sunni and Shi'a, Arab and Kurd, 211; Iraqi Constitution 2005, 214; Iraqi Kurds and Arabs, deep divide between, 214; Lebanon's civil war, 213; minority groups, intolerance and war-induced dispersion of, 214; Obama and withdrawal strategy, 217; primordial institutions of family, tribe, kin network and sect, 213; seeking way forward: priorities for international engagement, 216–18; US invasion and collapse of shared national visions, 213; US invasion and little advancement of popular sovereignty or democratic rule in region, 215

Iraq Center for Research and Strategic Studies, 44

Iraq Commission for Resolution of Real Property Disputes (CRRPD), 194

Iraq Core Group, 136
Iraq Debt Reconciliation Office (IDRO), 165
Iraqi asylum seekers, destination countries for, 205
Iraqi Civil Defense Corps (ICDC), 88
Iraqi Communist Party, 23
Iraqi Constitution 2005: Iraqi federalism at year four, 35, 38–41, 46–47, 49; Iraqi Kurdistan and, 53–54, 57–58, 61, 68; Iraqi minorities and, 110; reinventing Iraq, 214; roundtable report, 191, 195, 199, 207
Iraqi federalism at year four, 35–36; *balanced federation* option, 47; central institutions, growing strength of, 41–43; Chaldo Assyrians, 40; cleavage, social and economic, 41; conclusion, 49–50; constitutional government and federal government, 36–40; Constitutional Review Committee, 38–39, 49; Constitution of 2005, 35, 38–41, 46–47, 49; election in 2010, general, 43–44; elections, both national and provincial, 39, 43, 48; elections, democratic, 36; elections in 1992, 56; elections of January 2005, 37; elections of January 2009, provincial, 44, 48; equal citizenship, 68; federal arrangements, asymmetry in Iraq's, 48; federal consciousness, growth in, 45–47; federal developments, post-constitutional, 41; federalism, Iraq's experience with, 40–43; federal system, future evolution of new, 47–49; human cost of conflict, 44; human rights, respect for, 36, 40, 68–70; Iraqi National Police, 42, 54; KRG Constitution, 42–43; Kurds, 40, 42, 44–48, 50; national identification, 44–45; new regions, no strong desire to create, 44–45; partial federalism option, 47; political parties, sectarian, 43, 46; regions and governorates, differentiation between, 49; rule of law, 36, 39, 138, 141, 196, 217; sectarian conflict and emergence of cleavages, 43–44; sectarian conflict within Arab community, 39, 41, 43–44; Shi'a, 37, 39, 45–46, 54; Sunni, 37–39, 42–43, 45–46; Sunni insurgents, 43; Sunni leadership turned against al-Qaeda in Iraq, 45; survival concerns vs. niceties of constitutional government, 38; Turkmen, 40, 56, 58, 61, 68, 106–7; warring communities and wait for US exit, 43

Iraqi Kurdistan, 53–55, 75–77; Algiers Accord, 79; al-Maliki, Nouri, 58–59, 63–65, 83, 88; anti-terrorist techniques learned from US Army, 82; Arab-dominated federal government in Baghdad, 63; Arab–Iraqi political parties, 54, 58, 63; Arab–Kurdish conflict and 2009 provincial elections, 58–62; Arab–Kurdish distrust, 69; Arab–Kurdish relations, 55–56; Arab leadership of new Iraqi army, 90; Arab leaders in Baghdad intent on centralizing Iraqi state power, 70; Autonomy Accords 1970, 53, 56; Baathification of the Iraqi army, 76; Bazaaz Declaration 1966, 53, 56; chemical weapons massacres and *Anfal* campaigns, 56; Coalition Provisional Authority (CPA) disbanded Iraqi army, 81; conclusion, 89–90; Constitution 2005, 53–54, 57–58, 61, 68, 77, 91n7; "ethnic federalism," human rights and equal citizenship for all Iraqis, 68; genocidal campaigns of the 1980s, Baghdad's, 56, 60; governorates, uprising in the southern and northern, 75; "Green Line," 60;

human rights abuses against, 54; identity-based conflict in Iraq, 69; International Crisis Group (ICG), 65; Iraqi army, progressive deterioration of, 76; Iraqi state, preventing another failed, 62–68; Islamic Supreme Council of Iraq (ISCI), 58–59, 61–65, 67, 71n5; Joint Anglo–Iraqi Statement of Intent Regarding the Kurds, 55; KRG leaders intent on maintaining Kurdish autonomy, 70; KRG oil exports via Turkey, 70; KRG oil revenues, 70; Kurdish–Arab competition as political struggle in central institutions of government, 90; Kurdish autonomy, 53–54, 56–57, 67–70, 83, 89; Kurdish autonomy and implications, 68–71; Kurdish bid for statehood, 67; Kurdish Front (Democratic-Patriotic Alliance), 54; Kurdish minority, 53–54; Kurdish participation in rebuilding Iraqi army, 77; Kurdish re-engagement with Iraq: de jure autonomy and the 2005 Constitution, 57–58; Kurdish Regional Government (KRG), 76–77, 81, 83, 85, 87; Kurdish resistance movement, 79; "Kurdish special forces," 81; Kurdistan Democratic Party (KDP), 56–57, 69; Kurdistan National Guard, 63; Kurdistan Regional Government of Iraq (KRG), 54–55, 57–70; Kurds, 40, 42, 44–48, 50; League of Nations Commission, 55; military intelligence personnel (*asaysh*), 80; Mosul, 88–89; new Iraqi Army, 76–78, 81, 84–90; Nouri al-Maliki's "State of Law" party, 58; "Oil for Soil" report, 65; Patriotic Union of Kurdistan (PUK), 56–57, 69, 79–80, 82–83, 88, 91n14; Peshmerga (Kurdish fighters), 57, 59–60, 62–63, 76–90, 90n1, 91n9, 91n14, 92n18; Peshmerga movement, 76–79, 82, 89, 91n9; Peshmerga pensions paid from Baghdad, 63; Peshmerga Security Forces, 77–83, 87; populations, Kurdish, Arab, Turkmen and Christian, 61; Republican Guard forces and Saddam Hussein's army, 57; Republican Guards, Saddam's, 19–20, 24, 27, 57, 80–81; Rustamiyah Military Academy in Baghdad, 78–80, 84, 88, 91n10; Sunni, 37–39, 42–46, 54–55, 70; Sunni Arab Hadba party, 61; Sunni Awakening Councils, 32n22, 54, 59, 62, 184; Talabani, Jalal, 22, 31n14, 79; Tawafuq Sunni Arab Iraqi Islamic Party, 54, 61, 196; training centres in Erbil, Dohuk, Sulaymaniyah and Kirkuk, 79; US security guarantees for the KRG, 65; US Special Forces Group, 81; Washington Institute for Near East Policy, 62–63, 65; Zakho and Sulaymaniyah military academies, 77, 85, 88; Zakho Military Academy, 80, 85–88; Zerevani Peshmerga Security Forces, 81–83

Iraqi minorities, 95–97; al-Qaeda and suffering of Shi'a Shabak and Shi'a Turkmen, 108; "Arabization" and "correction" campaigns, 107; Armenians, 105; Assyrians, 40, 68, 98–99, 105; Chaldeans, 68, 105; Christians, 98–99, 101–2, 105–6, 108–9, 111; Christians in Mosul, violence against, 99; conclusion, 111–14; Constitution 2005, 110; election law crisis pushed minorities out of political process, 111; ethnic identity, "correcting," 99; ethnic/religious composition, estimates of pre- and post-2003, 109; ethno-religious groups and major tribes, 113; extremism threatens minorities to point of extermination, 112; human rights protection mandated by UN conventions, 110; Imam Mullah Farzanda and "good Muslims to kill any Yezidis in Iraq," 102; Iraqi Minorities Council, 104; Iraqi Turkmen Human Rights Research Foundation, 107; Islamic extremists attack Yezidi, 102; Jewish population, 108; Kurds, 20, 98, 194, 196–97, 200; Mandaeans, 98, 101, 103–5, 109; Middle Eastern minorities and hostility from extremist groups, 96; minorities and lack of access to basic necessities, 100–101; minorities since 2003, 97–101; minority communities vs. major political parties, 110; minority groups, other, 108–9; Oil-for-Food program and Assyrian prohibited from using their ration cards, 99; refugees, internally displaced, 100; sectarianism in Iraqi society, post-2003 rise of, 98; sectarian violence between Sunnis and Shi'as, 103; sectarian violence vs. national reconciliation, 95; socio-political challenges, 109–11; Sunni al-Qaeda militants targeted Yezidi, 101; Syriacs, 105; Turkmen, 98, 101, 106–9; Turkmen, forced removal and deportation of, 107; US invasion and occupation destroyed Iraq's social tissue, 111; US invasion and occupation exacerbated the vulnerable of Iraq's minorities, 99; US invasion and sectarian violence against Iraqi Christians, 105; violence, intra-sectarian and extremist, 109; violence and forced displacement, 99–100; violence may lead to extinction of ancient groups, 103; Yezidis, 68, 98, 101–3, 109

Iraqi Minorities Council, 104
Iraqi National Police, 42, 54
Iraq International Conference, 141
Iraqi Shi'is in exile in Iran, 25
Iraqi Strategic Review Board (ISRB), 139, 148; Chair of the, 139, 148
Iraqi Transitional Government, 144, 168
Iraqi Turkmen Human Rights Research Foundation (SOITM), 107
Iraq Living Conditions Survey (ILCS), 204
Iraq's economy and brain drain: academics and doctors flee, 123–25; academics and professionals assassinated, 123–24; academics and terror and violence on campus, 126; Bremer and dissolution of Iraqi Army, 121; Bremer and need for "vibrant private sector," 119, 127; Bremer's decree of de-Baathification, 4, 42, 119, 121, 124; Commission on Public Integrity, 123; Congress had allocated $21 billion for Iraq's reconstruction, 119; corruption and wasteful reconstruction efforts, 122–23; corruption as part of Iraq, 122; corruption pervasive, 120; emigration of highly skilled, 129–30; enterprises, closure of small and family-oriented, 120; government's incompetent management and corrosive corruption, 129; health sector brain drain, 124; higher-education institutions damaged, 125–26; humanitarian crisis, Iraqi officials reluctant to recognize, 127; hyperinflation and collapse of Iraqi dinar, 117; internal displacement of more than 2.7 million people, 120; Iraqi exiles post-2003 invasion, estimates of, 117; Iraq's resources, political parties want control of, 129; kidnappings

connected to sectarian strife, 123; Kurdistan benefits from exodus of skilled professionals from central and southern Iraq, 130; looting of ministry buildings, universities, 118–19; middle class as driver of democratization, 126; Oil-for-Food Program, 14, 99, 119; oil prices and inflation, 122; oil revenues, country's dependence on, 118; ORHA's planning for postwar period, false assumptions of, 118; professionals, urban middle class, 117; professionals, well-educated, 118, 211, 213; property disputes spark violence, 128; Special Inspector General for Iraqi Reconstruction (SIGIR), 122; unemployment and inflation, high levels of, 120, 127; violence and ethnic cleansing, 120

Iraq's National Development Strategy (NDS), 137, 139–40, 144–45

Iraq under siege (1990–2003), 13–15; Ahmad, Ibrahim, 22; Ahmad Chalabi and secular Shi'is in exile in Washington, 14–15; al-Hasan, Abd, 27; Ali Hasan al-Majid ("Chemical Ali"), 27; arms support from Soviet Union, 17; arms support from West, 17; Badr brigades tortured Iraqi prisoners, 25; Barzani, Mas'ud, 22–23; Ba'th against communism and Iran, 17; Ba'th Party in power since 1968, 26; CIA funding of organizations, 23; Compensation Commission and levy on oil revenues, 14; conclusion, 28–30; coup attempts in 1992, 26–27; demobilization of army and limited employment opportunities, 16; Desert Storm in 1991, failure of, 29; genocide waged against Marsh Arabs, 24; human rights record, 17; Hussein, Kamil, 27; Hussein, Saddam Kamil, 27; Hussein, Udayy, 27, 29; internecine family feuding, 27; Iran in 1988, defeat of, 17; Iran–Iraq War, 28; Iraqi Communist Party, 23; Iraqi intelligence sought and executed opponents of regime, 23; Iraqi politics 1991–2003, 26–28; Iraq invasion of Kuwait, background to, 16–19; Islamic Supreme Council of Iraq (ISCI), 24–25; Kurdish and Shi'i uprisings of 1991, 15; Kurdish autonomous region, creation of, 22; Kurdish autonomy and concerns of Turkey and Iran, 23; Kurdish politics since 1991, 22–24; Kurdistan Democratic Party (KDP), 22–23; Kuwait invasion in 1990, 7, 13–18, 26, 28, 56, 121; Kuwait's Rumayla oilfield takeover, 18; law and order break down, 14; Mahdi Army and Muqtada al-Sadr, 24–25; oil exports to United States, 17; oil-for-food program as intrusion on Iraq sovereignty, 14, 21; oil prices, 26; oil revenue, national revenue from, 13; Patriotic Union of Kurdistan (PUK), 22–23; Republican Guard brutality against uprisings in southern Iraq and Kurdistan, 19–20; Saddam Hussein, Shi'i parties opposed, 14; Saddam Hussein as anti-imperialist, 16; Saddam Hussein's fortune, sources of, 21; Saddam Hussein's posturing on liberation of Palestine, 26; Saddam Hussein used coercion and patronage, 29; Sadrist Movement, 15; sanction and UN inspections, 20–22; sanctions and indiscriminate punishment of the innocent, 21; sanctions and the regime's Machiavellian purposes, 28; sectarianism in Iraqi politics, 15; Shi'i politics since 1991, 24–25;

Shi'is close relationship with Iran, 24; Shi'is discriminated against by Iraqi government, 24; Shi'is objective for an Islamic state in Iraq, 24; Shi'i society, 15, 31n16; Shi'i south and Kurdistan, rising in, 19–20; strategic arsenal built by US and West, 17; Supreme Council for the Islamic Revolution in Iraq (SCIRI), 24–25; Talabani, Jalal, 22–23, 31n14; Tariq 'Aziz, 28; UN agencies charged with weapons inspection and supervising sanctions, 22; UN High Commissioner for Refugees (UNHCR), 22; United Nations Resolution 661, 20, 30n4; United Nations Resolution 678, 19; United Nations Resolution 687, 30n4; United Nations Resolution 986, 21; United Nations Resolution 1153, 21; United Nations resolutions, 13–14; United States and Israel, campaign against, 18; UN Security Council's resolutions condemning invasion of Kuwait, 19; UN Special Commission on Disarmament (UNSCOM), 21–22; US and Britain encouraged uprisings against Iraqi regime, 19; US-organized anti-Iraq coalition of 30 states, 19; weapons of mass destruction, US false claims of, 14, 21, 29

Iraq war and (non)democratization in the Arab world, 175–78; "Anbar Awakening" in Iraq, 184; Arab news networks report violence and other negative aspects of US policy, 182; Arab regional perceptions of Iraqi events, 178; Bush Administration and new Hamas-led government, 185; Bush Administration and US policy, region harbours suspicion toward the, 180; *democratic good governance* option, 186; *descent into violence* option, 186; *increasing authoritarianism* option, 186–87; Iraq and Islamist mainstream, 184–85; Iraq and jihadist movements, 182–85; Iraq conflict as *cause célèbre* for jihadists, 183; Iraqi government as puppet installed under US occupation, 180; Iraqi insurgencies against Coalition forces, 183; Iraqi Sunni insurgent movements, 184; Iraqi violence conducted by al-Qaida in Iraq (AQI), 181; Islamist political parties opposed to US foreign policy, 184–85; jihadist movements, growth of violent, 183; Justice and Development Party (Morocco), 184; Kurdish autonomy under protection of US no-fly zone, 178; looking back and ahead, 185–88; Middle East Partnership Initiative, 176; Muslim Brotherhood (Egypt), 184; Muslim Brotherhood/Islamic Action Front (Jordan), 184; "Plan of Support for Reform," 176; political rights and civil liberties, comparative, 177; political rights and civil liberties for Middle East and North Africa, 177; regime transition in Iraq, 179–82; regional environment hostile to US reformism, 182; resentment of US involvement in Muslim world, 183; sectarian violence and terrorism of AQI, 184; US agenda of regime change, 181; US invasion increased radical Islamist recruitment, 183; US invasion radicalized militant Islamist movements in Middle East, 182–83; weapons of mass destruction, 14, 26, 29, 176

IRFFI. *See* International Reconstruction Fund Facility for Iraq (IRFFI)

IRIN. *See* Integrated Regional Information Networks (IRIN)
ISCI. *See* Islamic Supreme Council of Iraq (ISCI)
Islamic Republic of Iran, 25
Islamic Supreme Council of Iraq (ISCI), 24–25, 57–59, 61–65, 67, 71n5
ISRB. *See* Iraqi Strategic Review Board (ISRB)
Istanbul Donor Committee meeting, 145

J

Jewish population, 108
jihadists, 38, 138
Joint Anglo–Iraqi Statement of Intent Regarding the Kurds, 55

K

KDP. *See* Kurdistan Democratic Party (KDP)
KDPI. *See* Iranian Kurdish Democratic Party (KDPI)
Khomeini, Ayatollah, 25
kidnappings, 104, 123, 147
KRG. *See* Kurdish Regional Government (KRG)
KRG Constitution, 42–43
Kurdish: autonomy, 23, 53–54, 56–57, 67–70, 83, 178; identity, 22, 107, 196; politics since 1991, 22–24; population in Iran, 31n15, 67–68, 70; separatism, 196; and Shi'i uprisings of 1991, 15
Kurdish Alliance, 61, 196
Kurdish Regional Government (KRG), 7–8, 22, 40, 42, 56–57, 60, 76, 84, 126, 214
Kurdistan Democratic Party (KDP), 22–23, 56–57, 78–90, 92n17
Kurdistan new oil law, 2
Kurds, 20, 98, 194, 196–97, 200; Iraqi federalism at year four, 40, 42, 44–48, 50; population of, 31n15; pursuit of a decentralized Iraq, 7
Kuwait, 156, 159–60, 167–79

Kuwait invasion (1990), 7, 13–18, 26, 28, 56, 121
Kuwait's Rumayla oilfield takeover, 18

L

Law of Administration for the State of Iraq for the Transitional Period (TAL), 51n4
LCCG. *See* London Club Coordination Group (LCCG)
Lebanon's civil war, 213
London Club, 9, 155, 165–66
London Club Coordination Group (LCCG), 165

M

Makiya, Kanan, 15
Mandaeans, 8, 98, 101, 103–5, 109
MDTF. *See* Multi-Donor Trust Fund (MDTF)
Mesopotamian region, 95–96
Middle East Partnership Initiative, 176
Ministry of Planning and Development Cooperation (MoPDC), 121, 138, 140, 145
MNF. *See* multinational force (MNF)
MoPDC. *See* Ministry of Planning and Development Cooperation (MoPDC)
Multi-Donor Trust Fund (MDTF), 135–36, 149
multinational force (MNF), 92n20
Muslim Brotherhood (Egypt), 184
Muslim Brotherhood/Islamic Action Front (Jordan), 184

N

Nasser, Gamal Abdel, 18
National Development Strategy (NDS), 137, 139–40, 144
NATO. *See* North Atlantic Treaty Organization (NATO)
NDS. *See* National Development Strategy (NDS)
Netanyahu, Binyamin, 26
9/11. *See* September 11, 2001 (9/11)

238 INDEX

non-governmental organizations (NGOs), 22, 136, 203
non–Paris Club creditors, 161–62, 167
North Atlantic Treaty Organization (NATO), 141, 147, 194, 199

O

OAS. *See* Organization of American States (OAS)
Obama, President Barack, 50, 112, 188, 201, 204, 217
Office of Reconstruction and Humanitarian Assistance (ORHA) [US], 118
Oil-for-Food Program, 14, 21, 99, 119
"Oil for Soil" report, 65
OPEC. *See* Organization of the Petroleum Exporting Countries (OPEC)
"Operation Iraqi Freedom," 81
Organization of American States (OAS), 180
Organization of the Petroleum Exporting Countries (OPEC), 17
ORHA. *See* Office of Reconstruction and Humanitarian Assistance (ORHA) [US]
Ottoman Empire, 1

P

Palestine Liberation Organization (PLO), 18
Paris Club, 8–9, 155–70
Patriotic Union of Kurdistan (PUK), 22–23, 56–57, 79–80, 82–83, 88, 91n7, 91n14, 92n17–18
People, State, and Fear (Buzan), 5
Persian Gulf states, 156, 167
Plan of Attack (Woodward), 3
"Plan of Support for Reform," 176
PLO. *See* Palestine Liberation Organization (PLO)
private commercial creditors, 156–57
private creditors, 155–56, 165–66, 170
PUK. *See* Patriotic Union of Kurdistan (PUK)

Q

Qatar, 151, 156, 159–61, 168

R

"Rebuilding Iraq: US Mismanagement of Iraqi Funds" report, 130n6, 201
Republican Guards, 19–20, 24, 27, 57, 80–81
roundtable report: debating the issues, 191; Bosnia and Herzegovina, 198–99; Bosnia-Herzegovina government, 197; Canada, 202–4, 206–7; humanitarian crisis in Iraq, 192; Centre for International Governance Innovation (CIGI), 191; citizenship and federalism, 195–98; civil planning lacking, mismanagement of economy, 201; conclusion, 206–8; displacement, sectarian violence as major cause of, 192; federalism in Iraq, 196–97, 204, 207; human rights, 196, 206; internally displaced persons (IDP), 191–95, 198–99, 204, 206; Iraq Commission for Resolution of Real Property Disputes (CRRPD), 194; Iraq Constitution and powers of central government, 200; Iraqi asylum seekers, top destination countries for, 205; Iraqi Constitution 2005, 191, 195, 199, 207; Iraqi funds under Coalition Provisional Authority Control, 202; Iraqi voter turnout for January 2005 elections, 198; Iraq Living Conditions Survey (ILCS), 204; Kurdish Alliance, 196; Kurdish separatism, 196; lessons from like cases, 198–202; middle powers, role for, 202–6; Ministry of Displacement and Migration, 194; Norway, 202–5, 207; oil revenue sharing, 200; policy of enticing refugees back to Iraq, 194; "Rebuilding Iraq: US Mis-

management of Iraqi Funds," 201; Refugees International report, 195; rule of law, 196, 217; Special Inspector General for Iraq Reconstruction findings, 200–201; Sweden, 202–5, 207; Swedish International Development Cooperation Agency (SIDA), 204; Swedish Migration Court and asylum claims, 205; UN estimates of refugees in Jordan and in Syria, 193; UN High Commission for Refugees (UNHCR), 192–93, 198–99, 205; United Iraqi Alliance, 196; UNSC Resolutions 1483 and 1511, 204; US army facilitated ethnic reorganization of Iraq into sectarian enclaves, 193; US-run Coalition Provisional Authority (CPA) transferred power to interim Iraqi government, 201

rule of law, 36, 39, 138, 141, 196, 217

Rustamiyah Military Academy in Baghdad, 78–80, 84, 88, 91n10

S

Sabian Mandaean Association of Australia (SMAA), 103–4

Sadrist Movement, 15

sanctions: punishment of the innocent, indiscriminate, 21; regime's Machiavellian purposes and, 28; twelve years of economic, 6; UN inspections and, 20–22, 156

Saudi Arabia, 156, 159–60–161, 167–70

SBA. *See* Stand-by Agreement (SBA)

Schwarzkopf, General, 20

SCIRI. *See* Supreme Council for the Islamic Revolution in Iraq (SCIRI)

September 11, 2001 (9/11), 35, 37, 176; post, 183, 185

Sharon, Ariel, 26

Shi'a: Iraqi federalism at year four, 37, 39, 45–46, 54; leaders in Iraq, Iran's influence over, 169, 171, 215, 217; uprising in Iraq south and in Kurdistan, 7

Shi'i (Shi'is): close relationship with Iran, 24; Iraqi government, discriminated against by, 24; Islamic state in Iraq, objective of an, 24; politics since 1991, 24–25; Saddam Hussein, parties opposed, 14; society, 15, 31n16; south and Kurdistan, rising in, 19–20

SIDA. *See* Swedish International Development Cooperation Agency (SIDA)

SIGIR. *See* Special Inspector General for Iraqi Reconstruction (SIGIR)

Sistani, Ayatollah, 25

SMAA. *See* Sabian Mandaean Association of Australia (SMAA)

Snow, Treasury Secretary John, 158

SOITM. *See* Iraqi Turkmen Human Rights Research Foundation (SOITM)

Solana, High Representative Javier, 142

sovereignty transferred back to the Iraqi government, 120

Special Inspector General for Iraqi Reconstruction (SIGIR), 119, 122, 124, 130n4

Special Inspector General for Iraq Reconstruction, 200–201

Stand-by Agreement (SBA), 163–64

Sunni, 37–39, 42–46, 54–55, 70

Sunni Arab Hadba party, 61

Sunni Awakening Councils, 32n22, 54, 59, 62, 184

Sunni resistance movement, 197

Supreme Council for the Islamic Revolution in Iraq (SCIRI), 24–25

Sweden, 202–5, 207

Swedish International Development Cooperation Agency (SIDA), 204

Swedish Migration Court and asylum claims, 205

Syriacs, 105

T

Taha Yasin Ramadan, 28
Takatoshi, Kato, 163
TAL. *See* Law of Administration for the State of Iraq for the Transitional Period (TAL)
Talabani, Jalal, 22, 31n14, 79
"Tanzimat" policies, 1
Tariq 'Aziz, 28
Tawafuq Sunni Arab Iraqi Islamic Party, 54, 61, 196
Terms of Reference (TOR), 134, 137–39
TOR. *See* Terms of Reference (TOR)
Tripp, Charles, 6, 26–27, 30n1, 31n20, 79
Turkmen, 8, 98, 101, 106–9

U

UAE. *See* United Arab Emirates (UAE)
UBAF. *See* Union de Banques Arabes et Françaises (UBAF)
UK. *See* United Kingdom (UK)
UN. *See* United Nations (UN)
UNAMI. *See* United Nations Assistance Mission for Iraq (UNAMI)
UNDG. *See* United Nations Development Group (UNDG)
UNDG-ITF. *See* United Nations Development Group Iraq Trust Fund (UNDG-ITF)
UNDP. *See* United Nations Development Programme (UNDP)
UNESCO. *See* United Nations Educational, Scientific and Cultural Organization (UNESCO)
UNHCR. *See* United Nations High Commissioner for Refugees (UNHCR)
UNICEF. *See* United Nations Children's Fund (UNICEF)
UNIFEM. *See* United Nations Development Fund for Women (UNIFEM)
Union de Banques Arabes et Françaises (UBAF), 165
United Arab Emirates (UAE), 50n1, 152n1, 156, 159–60, 167–68, 188n2
United Kingdom (UK): debt forgiveness, 162; International Donor Pledges for Iraq, 160–61; IRFFI donor commitments to World Bank Iraq Trust Fund and United Nations Development Group Iraq Trust Fund, 151; major power, 201; Muqtada, followers of, 25
United Nations (UN): Declaration on the Rights of Indigenous Peoples, 110; Development Group Iraq Trust Fund, 151; estimates of refugees in Jordan and in Syria, 193; General Assembly, 110; Oil-for-Food program, 14, 21, 99, 119; presence in Iraq, lack of, 136; representatives in Iraq, 65; sanctions, 156, 191–92; Universal Declaration of Human Rights, 110; University report on Iraq's higher-education institutions, 125; US urged nations to join International Compact for Iraqi debt forgiveness, 167; war reparations by Iraq, 31n11; weapons inspection and supervising sanctions, 20–22
United Nations Assistance Mission for Iraq (UNAMI), 49, 65, 192
United Nations Children's Fund (UNICEF), 140–41
United Nations Development Fund for Women (UNIFEM), 204–5
United Nations Development Group (UNDG), 135, 137–40, 144–45, 149, 151
United Nations Development Group Iraq Trust Fund (UNDG-ITF), 137–38
United Nations Development Programme (UNDP): brain drain and survey conducted by, 121; goals of multi-donor initiative, 137; Group Iraq Trust Fund

(UNDG-ITF), 137–38; International Donor Pledges for Iraq, 160–61; Iraq Core Group, 136; Iraq Living Conditions Survey (ILCS), 204; IRFFI and, 137–39, 151; IRFFI Donor Commitments to World Bank Iraq Trust Fund and United Nations Development Group Iraq Trust Fund, 151; Ministry of Planning and Development Cooperation, 121

United Nations Educational, Scientific and Cultural Organization (UNESCO), 140

United Nations High Commissioner for Refugees (UNHCR), 22, 98, 180, 192–93, 198–99, 205

United Nations Office for the Coordination of Humanitarian Affairs (UN OCHA), 121

United Nations Security Council (UNSC): Resolution 661, 20, 30n4; Resolution 678, 19; Resolution 687, 20; Resolution 986, 21; Resolution 1153, 21; Resolution 1483, 135, 138, 171n1, 204; Resolution 1511, 138, 204; Resolution 1770, 138; Resolution preventing creditors from resolving debt claims by litigation or attempting to attach liens on Iraqi energy resources, 156, 161, 166, 170; resolutions condemning Iraq and calling for withdrawal from Kuwait, 13–14, 19

United Nations Special Commission on Disarmament (UNSCOM), 21–22

United States (US): anti-Iraq coalition of 30 states, assembled, 19; Army, teaches anti-terrorist techniques, 82; Barzani's ties with, 23; bombing of "strategic" targets in Iraq, 19; burden of reconstruction, need to share, 158–59; Bush Administration and new Hamas-led government, 185; Bush Administration and US policy, region harbours suspicion toward the, 180; Bush Administration's rush to implant democracy as premature, irrelevant, 2; cable news networks present Iraq war in sanitized form, 3; Coalition Provisional Authority transferred power to interim Iraqi government, 201; coaxed creditors to forgive Iraqi debt on moral grounds, 156; Congress allocated $21 billion for Iraq reconstruction, 119; Congress approved $18.4 billion for Iraq's reconstruction, 119; Congress organized debtor and donor conference, 157; Congress pressured IMF to cancel outstanding claims, 158; Debt Sustainability Assessment, pressure to give favourable, 8, 170; Desert Storm, greatest mistake of, 29; Federal Reserve Bank, no financial controls to account for $12 billion from, 201; Government Accountability Office (GAO), 124, 202; humanitarian crisis in Iraq, catastrophic, 192; IMF, pressures placed on, 170; IMF pressured to give Iraq favourable debt sustainability assessment, 8; IMF pressured to underestimate Iraqi ability to repay debt, 156, 170; insurgency movements and loss of civilian life, 5; International Donor Pledges for Iraq, 160–61; intervention in IMF staff's DSA analysis, 170; invasion, Bush administration's justification for, 175; invasion, manipulated information to make case for, 3; invasion and collapse of national visions, 213; invasion and occupation destroyed Iraq's social tissue, 111; invasion and occupation exacerbated vulnerable of Iraq's minorities, 99; invasion and occupation of Iraq in 2003, 1, 13, 35, 96, 117, 175, 192; invasion and sectarian violence against Iraqi Christians, 105; invasion radicalized militant Islamist movements in the Middle East, 9, 182–83; Iraqi Christian identity, 106; Iraqi debt relief, 157–58; Iraqi debt relief as prerequisite to American "success" in Iraq, 156; Iraqi debts, used substantial leverage to settle outstanding, 215; Iraqi exile community in Amman, 27; Iraqi funds under Coalition Provisional Authority Control, 202; Iraqi government economic objectives, 120; Iraq International Conference in Brussels, 141; Iraqi regime, encouraged uprisings against, 19; Iraqi state, collapse of the, 37; Iraqi state-building and internal Iraqi divisions, 5; Iraq's accumulated debt, 156; Iraq's agricultural needs, supplied large portion of, 17; Iraq's diplomatic relations with, 16; Iraq's invasion of Kuwait, approval for, 18; Iraq's oil exports to, 17; Iraq's strategic arsenal, built up, 17; Iraq withdrawal and regional chaos, 4; IRFFI Donor Commitments to the World Bank Iraq Trust Fund and United Nations Development Group Iraq Trust Fund, 151; "Islamic Republic of Iraq" embraced by, 24; Kurdish region, encouragement from, 56, 67; Kurds and, 22; Mandaean families, 104; Muqtada, followers of, 25; nations urged to join the International Compact for Iraqi debt forgiveness, 167; occupation of Iraq, follies and challenges of administering, 4; occupation of Iraq, international opposition to US, 135; Office of Reconstruction and Humanitarian Assistance (ORHA), 118; organized anti-Iraq coalition of 30 states, 19; Paris Club and Iraqi debt relief, 164, 167, 170; Paris Club meeting of Iraq's official creditors, 158; Peshmerga Security Forces, 78; post-Saddam state-building and regime consolidation, 53; reconstruction aid for Iraq, pledged of US $48 billion in, 143; regime change, military worked to implement, 4, 181; Saddam Hussein, covert support of, 13; Saddam Hussein's campaign against, 18; Saudi Arabia and Kuwait and debt relief for Iraq, 170; security guarantees for KRG, 65; sovereignty and democratic rule in region, little advancement of, 215; Special Forces Group, 81; unilateralism, 142; United Nations Security Council used to limit Iraq's reparation payments to creditors, 156, 161, 166, 170; UN Security Council for debt relief, influenced, 170; UN Security Council Resolution 1483 to decrease Iraqi reparations, sponsored, 165–66, 171n1; US national security undermined by Iraq invasion, 4; weaponry made available to Iraq, high-tech, 17

UN OCHA. *See* United Nations Office for the Coordination of Humanitarian Affairs (UN OCHA)

UNSC. *See* United Nations Security Council (UNSC)

UNSCOM. *See* United Nations Special Commission on Disarmament (UNSCOM)

UN Special Commission on Disarmament (UNSCOM), 21–22

US. *See* United States (US)

V
Vatican, 206

W
war crimes, 198
Washington Institute for Near East Policy, 62–63, 65
WB-ITF. *See* World Bank Iraq Trust Fund (WB-ITF)
weapons of mass destruction, 14, 26, 29, 176
Western Europe, 165–66, 177
WHO. *See* World Health Organization (WHO)
Wolfowitz, Paul, 158
Woodward, Bob, 3
World Bank: Chair of the Donor Committee, 145; disbursement of funds, cautious approach to, 141; Donor Committee, 139; Executive Committee, 139; Facility Coordination Committee (FCC), 139; International Compact for Iraqi debt forgiveness, 167; International Donor Pledges for Iraq, 160–61; International Reconstruction Fund Facility for Iraq (IRFFI), 135–41, 144–45, 149, 151; Iraqi debt to, 158; Iraqis and determination of development priorities, 145; Iraq's external public debt, 162; loans by international financial institutions (IFI), 159; locals employed to execute projects, 149; management of funds administered by, 140; National Development Strategy (NDS), 144; needs assessment by, 137, 149; personnel in Iraq, lack of, 140–41; physical security in Iraq, lack of, 141; pledged funds in form of loans, 159; Secretariat, 140; total reconstruction costs for all priority sectors, 144; US Congress pressured IMF to cancel outstanding claims, 158; World Bank Iraq Trust Fund, 151
World Bank Iraq Trust Fund (WB-ITF), 137–38, 151
World Health Organization (WHO), 125, 140

Y
Yezidis, 8, 68, 98, 101–3, 109

Z
Zakho Military Academy, 80, 85–88
Zerevani Peshmerga Security Forces, 81–83

Books in the Studies in International Governance Series

Eduardo Aldunate, translated by Alma Flores
Backpacks Full of Hope: The UN Mission in Haiti / 2010 / xx + 232 pp. /
ISBN 978-1-55458-155-9

Alan S. Alexandroff, editor
Can the World Be Governed? Possibilities for Effective Multilateralism / 2008 / vi + 438 pp. /
ISBN 978-1-55458-041-5

Hany Besada, editor
From Civil Strife to Peace Building: Examining Private Sector Involvement in West African Reconstruction / 2009 / xxiv + 288 pp. / ISBN 978-55458-052-1

Jennifer Clapp and Marc J. Cohen, editors
The Global Food Crisis: Governance Challenges and Opportunities / 2009 / xviii + 270 pp. /
ISBN 978-1-55458-192-4

Andrew F. Cooper and Agata Antkiewicz, editors
Emerging Powers in Global Governance: Lessons from the Heiligendamm Process / 2008 /
xxii + 370 pp. / ISBN 978-1-55458-057-6

Jeremy de Beer, editor
Implementing WIPO's Development Agenda / 2009 / xvi + 188 pp. /
ISBN 978-1-55458-154-2

Geoffrey Hayes and Mark Sedra, editors
Afghanistan: Transition under Threat / 2008 / xxxiv + 314 pp. /
ISBN-13: 978-1-55458-011-8 / ISBN-10: 1-55458-011-1

Paul Heinbecker and Patricia Goff, editors
Irrelevant or Indispensable? The United Nations in the 21st Century / 2005 / xii + 196 pp. /
ISBN 0-88920-493-4

Paul Heinbecker and Bessma Momani, editors
Canada and the Middle East: In Theory and Practice / 2007 / ix + 232 pp. /
ISBN-13: 978-1-55458-024-8 / ISBN-10: 1-55458-024-2

Mokhtar Lamani and Bessma Momani, editors
From Desolation to Reconstruction: Iraq's Troubled Journey / 2010 / xii + 246 pp. /
ISBN: 978-1-55458-229-7

Yasmine Shamsie and Andrew S. Thompson, editors
Haiti: Hope for a Fragile State / 2006 / xvi + 131 pp. / ISBN-13: 978-0-88920-510-9 /
ISBN-10: 0-88920-510-8

Debra P. Steger, editor
Redesigning the World Trade Organization for the Twenty-first Century / 2010 / xx + 478 pp. /
ISBN 978-1-55458-156-6

James W. St.G. Walker and Andrew S. Thompson, editors
Critical Mass: The Emergence of Global Civil Society / 2008 / xxviii + 302 /
ISBN-13: 978-1-55458-022-4 / ISBN-10: 1-55458-022-6

Jennifer Welsh and Ngaire Woods, editors
Exporting Good Governance: Temptations and Challenges in Canada's Aid Program / 2007 /
xx + 343 pp. / ISBN-13: 978-1-55458-029-3 / ISBN-10: 1-55458-029-3